The Hillwalking Bible

CONWAY
Bloomsbury Publishing Plc
50 Bedford Square, London, WC1B 3DP, UK
29 Earlsfort Terrace, Dublin 2, Ireland

BLOOMSBURY, CONWAY and the Conway logo are trademarks of Bloomsbury Publishing Plc

First published in Great Britain 2024

This book is a guide for when you spend time outdoors. Undertaking any activity outdoors carries
with it some risks that cannot be entirely eliminated. For example, you might get lost on a route or
caught in bad weather. Before you spend time outdoors, we therefore advise that you always take
the necessary precautions, such as checking weather forecasts and ensuring that you have all the
equipment you need. Any walking routes that are described in this book should not be relied upon
as a sole means of navigation, so we recommend that you refer to an Ordnance Survey map or
authoritative equivalent.

This book may also reference businesses and venues. Whilst every effort is made by the author
and the publisher to ensure the accuracy of the business and venue information contained in our
books before they go to print, changes to such information can occur during the production and
lifetime of a publication. Therefore, we also advise that you check with businesses or venues for
the latest information before setting out.

All internet addresses given in this book were correct at the time of going to press. Bloomsbury
Publishing Plc does not have any control over, or responsibility for, any third-party websites
referred to or in this book. The author and the publisher regret any inconvenience caused if some
facts have changed or sites have ceased to exist, but can accept no responsibility for any such
changes.

A catalogue record for this book is available from the British Library
Library of Congress Cataloguing-in-Publication data has been applied for.

ISBN: PB: 978-1-8448-6655-7; ePDF: 978-1-8448-6653-3; ePub: 978-1-8448-6656-4

10 9 8 7 6 5 4 3 2 1

Typeset in IBM Plex Serif
Designed by Austin Taylor
Printed and bound in UAE by Oriental Press

To find out more about our authors and books visit www.bloomsbury.com
and sign up for our newsletters

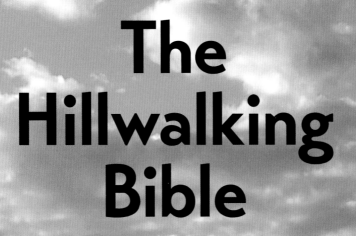

The Hillwalking Bible

Where to go, what to take, how to not get lost

Ronald Turnbull

CONWAY

LONDON · OXFORD · NEW YORK · NEW DELHI · SYDNEY

BELOW Stob Coire nan Beith, Glen Coe.

PREVIOUS PAGE Blackmount Hills seen across Rannoch Moor.

FRONT COVER Above Hawes Water, Lake District.

CONTENTS

ROUTES ROUND-UP 9

FOREWORD 10

INTRODUCTION 12
Mistakes, and how to make them 16
How to use this book 18
WALK 1 Walla Crag 20

FIRST STEPS 27

1 GEARING UP 28
Item No. 1: map 29
Item No. 2: compass 31
Item Nos 3 and 4: boots 33
Item No. 5: waterproof jacket 34
Item No. 6: rucksack 36
Other stuff to stuff in the sack 36
Things to ask for for Christmas
(maybe) 37
Ronald's rucksack 41

2 UNDERSTANDING MAPS 43
The shape of Schiehallion 43
Contour lines 44
Summits and saddle points 46
Re-entrants and spurs 48
Different sorts of mapping 49
Means and ways: path markings
on maps 52
Access and rights to roam 54

3 CHOOSING THE RIGHT ROUTE 55
Low-level routes 56
Mountain ground 62

4 ON NOT GETTING LOST 65
Finding the way with compass
and map 66
Don't stand next to the synchrotron 68
Finding the way with a mapping app 68
App happy 69
Phone for navigation 70
Following a pre-set route 73
Or let the phone take control 74
Devouring the hamburger: the rest
of the menus 75
Other appropriate apps 75
On getting lost 77

5 LOOKING AFTER THE MOUNTAIN 86
Path masters 87
Cars and effect 87

6 CHILDREN AND/OR DOGS 90
Children on hills 90
Adventuring again 92
Dogs 94

7 GETTING SERIOUS: SCRAMBLING 97
Going high with the Pumpkin Person 97
WALK 2 Blencathra by Halls Fell 104

8 GETTING SERIOUS: WINTER WALKING 107
No snow go 108
Let it snow 110
A bit of snow-how 112

9 WHEN THINGS GO WRONG 114
Awkward moments for those
left at home 117

WHERE TO GO 121

ENGLAND 122
Peak District 122
WALK 3 White Peak: Hartington valleys 126
WALK 4 Dark Peak: Kinder Scout 130
Lake District 133
WALK 5 Great Gable 137
Yorkshire Dales 143
WALK 6 Ingleborough 146
England's coastlines 152
WALK 7 Jurassic fantastic, Durdle Door to Osmington 154

WALES 158
Snowdonia 160
WALK 8 Moel Siabod 165
The great scarp: Brecon Beacons 169
WALK 9 Pen y Fan horseshoe 171
Welsh coast 175

SCOTLAND 177
Southern Uplands and other lower-level walking 177
The Munros 181
Loch Lomond and the Trossachs National Park 183
WALK 10 A first Munro: Ben Lomond 184
More Munros 187
WALK 11 A second Munro: Meall nan Tarmachan 191
The Cairngorms 195
Wester Ross 196
The Cuillin 199
Scotland's other islands 199

NORTHERN IRELAND 202
Mountains of Mourne 203
Antrim coast 204

WIDER HORIZONS 207

10 LONG-DISTANCE WALKING ROUTES 208
My favourite multiday walks 209
WALK 12 In the steps of Cuthbert's Corpse 213
Hiking hostel to hostel 217
WALK 13 Tour de Scafell Pike 220

BELOW Am Bodach (left) and Stob Coire a' Chairn, seen from Coire na Ba (Walk 16).

11 BACKPACKING AND WILD CAMPING 224

Tent or bivvy bag? 226
Packing light 228
Making backpacking bearable 228
Site specific 229
Routes round-up 229
WALK 14 West of the West
   Highland Way 232

12 RUNNING UP THAT HILL 240

13 WALKING ABROAD 244

Boots and bathing costumes 244
Ways and means 244
Hut-to-hut hiking 245
WALK 15 Stubaier Höhenweg 250

14 LISTS OF HILLS 254

The Munros 255
The Corbetts 255
Other Scottish lists 256
The Wainwrights 256
The English 2000s 257
The Welsh 2000s 257
The Marilyns 258

15 MORE APP AND MAP 259

Clicking out routes on the
computer 259
Snapping to your path 261
A walk in the Mamores 261
WALK 16 Stob Coire a' Chairn and
   Am Bodach, Mamores 269

16 MORE MAP AND COMPASS 272

So, how to take a bearing? 275
Grid references 280
Finding the way Stone Age style 281

17 WINTER SKILLS 283

Crampons 285
Winter and rough weather 286

18 A BIT ABOUT BEDROCK 288

Different sorts of stones 289

Final words 298
Glossary 299
Index 302

ROUTES ROUNDUP

		Area	Type	dist (km)	dist (miles)	ascent (m)	Page
1	Walla Crag	Lake District	small hill	11.5	7.2	450	20
2	Halls Fell, Blencathra	Lake District	scramble	9.5	6	750	104
3	Hartington valleys	Peak District	valley	10	6	200	126
4	Kinder Scout	Peak District	hill	13	8	650	133
5	Great Gable	Lake District	hill	9	5.5	850	137
6	Ingleborough	Yorkshire Dales	hill	21	13	800	146
7	Durdle Door to the Smugglers' Path	Dorset	coast	19	12	750	154
8	Moel Siabod	Snowdonia	hill	12	7.5	900	165
9	Pen y Fan	Brecon Beacons	hill	20	12.5	1,000	171
10	Ben Lomond	Lomond NP	hill	11	7	1,050	184
11	Meall nan Tarmachan	Perthshire	hill	15	9.5	850	191
12	St Cuthbert's Way	Scottish Borders	long-distance path	100	62	2,300	213
13	Tour de Scafell Pike	Lake District	multiday	65	40	3,200	220
14	A West Highland Walk	SW Highlands	backpack	96	60	2,500	232
15	Stubaier Höhenweg	Austria	hut-to-hut	80	50	6,500	250
16	Am Bodach, Mamores	SW Highlands	hill	15	9.5	1,200	269

FOREWORD

I'd been on a course in Barnsley, and had to take the train from Manchester to Sheffield. The one that goes through all those tunnels, and the little villages at the bottom of the Peak District. I was at a low point in my life, I know that, all kinds of issues with my mental health. And I noticed all these people getting off at Edale, people with rucksacks and walking poles and all the gear. They weren't people like me, they didn't look like me. But something inside me went: that looks like fun. I'm going to try it.

So that's how I got started. I went into it without really knowing what I was doing. I'd never led a walk, I'd never even been on a walk. But I posted on a forum that I was going to lead a walk and did anybody want to come. I didn't know how to read a map, so I Googled walks in Greater Manchester and tried to memorise a route for our first walk. I was just winging it! I didn't know if anybody would come but 14 women turned up, and that was the beginning of Black Girls Hike (www.bgh.com).

And do you know what? It was easier than I thought. A lot of people have an idea that the countryside is not welcoming to people of colour. But we've found that it's a lot more welcoming than you think. We have some lovely conversations with people we meet on our hikes.

When I started BGH I couldn't read a map or use a compass. I've been lost – I've got the group lost, too, out on Saddleworth Moor in low cloud and horizontal rain. But through adventures you learn so much about yourself. It changes your mindset. I used to have loads of reservations about going out into the countryside, but when you actually go there and realise it's overwhelmingly positive and friendly, then you start thinking about all the other barriers you've created in your mind to trying things. It opens doors.

Since then I've learned hill and mountain skills and learned to navigate and plan routes. It's not brain surgery! Which is why I'm glad to see that Conway has brought out this book. A couple of months back, I got to share a walk with Ronald. We were walking to the top of Cumbrae, a little island in the sea just outside Glasgow. It was a whole gang of people from the Outdoor Writers and Photographers Guild. Some of those writers are very fit and strong walkers I could tell, some of us quite slow and pottering about. But there we all were, walking together, chatting, taking photos of the sea and the Isle of Arran, trying to crouch down behind the trig point when the cold rainshower came through. Which is what it's all about, really.

And when you're with him on a hilltop, Ronald's just the same as he is in this book, friendly, cheerful, not too full of himself. And the same slightly sharp-edged sense of humour. You need to watch out for that.

It would have been handy, when I was starting out, knowing the stuff in Ronald's book. You don't need all that special high-tech equipment, but you do need a decent waterproof jacket. How you can find your way around using your phone. But mainly, yes, to just go out there, up on the moors, or round a reservoir, or out along the coast. And just do it.

It's probably a whole lot easier than you think.

Rhiane Fatinikun MBE
FOUNDER OF BLACK GIRLS HIKE

RIGHT Rhiane Fatinikun and Ronald Turnbull on Great Cumbrae Island

INTRODUCTION

It's one of those cold, clear November mornings. At 7.30am, primrose-coloured light is seeping up into the bottom of the sky. As I lock the house behind me, an owl hoots somewhere in the dark woods. Cold air on my face, cold air in my nose every time I take a breath, my footsteps crunchy in the frost along the empty road. After half an hour, the first sun lights up the hillside above me. The dead bracken glows like a fox who's just had a shampoo and blow dry. Sunlight creeps downwards, lies in streaks across the fields, highlighting a white cottage, laying grey-blue shadow along the dip of a stream.

Against the horizontal sunlight, the ruined Morton Castle is an old painting that's just had the varnish scraped off back to its original colours. And again, upside down, in the mirror-flat lochan. Fifteen minutes up the hill, the wide valley is spread below, the woodlands chocolate brown, the fields the green of peppermint icing, farm ponds gleaming like silver foil. Today, in the second autumn after

lockdown, there'll be queues for the cairn on Snowdon and Scafell Pike. But here on Morton Mains Hill, it's Margo in the yellow jacket and Julie in the red one, two neighbours from the nearby town – and jolly surprising to see any other people at all up here. They're surprised as well, and we chat for a minute before they head round to the little reservoir behind the hill and I head up along the ridge.

It's a tiny one, Morton Mains Hill, just 328m high. But it sticks into the curve of the valley so you see all the way down to Criffel hill behind Dumfries, the shine of the Solway Firth, a bumpy blue shadow that's the hills of England on the other side. Up here on East Morton there are clumps of sedge grass going ochre brown,

ABOVE Crummock Water and Grasmoor, as seen from High Stile, western Lake District.

and the grass path of a shepherd's quad bike, and the bank of an Iron Age hillfort. And high above the reservoir, a bird-shape that's big, and never moves its wings – long finger-shaped wings, slightly splayed at the ends – can it be the Southern Upland eagle, reintroduced last summer in the higher hills away in the east? No, silly – it turns, much too quick for an eagle, and shows its slightly forked tail. It's a red kite; they've been back in our valley for the last five years now.

Two more little hills ahead of me, and I'll still be home in time for lunch.

Walking. By the time we're five years old, most of us are pretty good

ABOVE Loch Coruisk in the heart of the Cuillin range, Isle of Skye.

Walking as a form of fun is more recent. I date it from Monday 2 August 1802, when the poet Samuel Taylor Coleridge tore the twigs off his wife's besom broom to make a walking stick and set off for a nine-day hike around the Lake District. Before that Monday morning, the hills and the long-distance paths weren't a form of fun because they were just everyday life. Across the Southern Uplands to Edinburgh to get an education. Down the Great North Road to get a job. Across the Pennines in a snowstorm to visit your best female friend in the Vale of York.

But our ancestor of 50,000 years ago, who picked her way up the icefield and reached the rocky ridgetop – looked out over the undiscovered valley, with its lake and its fish, its grasslands and woods, its river running down just so and its small hills arranged just so – we know that a little flame of delight burned in her heart. We know because, standing on Ben Lomond or Snowdon or the Old Man of Coniston, the same little flame will burn in us as well.

Hillwalking, or walking along the coastline or over the bleak, empty moors: this is a natural, non-technical form of fun. It doesn't need much specialist kit, and the knowledge and skills you require are ones you'd already have if you'd only been born in the Stone Age. Maybe, living in cities, we've lost the habit of using our legs to get about the place. We may have forgotten how to head out into unknown country with only our brains and eyes to guide us. But those skills are still there, written into our minds

at it. As humans, we've been at it for the best part of two million years. If you wanted to gather some berries that just came into season over in the next valley, or track down a tasty elk, or explore the villages down the river and, who knows, meet your future life partner – you went for a walk. And if you were good at walking – not just strong in the legs and lungs, but clear-eyed in understanding the country, cunning in working out your way, logistically skilled in the simple art of packing a rucksack – if you were good at walking, you were good at life.

by two million years of evolution. Plus, we've got our mobile phones and some excellent Ordnance Survey (OS) maps.

They don't know it, but three people I talked to a few weeks ago got me to write this book. The first is a neighbour who likes to go running. Not fast running, but quite a long way, 16km (10 miles) or more on the farm tracks and little country roads. Now, the Southern Upland hills above where we live, they're just ideal for that sort of sport. Southern Uplands are grassy on top, with helpful grouse-shooter tracks, one hill linked to the next in wide, gentle ridgelines. No pools of tractor slurry, no muck spreaders trundling past, and great views out over the glens. Why doesn't she go

ABOVE Upper Eskdale and Scafell Pike.

BELOW Two neighbours heading up Morton Mains Hill.

running up on the Southern Uplands?

'Oh, no,' she says. 'Because I might get lost.'

The other two were above Burnmoor Tarn, on the old corpse road from Wasdale Head. They were heading back round to Eskdale after a day up Scafell Pike. They'd enjoyed their day up and down the busiest path on England's highest hill. However, starting from Eskdale, there are some deeply wonderful and quiet ways on to Scafell Pike. You go by the huge, empty place that's the Great Moss, up beside the long waterfall called Cam

Spout, to the dramatic little saddle below England's biggest crags. In the huge emptiness of the Great Moss you might meet two or three other people. Then again, you might not. Instead of all that, the two people on my path chose to hike around the hill to one of England's busiest car parks, so as to head up the wide, rebuilt path behind a hundred other people.

Walking up Scafell Pike from Wasdale (and then back down again the same way); Snowdon from Pen-y-Pass (if you can get into the car park, which you can't); the Yorkshire Three Peaks, or even only one of them. Yes, these are enjoyable; and you almost certainly won't get lost. But I'm hoping this book will take you a little farther. Or a whole lot farther, over the hundreds of other hills the UK has to offer. The downlands of the South, the windy seacliffs, the grim peat moors of the Pennines, the craggy corners of the Lake District, the harsh, romantic glens of Scotland. Using the wild country navigation embedded in your brain, along with a compass (costs £15), a map (about the same), and the mapping app on your mobile phone.

Walking up hills. It's what legs, and lungs, were made for.

Mistakes, and how to make them

Danger and difficulty doesn't have to mean freezing to death in a snowstorm on Everest's South Col. It's more like, dropping the map on a windy day

and watching it flap away down the slope like a wounded heron. Dropping a different map in the woods below the Mamores and not noticing until two hours later. When it starts to rain, halfway round a two-day winter trek, opening the sack to take out the waterproof jacket and realising the waterproof jacket got left behind at home. Pitching the tent in a cosy hollow that two hours after midnight turned into a stream. The two-car ridge-run along the Rhinns of Kells, to find the car keys are still locked inside the other car back at the other end…

Yes, these are all mistakes I've made myself. If you do get serious as a wild-country walker, you're going to make some of them as well. And if you're laughing at the silly fellow trying to hitchhike 27km (17 miles)

back to his car while wearing sky-blue Lycra leggings – well I'm glad someone's getting some fun out of that one.

With greater experience and knowledge comes greater confidence. And with greater confidence comes new and more interesting mistakes, and different ways of getting it all a bit wrong. Which, sometimes, can provide some of the best days of all.

So the reason for this book (apart from paying for my next shortbread biscuit at Keswick's Laura in the Lakes) is to share the knowledge, and confidence, so you can go to places that aren't on Instagram.

RIGHT Y Lliwedd – the less crowded but more challenging way up Snowdon.

BELOW Autumn day on Cross Fell, North Pennines.

The knowledge is mostly about how to understand a map, pick an interesting route, and avoid getting lost. And the confidence is about giving yourself permission to make a few mistakes, and get lost anyway...

Because walking in the hills and the wild places isn't just about the benefits to your physical and mental health. It isn't just about the summit photo on Cat Bells for your WhatsApp. It's about those things, yes. But it's also about the freedom of the hills. Finding your own way, taking yourself a little farther, widening your horizons. And yes, making your own mistakes.

You can't really get it right – until you're prepared to get it wrong.

How to use this book

My first hope here is to get you out of the house and walking up some small hill – or maybe along the top of a seacliff – or any bit of open country that's easy to get to starting from where you're starting from. The idea being just to find out whether it's fun.

Which it is, of course. So then you'll be thinking about some of the wild and lovely hill country the UK has to offer. Snowdonia or the Scottish Highlands or Bannau Brycheiniog

(the Brecon Beacons) or Dartmoor or even the South Pennines. What sort of kit do you need? Perhaps a bit less than you think. How shall you find the way? Are some bits even better than the others? How scared should you be? Is it absolutely necessary to join the crowds on Cat Bells?

There will be one or two specific routes to get you started. The first of them is a boat trip to Walla Crag, which is a wonderful wee hill and lets us look across in a superior way at busy Cat Bells. But mostly I want to pass on the skills that let you explore on your own. Make up a route line off the map, find your way along it with a compass and your mobile phone, get lost a little, and still get back to the teashop in time for tea.

That's the first part of the book. Then there's a rundown of where you might like to go, in England, Wales, Scotland and Northern Ireland.

There's also some clever stuff with compasses. Magnetic bearings, the use of the fall line, handrailing and aiming off – I like that stuff myself; maybe you will as well.

At the back of the book is a glossary: a list of the fancy words that fellwalkers use and people like me write down without even thinking about it. Some of them are just to mystify outsiders or show off how clever we are with the Gaelic inflections and the Welsh pronunciation. But knowing what a col is, and which direction you're going in when you're contouring – these do make it easier to think about what you're up to when you're up on a hill.

And maybe, by the end of next summer, you'll find yet another way to use this book. A paperweight for some unruly invoices, perhaps. Tear out the pictures to use as picture postcards. Because you'll be off in the hills, with your map and your mobile phone, and your head full of plans and ambitions. Perhaps this little path you've spotted on Glaramara? Ronald's a bit sneery about the South Pennines, so let's just go to the South Pennines. And what about that Welsh Coast Path?

The weather forecast's sort of showery. It's December now, and the wind will be singing in the fence wires. Maybe the English hills across the Solway will even have some snow on them. Chapter 1 can wait. I'm not going to spot that Southern Upland eagle unless I get up there on the Southern Uplands, right now.

BELOW Evening walkers on High Rigg, Lake District.

WALLA CRAG

But first of all, the question I know you're asking: why aren't we climbing Cat Bells? Cat Bells is a small hill above Derwent Water in the English Lake District. For a first-ever fellwalk, Cat Bells is just about perfect.

There's the shape of it. Take a thick crayon, draw an upside-down V, and that's the shape of Cat Bells. There's the size, 451m, taking about an hour and a half to get up it. There are a couple of little rocky bits on the path, and one flat shoulder for a bit of relaxation. And on top of all that, there are the literary associations. Yes, Cat Bells is the home of Mrs Tiggy-Winkle, Beatrix Potter's hedgehog washerwoman. Altogether, for a mini-mountain that's not too demanding but gives a whole lot more than it takes, Cat Bells is pretty much perfect.

Which is precisely the problem with Cat Bells. Well, two problems really. There's the parking – or rather, there isn't. The small parking area at the bottom of Cat Bells fills up by breakfast time. After that, you're squashed up along the lane edge, and with luck you won't come down to find a parking ticket on your windshield, and with even more luck you won't find your wing mirror snapped away by a tractor or the Mountain Rescue Land Rover or the Number 77 bus.

At the time of writing, the National Park Authority is applying for a bigger, better car park for Cat Bells. Which if they get it will simply worsen problem number two. The queues at the little

BELOW Derwent Water from the Keswick Launch.

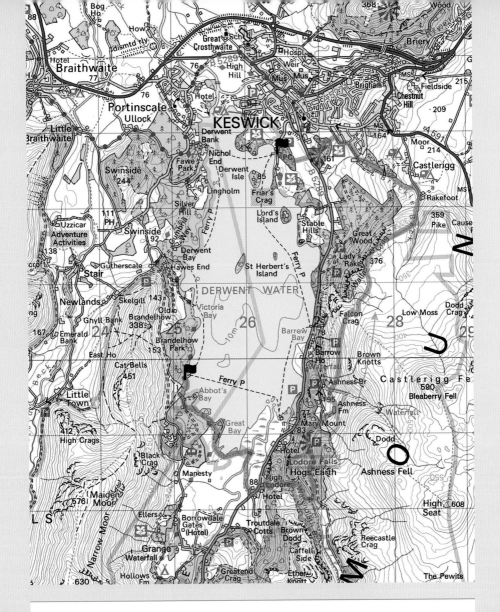

WALK 1 **Walla Crag**

START/END **Keswick landing stages for boat to High Brandelhow (NY264226)**

DISTANCE **11.5km (7.1 miles)**

ASCENT **450m**

APPROX. TIME **4 hours 30 minutes (+ lake cruise and cafe stops)**

HIGHEST POINT **Walla Crag, 376m**

TERRAIN **Shoreline and hill paths, steep and rugged in one or two places**

PARKING **Keswick Lakeside (postcode CA12 5DJ)**

CAR-FREE **Buses to Keswick from Penrith (station); Keswick Launch on Derwent Water, book at keswick-launch.co.uk**

TOILETS **Lakeside car park**

PUBS & CAFES **Cafe at Theatre by the Lake (walk start), two more on the walk itself**

scrambly sections aren't quite as bad as the Hillary Step on Everest. But Cat Bells is still a busy place.

And yes, Cat Bells is a lovely place to be at the end of a long day around Borrowdale, with the last light caressing the slopes across the lake and the lamps coming on in Keswick's pubs. But in the middle of the day, in the middle of summer, I'll be on one of a hundred other summits that are just as nice as Cat Bells in their various different ways. One of them is Walla Crag.

Walla Crag doesn't have the pointy perfection of Cat Bells, being merely a high point at the top of a crag. What it does have is a wander along lakeshore woods; a moment of ruggedness on the way up to Surprise View; its own Instagram hotspot at Ashness Bridge; a ramble along the rocky edge above Derwent Water; and an ice cream to finish at Annie's Pantry.

But what makes this one extra special is the Derwent Water boat trip

BELOW The path above Falcon Crag.

at the beginning. Starting from Keswick landing stages means no parking problems, plus not even needing the car in the first place.

Take the Derwent Water Launch either clockwise or anticlockwise. From the landing stage at Brandelhow, turn left on a wide lakeside path.

BELOW On Walla Crag at sunrise.

If you just gotta climb Cat Bells, a turn uphill here gets you up towards the hill's north ridgeline. You'll descend south, swerve the crowded car park, and bag a second Beatrix Potter location by passing through Squirrel Nutkin's wood and past Mr McGregor's Garden on the way back to Keswick via Portinscale.

Fork left along the water's edge over mine tailings. At Manesty, keep ahead on a tarmac lane. Ignore a private driveway on the left, but then take a wide path to the left signed for Lodore. This has long duckboard sections on recycled plastic planks, plus grand views of Castle Crag on your right.

Cross the River Derwent on a high footbridge and turn right on a faint path alongside the river to a gate. Now fork left (south) across open grassland, then with the fence and creek on your left, to a short track out to the B5289 road.

Turn left on the roadside footpath past the Borrowdale Hotel, then cross to an inconspicuous path signpost. High Lodore Farm Cafe is just to the left. Pass through a small

BELOW Ashness Bridge. A path higher up the hill lets you avoid this Instagram hotspot if preferred.

car park, then bend left on a stony path above a house. Where the path turns uphill, at once fork right at an unsigned junction – the left fork is for climbs on Shepherd's Crag. The right fork passes a bench and runs up through woods, steep and stony. It's in a deeply eroded trench at one point, before arriving above Watendlath Beck.

The main path runs a little above the beck, to a gate above a high footbridge. Cross this and turn left through a wall on a well-made path through woods. After 400m (¼ mile), the path is about to join the small but rather busy Watendlath road. Instead, fork left on a small path through woods to the left of the road, to Surprise View high above Derwent Water.

Turn right to join the road.

For the busy photo-spot at Ashness Bridge, you'd just continue down this road. Take the photo (at busy times, you'll have to queue), cross the bridge and turn uphill to the left of the stream. When you see a footbridge on your right, that's the point at which to take the path turning left. It may be better →

to enjoy it on Instagram, as the lake glimpse, essential to the composition, is now almost hidden by trees. So I prefer a bypass route running above it – the permissive path via Ashness Farm.

For the upper option, follow the road below Surprise View just until it leaves the wood, and take a gate on the right. A rough track runs gently downhill to join the concrete driveway to Ashness Farm. Pass below the farmhouse to a small gate on the right. Pass along above buildings (faded green waymark arrows here) and along the foot of a field to a gate on the left. Go through this then pass along the top edge of the next field to a small gate in a wall and drop to a footbridge under trees across Barrow Beck.

The path ahead slants up the grassy hillside, through a gate. It continues along the top of Falcon Crag with wide lake views. Then it bends in to the right around the top of Cat Gill hollow and

BELOW View to Blencathra while descending from Walla Crag.

ABOVE Cockshot Wood by Derwent Water.

from the clifftop.) The rougher path runs between trees along the brink of the crag, with a few rocky steps, to emerge over a stile on to open grassland. Head left down a wide path above a wall, until a footbridge leads to the lane end near Castlerigg Farm.

Follow the lane down to the left, over a stream, to a gate where you turn back sharp left, down through woods. At the wood foot is another good cafe, Annie's Pantry, which also serves ice cream.

Continue ahead on a street (Springs Road) into the edge of Keswick. After 400m (¼ mile), turn left on a hedged path, across a field into Castlehead Wood. At the first fork, bear right, at the next one, turn left, up to Castle Head summit.

reaches a stile in a fence on the left. Go over this and up through heather to the trampled bare rock summit of Walla Crag.

You now have the view across Derwent Water that you would have got from Cat Bells, but the other way round. If you've already been studying the map reading chapter, the Grasmoor group of hills opposite offers a tangle of tops and ridges. See whether you can work out which of the summits is Crag Hill (Eel Crag on Harvey maps) and find the gap north of it called Coledale Hause. Next, check with the compass. If you've got it right, Coledale Hause is due west from the top of Walla Crag.

A popular viewpoint since the 18th century, this is where the first 'tourists' would turn their backs on the lake and examine it via a tinted Claude glass, a curved mirror designed to show the scenery stretched and tinted, and framed the way it really ought to be framed.

Today, we're so much more sophisticated. We turn our backs on the view in order to wield a selfie stick.

From the bare rock above the lake view, drop towards Keswick to find the start of a rough path just below. (An easier and less exciting path runs farther to the right, a little way back

From the viewpoint here, return on the same path briefly. Turn left above the corner of an open field and head down to the Borrowdale road at the wood's foot.

Cross into the path opposite, which turns left along the roadside hedge, then turns right across a field into Cockshot Wood. Keep ahead for the landing stages or turn right along the wood's near edge for Lakeside car park.

BELOW Two experienced walkers (with good boots!) tackle a scrambly ridge, Meall Garbh on the Tarmachan ridge, Scottish Highlands (Walk 11).

FIRST STEPS

‘ *The language of hiking and the outdoors can be off-putting –*
it makes it sound like you've got to go up Everest, but it's just walking. ’
RHIANE FATINIKUN, FOUNDER OF BLACK GIRLS HIKE (*THE OBSERVER*, 2023)

1

GEARING UP

One great advantage of going up hills – yes, it's good for your heart, it's good for your mental health – but it also opens up a whole new world of shopping. Take your credit card up to the Outdoor Capital of England, which is Ambleside, or the UK's Capital of Adventure, which is Fort William. And within a couple of hours, you can be a complete outdoor person, owning everything from a bobble hat to incised rubber boot soles.

There's one odd thing about these outdoor stores, though. Did you spot it? They are – every single one of them – indoors.

Shopping is satisfying. Shopping is what drives our economy. But if what you want is to go for a walk, in some comfortable old clothes, in some rather rugged hilly country, there are six extra items that you actually need. Plus a few more you might like to ask for, eventually, in your breathable Merino-knit Christmas stocking.

When you've been up your first few hills, you'll work out for yourself what you need, or more importantly, what you want, to feel comfortable and stylish in the sort of wild places you

ABOVE For coastal walking with a settled forecast, kit can be quite informal. Quinish Point, Isle of Mull.

find you like to be in. The suggestions here are to help you get started. And if you're already kitted out, you can read my suggestions anyway and have fun not agreeing with them and draft me an icily polite email about how I forgot to mention gaiters.

Gaiters, yes. A lot of us go around in gaiters. Someday, I'll maybe get a pair and wonder how I've gone so long without any gaiters. On the other hand, after 50 gaiterless years, I suspect I probably shan't.

Item No 1: map

Satnav is extremely useful when you're driving in a car, on your own, trying to find the youth hostel in the centre of Bristol. But although you find things, including that youth hostel in its nest of one-way streets, there's also a lot you miss. Like the time I drove right down through Wales to the Gower Peninsula with its wonderful limestone arch – and never even noticed that I'd passed right through the Black Mountain range on the way.

ABOVE Plenty to choose from at the Tiso shop, Perth.

LEFT The author (left) on my first ascent of Scafell Pike sporting a Mackintosh and school sandals, while my Dad models an early anorak.

When you go for a walk with someone else finding the way – well was that Great Gable we just went up? Oh, it was Bow Fell? And did we really just go over Glaramara without even realising...

When we go up into the hills, we might be hoping for something a bit more than the satnav experience.

Yes, Google Maps on your phone can get you up to the top of the hill. And it'll get you safely down again – quite a lot of the time. But it won't show you where you are in the wider landscape. When you get to the top, you won't be able to point around the horizon and say which one's Snowdon away over there. And when you wander down to the wrong little lake, you won't be able to work out which is going to be the best way back to your bus stop. And when you've been lost and wandering in the rain for six hours, and you've used up all your battery, you'll be jolly glad you've still got that old-style paper map with its comforting Gill Sans typeface.

That last one works both ways, of course. When you've been lost and wandering and the wind just blew away your map, you'll be jolly glad you've got your phone...

So what sort of map? Google's great at where's the nearest coffee shop, and does it do vegan cream cakes. But it doesn't cut it when it comes to contour lines. In the mapping chapter, I'll analyse the options. But for a quick start, Bing's streetmap.co.uk website has the Ordnance Survey Landranger and Explorer styles. Take screenshots of the Landranger, paste them together, print them out and put them in an A4 file pocket to keep it out of the rain.

Because this is the Great Outdoors. We need more of it than we can see on 10cm of digital screen.

> **Start-up suggestion: OS Maps app on the phone. OS Landranger or Harvey British Mountain Map on paper.**

PHONE OR PAPER?

A phone app is a back-up to your paper map that:
→ shows where you actually are at this very moment
→ zooms in and out to different scales
→ is very small
→ may freeze, drop out, or lose its battery

Whereas a paper map is a back-up to your phone app that:
→ doesn't show where you are on it
→ is fixed at a single scale
→ is nice and big (on a windy day, too big)
→ may get dropped and blow away

Item No 2: compass

So what's the best way to get yourself to where you want to go, and even to know where you are once you've got there?

There's the innate sense of direction that we all have, as we wander through the city or around the hummocks of the hill, to know which way we're facing and where it was we started from. This can be amazingly effective – just so long as you happen to be an Arctic tern or a migrating wildebeest. In humans, not so good. As you already know from the last time you drifted around some city streets being quite sure you knew how to find the train station.

About 2,200 years ago, Chinese magicians discovered the south-pointing spoon, crafted from natural magnetite mineral. Ever since then, wayfarers and wanderers have been using ever more accurate maps, along with ever better balanced compasses, to find our way around the world.

That's until the year 1989. At that point the antiquated hand-held compass began to be replaced by a system involving 32 orbiting artificial satellites, atomic clocks and complex calculations involving Einstein's general theory of relativity.

For those of us who've spent a lifetime refining our skills with compass and map, 1989 counts as a slightly sad moment. Navigation by the compass and the contour lines is just so clever, and also so satisfying when you come down out of the cloud and find yourself exactly where you intended to be.

But for the rest of us, given we've spent £600 on our lovely smartphone, with the GPS chip and the Google mapping already inside it, is it time

ABOVE Map (Harvey Superwalker) and compass.

to give up on the compass and save ourselves £14.99?

When we get to the chapter about finding our way, the GPS on the phone will tell us with remarkable accuracy, powered by those billions of dollars of US military hardware, exactly where we're at. It's less good at telling us which way we're going. Of course, there is the 'compass' app, which tells your direction with an accuracy of one tenth of a degree. However, in my experience, it's telling you wrong.

So as a back-up to my phone, and a quick way of knowing which way's north, I like to tap into the natural power of the Earth's magnetic field. I spend that £14.99 and I carry a compass. It doesn't need to be booted up and take two minutes to find the satellite. It doesn't run out of battery. And it'll tell me which way north-west is even when it's raining.

BELOW Waterproof jacket, comfortable boots and perhaps a pole. High Snab Bank of Robinson, Lake District.

It also has a sophisticated chunk of rectangular plastic attached, whose lines and little numbers will tell us lots of important and exciting stuff. This is quite fun for those who find lines and little numbers quite fun, and I'll go into it much later on in the book (because yes, I'm one of those people who do find such stuff quite fun). But for now, we want to get down off this misty hill and we want to get down north-west towards Borrowdale not south into the valley of the Esk. Unzip pocket, compass out, job done. Well not, because you'll need to look at the compass again on the way down there. More about that in the following chapter.

So why in my list of six haven't I mentioned the mobile phone? Short answer: I'm assuming you've already got one. And if you haven't, and you're able to navigate your life without that

essential bit of electronics – then you'll be just fine navigating the hills the crafty way with just a compass and a paper map.

Start-up suggestion: Bottom-of-the-range Silva compass.

Item Nos 3 and 4: left boot and right boot

Back in the Old West, you had to tame your horse and break it to your will over months of suffering (especially for the horse). And as rugged outdoor types, the same used to be true of our boots. Only involving blisters rather than broken legs. I once had some, from the shop that supplied the early Everest expeditions. They came with a small piece of sandpaper for when the nails started to come through into your foot.

Sometime in the 1960s, a wise chap called Chris Brasher started wondering why his running shoes were seductively comfortable, at least for the first six or seven hours, so why did hill boots have to be a pain? And for that matter, did they really need to be so damned heavy? Thanks to Sir Chris, the boots of today – of whatever brand – will by default be lightweight, comfortable and blister-free.

Best brand? The one that fits your feet. Head to one of the larger outdoor stores, because it will stock lots of different

brands in lots of different shapes. Also, because it'll be on more than one floor, and you can try your boots up and down the stairs.

Fabric boots or leather? Fabric ones will be lighter, and cheaper, and more comfortable. Leather ones will last longer and will keep your feet fairly dry even after the Gore-Tex lining's been pierced by a tiny piece of gravel.

> **Start-up suggestion: Fabric boots from a proper outdoor shop – whichever brand feels comfortable.**

Item No. 5: waterproof jacket

There's no such thing as a waterproof jacket. Well, there is: it's a bin liner with two holes in it for the arms. But your body itself produces dampness, about half a litre a day. And if you're wearing a binbag, all of that half litre ends up still inside it with you.

So a jacket has to not only keep the outside water out; it also has to not keep the inside water in. It needs to be breathable.

A really expensive jacket will be pretty good at being both breathable

LEFT Well-equipped walkers heading into some dirty weather on Crib y Ddysgl, Snowdon.

make the rainwater outside bead into little droplets and drop off.

Even on a very cheap jacket, the silicone coating works really well the first time you wear it. Then, after that, less and less well. You can refresh it by washing it and then recoating the coat with its silicone coating. The washing must not be with detergent, which damages the semi-permeable membrane, but with soap or a specialised technical washing powder. The waterproofing can be sprayed on or washed in in your washing machine. This is quite expensive. But a lot cheaper than buying a new jacket every year.

In the olden days, way back in the 1970s, walking jackets came right down to the tops of your thighs. You could wear shorts underneath and the water would just drip past on to your bare legs. Nowadays, the manufacturers think we might want to suddenly start running, or jump on a bike, or clamber up the rockface. Or else they think we think we want to look like someone who does those things and not just a boring old walker. So the jackets all end at waist level. This is a pity, as it means you may need some waterproof trousers, which involve struggling your legs into them whenever it starts to rain.

and waterproof. It will have several layers, so will be a bit hotter, heavier and more expensive than you want.

A bottom-of-the-range jacket will be less effective, but still effective enough to keep you dry through the first hour or so of the rainstorm, and still alive through the next eight or ten. It'll be nice and light. It won't be terribly robust. And it may make an annoying rustling sound when it's windy.

Jackets work two ways. There's some sort of permeable membrane to let the condensation out – that could be expensive Gore-Tex, or it could be cheaper polyurethane-coated nylon. And then there's a silicone coating, to

Start-up suggestion: Second cheapest in the shop – just so long as you like the colour.

Item No. 6: rucksack

Finally, you need some sort of bag to put the waterproof jacket in whenever it's too warm to wear it, along with the other items you'll need on any walk more serious than a dog-stroll. Some food, some water, a woolly hat or sunhat or both, sunscreen and gloves – and yes, on hilltops it's quite possible to use all four of these on the same day, though nobody has yet designed the combined sunhat-balaclava for those icy-shiny perfect winter days. Small first aid kit.

Leaving aside the embarrassment factor of the Barbie branding, the rucksack your daughter carries her schoolbooks in will do the job just fine. Of course it won't keep the rain out. Once you're taking this hill business more seriously, you'll upgrade to something stouter, with the logo of some leading outdoor brand, and made in durable nylon.

And do you know what? That won't keep the rain out either. Well, it'll keep it out for a while, but not all afternoon. Truly waterproof boots are obviously a bit tricky, but you'd think it'd be easier to make a waterproof bag.

Not easy enough, it seems.

The answer is a plastic bag inside the rucksack. If you want one with outdoor-shop branding, it's called a rucksack liner. Other sorts are referred to as the Bag For (Outdoor) Life.

> **Start-up suggestion:** Your daughter's school rucksack, if she'll lend it to you, and a plastic bag inside to keep things dry.

Other stuff to stuff in the sack

FOOD The important thing about food, said a wise man on the 1953 Everest expedition: the one, important, thing about food is that there should be some. Scientifically formulated energy bars crafted from all-organic ingredients really are just as good as the traditional honey sandwich or even the confectionery bar made of cheap chocolate and sticky sugar paste and named after a well-known planet. (Other nutritionally suspect sugared snacks are available.)

WATER 1 litre is about right for a full day's walking – more if it's during a heatwave. Dehydration's an insidious beast, your blood thickens up and can't get through to your muscles quick enough. The most obvious symptom is tired legs going uphill; and this is quite a common symptom anyway. But the blood's also not getting to your brain, resulting in bad decision making and swearing at your zips and even your walking companions.

There is a possibility that drinking from mountain streams could mean you ingest infectious bacteria such as *Giardia*. I'm not aware of anyone actually catching these infections in the UK in open hill country. I avoid streams below busy footpaths or any human habitations. Otherwise, I've been drinking from mountain streams all my life. That's my choice though, so do use sterilisation methods if you prefer to or are especially vulnerable (children, pregnant women, those with

health conditions).

SPARE CLOTHES The top of a hill is one layer of clothing colder than the bottom, and may be two layers colder, not to mention a layer wetter. A cheap lightweight waterproof also provides very useful protection against cold winds.

HEADTORCH This becomes important on short winter days when you go a bit too far and get benighted. Two good things to check are the time of sunset and whether the torch is still working. I prefer one that's not too bright, to preserve my night vision.

FIRST AID KIT My one contains a wound bandage (never used), ibuprofen, petroleum jelly for chafing, and some specialised sticking plasters for blisters.

MISCELLANEOUS Back-up battery for the phone, spare battery for the torch, spare battery for the camera, spare bootlace, midge repellent, sunscreen, credit card, car keys. Mostly I manage to forget at least one of these essential items.

Things to ask for for Christmas (maybe)

WATERPROOF TROUSERS Once there were no such things as waterproof trousers. When it rained, our trousers got wet and when it stopped raining they dried out again. Now we have waterproofs, though it's surprising how often you don't get around to putting them on until after your legs have already been rained on.

Inside the waterproofs, your legs gradually get damp with condensation, and once they're damp they start to get smelly. This is still nicer than not having them on at all, but it does make it worth taking them off again at some point. Waterproofs for walkers are designed so you can put them on without taking your boots off. Even so, it's still a struggle.

SOME REALLY SNUGGLY SOCKS You know how you get given ever so many socks. Well, when they're hiking socks, that particular life problem is safely solved. Because you can't have too many nice, new, expensive sort of socks. Call me a fusspot, but I hand wash mine in proper soap then finish with conditioner. And do wash them rather often, for the sake of your feet. You wouldn't wrap any other part of your body in a poultice of stinky bacteria, would you?

WALKING POLES These make you feel a bit of a twit, especially when you're using two of them. Plus they leave you looking for a third hand to hold the map and a fourth one for the compass and camera.

ABOVE On steep, rough ground, poles can be useful. Ben Vane, Loch Lomond.

I bought my walking poles at the age of 57, when I was going to walk the John Muir Trail, because the John Muir Trail is very long and makes you carry seven or eight days of food through the mountains of California. I was walking with my son, and I thought the walking poles would help me to keep up and keep going. They were also useful for tapping against trees to make sure the bears knew we were coming. The poles

ABOVE A snowy day on the Grey Corries.

LEFT Measuring pole length settings with fingers and thumbs means you can adjust them without stopping to look at the little numbers.

worked. I kept up with Tom, and also we didn't see any bears.

Walking poles are useful if your knees hurt when going downhill, or when you're carrying a heavy load, or when you're going uphill and want to go a bit faster by getting your arms tired out as well as your legs. They're very useful when balancing across a stream. And yes, two poles are more than twice as useful as one of them.

However, human beings are perfectly capable of walking without any retractable aluminium aids. We've been doing it for nearly 2 million years now. And, of course, that clicky clicky noise: they do make you feel a bit of a twit, don't they?

The wrist loops reduce the effort when going uphill. The rest of the time, I take them off. If you fall over, the wrist loop can sprain or even dislocate your thumb. And if you fall over with the point jammed between the stones, the wrist loop grabs your wrist and pulls you away in a direction you don't want to go.

All this is starting to sound like a lot of stuff. The various items will make you a bit more comfortable. As your walks get more serious, some of them will be needed for your safety. And you've already got a plastic water bottle in your recycling bin.

> But for starting off, just those six. A map. A compass. Two boots. One waterproof jacket. And a sack to put them in.

Ronald's rucksack

Here, I'm going to describe the kit actually carried by a real-life hillwalker (me) on the Grey Corries ridge east of Ben Nevis. This was a snowy day in early May, but one with little wind and an encouraging weather forecast.

1 My very early **bivvy bag**, 280g (10oz) of fairly breathable green nylon, from Kathmandu Trekking, a pioneer company that consisted of a man called Julian Miles in a shed with a sewing machine. Now in honourable retirement as an emergency survival bag.

2 Camp Jolly **ice axe** in fairly lightweight aluminium. This replaced a classic axe in stout ash wood and steel weighing over 1kg (2.2lb). It now has a pleasingly battered look and won't ever be replaced.

3 Classic **crampons** by Salewa, a lifetime old. Heavy and strappy by today's standards. Supremely flexible: I've worn them under running shoes. And they took me up the Mittellegi Ridge of the Eiger so how can I abandon them now?

4 A **tripod** should be lightweight, inexpensive and compact but also sturdy and stable. This one has the first three virtues – which are the ones I need for taking pics of myself with the remote timer. I used it to take this photo and it also appears in it by digital trickery.

5 We're not supposed to wear jeans on the hills. But this is what the crampons wear – a **crampon bag** made from an old trouser leg.

6 In my fellrunning days, this would have been a bumbag. As a walker, I'm allowed to call it a 'waist pouch'. Quick access to gloves, hat, map, compass, snack bars and specs. OMM brand (Original Mountain Marathon) for nostalgic reasons.

7 **Map.** There are parts of the Highlands that Harvey maps don't cover but the Grey Corries isn't one of them so the map is a Harvey one.

8 **Fleece gloves.** From a little shop in Kinlochewe – still Scotland's top mountain resort in my book.

9 **Granola bar** – the Co-op only had the variety pack and my wife likes the maple syrup ones so this is the ginger flavour. And an Aldi Titan bar, which is a sort of Mars bar but with an intriguingly different taste – it's good to vary the diet.

10 Cheese and Marmite inside **wholemeal bread** I make myself in the woodstove. Plus more Mars bars. Food bag from Patties, Dumfries' now defunct outdoor store.

11 My **navigation system.** I have a phone app, and I do use it now and then. Otherwise, I tap into the natural power of the Earth's magnetism, for £17 from Silva.

12 **Waterproof trousers.** Folding them so's to display the brand name also shows the recently applied duct tape – no blame to Berghaus, they're five years old and had a bust-up with a barbed wire fence.

13 **Mobile phone**. Wrapped up in plastic and stuffed inside the stuffsack. (These days I keep it more accessible in case I want to do some lazy navigation on it.)

14 **Stuffsack**. I don't usually sport camo gear but it was a present from Julian Miles, my early bivvy bag supplier. And if war does break out, my spare fleece will be well hidden from the enemy.

15 Spare layer – **fleece shirt**, Graham Tiso own-brand. Good enough for Graham (who climbed the hard side of Everest with Dougal Haston and Hamish MacInnes) is good enough for me.

16 **Trekking poles**, carbon fibre, from Alpkit. I'm taking them to the actual Alps this summer, after which if they're worn out I'll get some more just the same.

17 **Camera case**, Jessops own-brand, with spare battery, SD card, polar filter and lens cloth. Camera – not in the picture because it's taking it – bottom of the range Nikon SLR, second-hand (£200 on eBay). I don't spend more on a camera because I like to be able to bash it about. But you don't need 1kg (2.2lb) of camera these days to take decent digital pics, so my current one's a Sony Alpha A6000 compact camera but with 24mm sensor, £400 reconditioned.

18 **Water bottle**, 99p including its first fill-up of sparkling tonic water. Lightweight, non-leak and transparent for fullness/emptiness viewing. Why pay more when this represents perfection in water bottle design.

19 **First aid kit and torch**, in the detachable pocket from an old 'Dougal Haston' rucksack (I'm a sucker for old-time climber branding). Torch is 3-LED, minimum brightness for map reading, otherwise I keep it switched off for night vision and moonlight. Carried even at midsummer as I may well want to stay high for sunset.

20 **Rucksack**, Lowe Alpine Yocton 35 litre. Outdoor writers don't get much money but we do have scrounging opportunities. Being (you might have noticed?) deeply disinterested in gear, I'm not a convincing scrounger. However, this was a gift from *Trail* magazine, as the 30-year-old Karrimor model looked scruffy in the photos I had taken.

21 **Sunspecs**. Stylish, huh? Picked them up in Langstrath. No, Langstrath doesn't have a shop – when I say picked them up, I mean if you dropped them tell me the year it was and I'll send them back.

22 **Breathable jacket** from The North Face. It's a good one, as its pockets are also my office.

23 **Fleece**, from a 'High Street Hillwear-type' shop. Very cheap, not very good.

24 **Hat**. Christmas present (hence the colour) from my mother-in-law. Thanks, Renate!

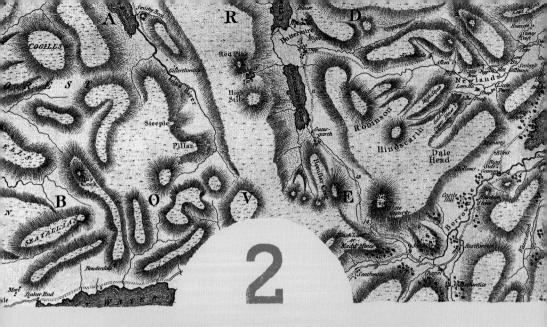

2

UNDERSTANDING MAPS

The shape of Schiehallion

In the year 1774, Nevil Maskelyne, the Astronomer Royal, worked out how to weigh the world. You do it using a plumb line, with a very large mountain as a counterweight.

The mountain they chose was Schiehallion, above Loch Tummel, because of its nice symmetrical shape. They built two small observatories,

halfway up each side of the hill. They pointed telescopes straight up the plumb lines and used the stars to work out how much the two angles diverged. That came out at 0.015 degrees. This meant that planet Earth weighed in at around 5 million trillion Schiehallions.

That was the easy bit. Next, they needed to work out the weight of Schiehallion, which meant measuring

ABOVE A fairly unhelpful map of the Buttermere fells from 1774, the year that Nevil Maskelyne was coming up with contour lines, © Carlisle Library.

ABOVE Admiring Schiehallion's symmetrical shape.

its shape and size. It would take two years of surveying and two more of calculations. As a starting point, they needed a way of recording hill shapes that actually worked. And so it was that Nevil Maskelyne invented the contour line.

Contour lines

Since 1774, reading a map has mainly been about reading the contours.

Once you've learned how to do that, the hill and valley shapes can leap from the map straight into your mind, in the same way the words on this page do without you needing to go, 'That's an A and that's an S, oh, Ronald's

trying to tell us about an astronomer.'

However, the basic shapes of the hills are a whole lot less than the 170,000 words of the English language. We'll start with this exotic tropical island. And the starter map, which is just its outline with a couple of spot heights marked on (see Island 1, below).

ABOVE Island 1: no contours.

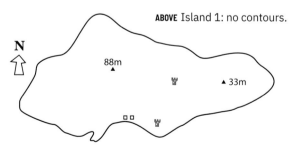

N

88m ▲

▲ 33m

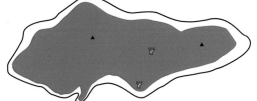

ABOVE Island 2: one contour.

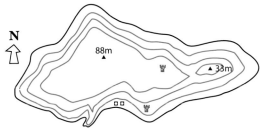

ABOVE Island 3: three contours.

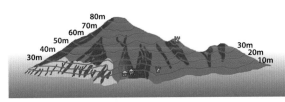

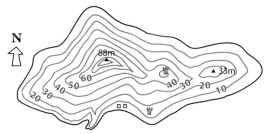

ABOVE Island 4: all contours.

Now we'll imagine some global warming, and the sea level rises by 10m (Island 2). The island shrinks: not by a lot at the cliffy western end, rather more over in the east. The houses in the bay have been lost, and the lower of the two castles is now standing on the seashore.

And we'll mark the new shoreline (in red) on the same map as the original one.

We continue the process. After three sea level rises (Island 3), the hill at the eastern end becomes a separate island. And as before, we mark up each of these shorelines on the original island map.

We'll keep going until the sea rises above 80m and the tip of the left-hand hill vanishes under the water (Island 4). The sea recedes again, and the various tide marks are inscribed on the landscape. Add some numbers to make it easier to work out that the upper castle stands about 52m above the sea.

The third line up, the 30m contour, connects all the points that are exactly that height above sea level. If you walked along it, you'd pass all around the island while staying at exactly the same level.

Now we can start working out some of the main features. A set of little rings one inside the other are marking a summit: there are three summits here, including the one with the upper castle on it. Between that castle and the small eastern hill, there's a white space of a special sort. It has two V-shaped contours leading away from it to the left and right, and two U-shaped ones to the north and south. This marks a saddle point, or col. Depending which way you're walking, this is either the low point on the ridge between the two summits, or the high pass between the southern shoreline and the northern one.

On the steep ground, to the west of the island, the contours are close together; where it's gentler, on the eastern slope, they're farther apart. Where it's flat, on top of the eastern hill, there are no contour lines at all. And at the south-west shore, where the cliffs are, the contours are almost on top of each other.

Summits and saddle points

Now for some real mapping of a real place: Great Gable above Wasdale Head. This is the Harvey British Mountain Map at 1:40,000 scale: 1cm on the map represents 40,000cm or 400m on the ground. (In Imperial units, that's 1 inch representing 5 furlong, 11 yards, 4 inches: one reason why, as you get used to using maps, you may start thinking in kilometres!) This 1:40,000 scale is large enough to give good, useful detail, but small enough to have the whole of the Lake District on a single large map. As on all walkers' maps, the grid squares drawn over it are 1km (0.6 miles) across.

As on all the Harvey maps, the interval between contour lines is 15m of height. It's an odd distance but it makes the contour lines easier to read. Higher ground is coloured in browns

BELOW Great Gable area, © Harvey British Mountain Map.

ABOVE Kirk Fell (left) and Great Gable, seen from the bottom-left corner of the map section.

and greys: most of this bit of map is higher ground.

You can pick out the closed-circle contours around various named summits and spot a fiercely steep slope on the south side of Great Gable, with some gentler ones north of Green Gable. There's flat ground down at Wasdale Head. The plateau is almost flat across the two summits of Kirk Fell: the top of Great Gable is much sharper. A wide, near-flat ridgeline runs north-east to the minor hump of Base Brown.

When it comes to saddle points, there's a major pass at Beck Head, west of Great

Gable, and another one above Stone Cove, between the two Gables. Less significant cols are between Base Brown and Green Gable, and between the two flat summits of Kirk Fell.

CENTRE RIGHT Pointy peak: Sgurr Choinnich Mor, Grey Corries.

RIGHT Saddle, or col: Mickledore, with Scafell beyond, Eskdale down left, Wasdale down right.

Re-entrants and spurs

Just to the west of Wasdale Head, Yewbarrow is shown here on the Ordnance Survey's Landranger map at 1:50,000 – a slightly smaller scale than the Harvey British Mountain Map, and with slightly less detail. The contours are at 10m intervals.

Yewbarrow itself is a near-level ridgeline, over 1km (0.6 miles) long, with formidable steep sides on both west and east. If you look closely at the index contours – the thicker ones at 300m, 350m, and so on – you'll see that on both these slopes, some of the thinner ones in between have been left out. Such missing contour lines on the Landranger map indicate really steep ground, awkward or impossible for walking, especially in descent.

There are just two general hill shapes still to identify, both of them marked by the contours.

Above the lakeside car park, there are V-shape contours, one above the other, up through the rocky feature named as Bell Rib.

If the sea level rose to one of those V-shapes, you'd be standing on the tip of a pointed peninsula sticking out into the sea. Such V-shapes, one above the other, indicate a spur line: a descending corner, like the corner of a hipped roof.

Immediately to the left, or west, there's another set of V-contours,

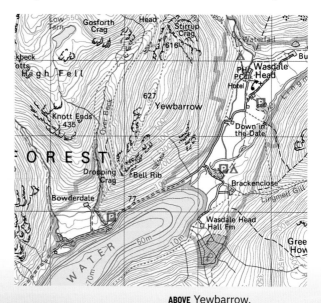

ABOVE Yewbarrow.

BELOW Yewbarrow with Bowderdale Farm, seen from the south west. The spurline of Bell Rib runs down between shadow and sunlight.

underneath the name of Over Beck. But this time, the points of the Vs are running uphill rather than down. This marks a re-entrant, which is the geography-type name for a narrow, descending valley. You can tell that these Vs are a descending re-entrant, rather than an ascending spur line, in two ways. At the re-entrant, the points of the Vs have a stream in them; and if you follow them in the direction they open towards, south in this case, you get down to the valley or indeed the lake.

Meanwhile, to the west of Over Beck, there's the less clearly defined spur line of Knott Ends. And this bit of map has just a single saddle point or col for us to try to find.

The first time you meet terms such as summits and saddles, ridges, spurs and re-entrants, they can be pretty perplexing. But if you keep looking at maps, with practice you should start to read the hill shapes without even thinking about them, in the same way you read words out of a book.

Different sorts of mapping

The Ordnance Survey have mapped the whole of Britain, to a very high standard, at the 1:50,000 scale (Landranger maps) for walkers. As well as that, for fussy walkers who want a higher level of detail, they've mapped it again at the larger 1:25,000 scale (Explorer maps). On top of that, the main hillwalking areas have been mapped, to a very high standard, by Harvey; again, at two different scales.

If you want to explore wild, unmapped country, sorry! The UK is the wrong place to be.

Ordnance Survey Landranger (1:50,000)

Landranger is the standard mapping familiar to most walkers and found on all paid-for mapping apps. For planning out routes it is first class. For navigation on the hill or moors

BELOW Great Gable area, Ordnance Survey Landranger.

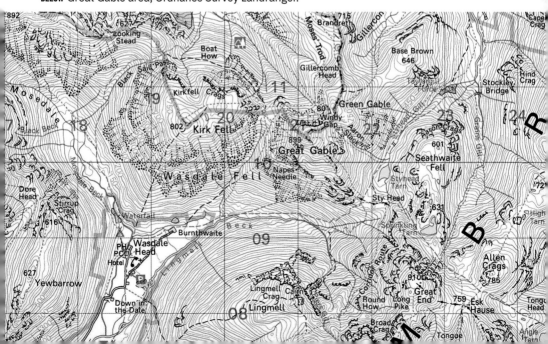

it is also good; but for exploration of craggy country off the paths you'll need more detail. In Northern Ireland, the equivalent map is the 1:50,000 Discoverer from Ordnance Survey of Northern Ireland (OSNI).

Ordnance Survey Explorer (1:25,000)

For exploration of craggy country off the paths, this is the level of detail that you need. The contour line accuracy is excellent – mostly. On the really

serious sort of ground, where you need it most, the rather faint brown lines are obscured by 'craggy ground' markings. As a spectacles-wearer, I also find this paper map difficult to read. On the smartphone, tiny text and faint little contour lines can be blown up to a more readable size.

An added advantage of this scale

BELOW Great Gable area, Ordnance Survey Explorer.

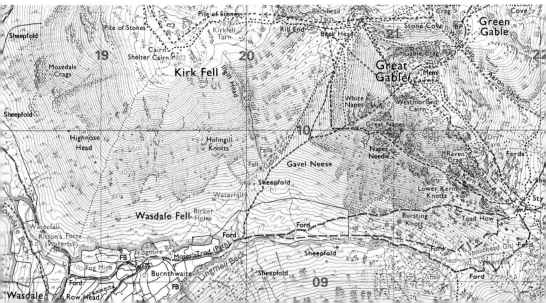

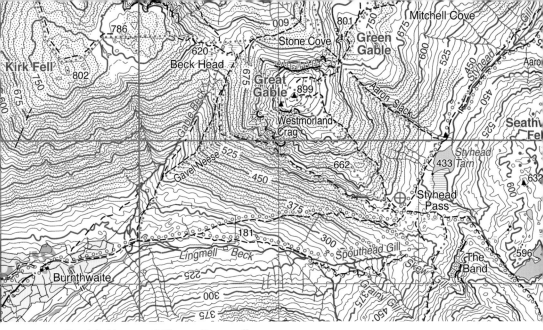

ABOVE Great Gable area, © Harvey Superwalker.

is the marking of field edges – walls and fences – across the lowlands. This is useful when you're tracing invisible field paths.

So, this is an excellent map. It's only on the most seriously craggy and demanding ground that it falls down; to avoid doing the same, I use the Harvey Superwalker on the mountains of Torridon, Glen Coe and, especially, on the Black Cuillin of Skye.

Harvey Superwalker (1:25,000)

In contrast to the massive 250-year-old organisation that is the Ordnance Survey, Harvey is a small group of hillwalkers and orienteers in Doune, Perthshire. Their maps, made with walkers in mind, are easier to read than the OS ones – on rocky ground, they switch the contours from brown to grey instead of covering them up with scratchy crag markings. Unlike the OS ones, they are printed on tough, waterproof plastic.

Against that, OS is the mapping that

most of us are familiar with, and some dislike Harvey's 15m contour interval, which makes it trickier to count your way up the hillside. They are also more expensive. They cover all the UK's main hilly bits, but not the lower ground in between.

An extract from a Harvey British Mountain Map (1:40,000) appears earlier in this chapter. It outpaces the OS on clarity of contours and by being printed on near-indestructible plastic. They've also done strip maps for the best of the long-distance paths, mostly at 1:40,000 scale.

OpenStreetMap

This mapping isn't meant to be printed out on paper: it's for digital use. The contour detail is weak, although it has hill shading to help us grasp the basic shapes. Paths and places are accurate and useful, and it's available free of charge. But I'd want something more detailed for actual navigation.

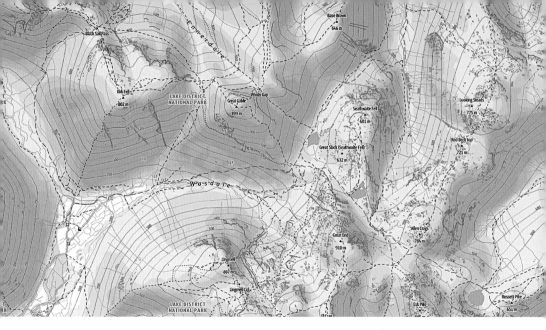

Best maps:
- **Established paths and well-used routes: OS Landranger or Harvey British Mountain Map.**
- **More difficult and challenging mountain ground; untrodden field paths: OS Explorer or Harvey Superwalker.**
- **Seriously craggy mountains in Scotland: Harvey Superwalker.**
- **Long-distance paths: Harvey Trail Map.**

BELOW When is a path not a path? Plenty of people take their phones up Swirral Edge, so it's a 'path' on OpenStreetMap.

Means and ways: path markings on maps

Paths are marked on maps in various different ways. Some of them also exist in real life. But there are some that don't.

Black-dashed path lines

On Landranger maps, a dashed black line marks a path. However, the Ordnance Survey has been at it since 1801, and some of those black-dashed paths are there for historical reasons. The one down the south-west spur of Lingmell (on the map section above)

by the local council. They *do not* necessarily involve any visible, or even walkable, route on the ground.

In the uplands, right-of-way lines should be considered merely as suggestions. Looking at Great Gable on the map extracts above, the right-of-way down the north-west spur is an actual, usable path. The one slanting down the western face is a steep and unpleasant stonefield. And the one on the White Napes actually goes over a cliff.

In the lowlands, among the fields and hedges, the right-of-way lines are more useful. Although there may be no visible path, the right of way means there will be a possible one. The stiles and footbridges will be where you need them, and there may even be some waymark arrows. Also, in the low

is, in real life, invisible in its upper sections. On Explorer maps, the little dashed lines for paths come in two levels of intensity. The very faint ones *possibly* exist on the ground: the rather darker ones *probably* do.

Harvey maps derive their path lines not from ancient history but aerial photography. Their dashed-line paths do exist and are there when you want to walk them.

Paths marked on OpenStreetMap are generated by people walking around with their mobile phones switched on. This means they are reliable guides to where people actually walk, and OpenStreetMap picks up paths not marked on other maps. Sometimes these open source-only paths can be rather wild, rugged and untamed.

Rights of way

Within England and Wales, walkers' maps have other sorts of path lines in various colours: pink on Landranger maps, green on Explorer maps, red on Harvey maps. These mark rights-of-way, legally defined on maps held

BELOW This effective, ranger-approved gate latch suggests we're on a public right of way.

ground of England and Wales, those rights-of-way lines are the only routes you're allowed to go on.

Maps in Scotland and Northern Ireland don't show rights of way.

Access and rights to roam

In Scotland, there's a legal right to roam in open country almost anywhere – the main exceptions being land immediately around houses and fields of growing crops. These rights must be exercised responsibly. The details of what 'responsibly' means are in the Scottish Access Code, which can be found online (www.outdooraccess-scotland.scot). It may be summarised as behaving with respect and consideration for other hill-goers, land managers and the environment.

The Scottish Access Code includes bikes and horses, and unobtrusive wild camping; though that wild camping right has been removed on valley floors in the Lomond and The Trossachs National Park because of persistent littering and open fires.

In England and Wales, your legal rights are more complicated. There's a 'right to roam' on most upland open country, established by the Countryside and Rights of Way Act of 2000 (the CRoW Act). These areas, known as CRoW access land, are marked on Explorer maps. On Harvey maps, 'enclosed' land is shaded in yellowish tints. The un-tinted ground more or less matches the CRoW access land.

These access rights do not include bikes, horses or wild camping. On most open upland country south of the Scottish border, unobtrusive wild camping is tolerated. But nowhere is it a legal right.

Away from the open access areas, down among the fields and houses, the rights of way come in two different flavours. Public footpaths are pink dots on Landranger maps, red ones on Harvey maps, and short green dashes on Explorer maps. These are open only to walkers and mobility scooters. (As I've said, they may not actually be 'paths' in the normal sense of the word.) Bridleways are pink dashes on Landranger maps, long green dashes on Explorer maps, and little red rings on Harvey maps. As the name suggests, these are also open to horse riders. And in this context, a bike counts as a horse – yes, even if it's a high-speed artificially assisted ebike.

On higher ground, bikes and horses don't have walker-type access to the access land; but they are allowed to go on the bridleways. So if a mountain bike whizzes past you on a public footpath, you're allowed to scowl at it and tut-tut under your breath.

Northern Ireland combines these two systems. There are no rights-of-way marked on the maps; and there's no right to roam either.

Oh, and that Yewbarrow map, a couple of pages back? If you didn't spot it, the single saddle point is on the high ridgeline, between the two tops of Yewbarrow itself.

3

CHOOSING THE RIGHT ROUTE

There are two basic techniques for deciding on a route to be walked along. The quick one was used by Bill Bryson in choosing to do the 3,500km (2,200 mile) Appalachian Trail.

'Looks neat! Let's do it!'

This strategy can lead to interesting days in the hills, even if it didn't work out that well for Bryson: he only completed a third of the thing. But when I'm taking other people on a walk – other people who, if they get wet or hungry or tired, are going to think it's my fault – I go about it the slow, thoughtful way. Sometimes I'll even spend more time plotting and planning a walk than it ends up taking to walk it. But when it works, when the eye for the map combines with a bit of research on the bookshelf or the internet, and the weather turns out OK, not only do I end up feeling quietly chuffed at my own skill and judgement, but companions may also be quite impressed as well.

ABOVE Consulting Wainwright on Bow Fell, Lake District. Scafell Pike on the skyline.

MILES OR METRIC?

The UK formally adopted the Metric system in 1965. You'd never guess, would you? Most of us still think in miles, and I've included mile distances all through this book. But when you get seriously sporty about it all, it gets more convenient to start thinking in metres: for one thing, the map has those 1km squares inscribed all over it.

As walkers, we necessarily use our feet. But the UK's maps stopped using them back in 1974. Given that I'm a bivvybag user and former fellrunner, I'm not discouraged by perverse and awkward ways of doing things. Even so, I gave up altitudes in feet about 50 years ago.

In case you're a serious feet fetishist – or perhaps a person from the US, or a traveller in the US who's using an American map: here's the useful rough conversion.

From feet to metres: *multiply* by 3 (NB, not divide) and then knock off the last digit.

1,000ft x 3 = 3,000, goes to 300m.

3,000ft (Munro height) x 3 = 9,000, goes to 900m. The actual figure is 914.4m.

From metres to feet: *divide* by 3 (NB, not multiply!) and then add a zero.

1,000m ÷ 3 = 330 (approx), goes to 3,300ft.

Low-level routes

The first question is: where are the usable paths?

England and Wales

In England and Wales, this isn't too difficult to answer. In the low country, the only routes you're allowed on are the rights of way, the dotted 'public footpaths' and dashed 'bridleways' marked on the maps. And as well as being permitted, these will also be possible. The necessary stiles and footbridges will almost invariably exist. There may be waymark posts and little arrows, and there really ought to be a small signpost where you leave the public road.

If you choose a right of way line that's also an attractive walk to walk on, then others will have chosen it before you. There will be a trodden way, a visible path to guide you. If you choose a line that leads from nowhere in particular to nothing much, by a way that's boggy and boring – well, the stile will be there, but you might have trouble finding it inside the head-high bed of nettles.

Here and there, there will also be (on Explorer maps) the brown-edged 'open access' areas of moorland, common land and unenclosed pasture, where you can go where you like. Actual paths marked on maps (grey dashed lines) will be the best guide here.

RIGHT A core path that's working its way up towards being a Great Trail: coast path south of Portpatrick, Dumfries & Galloway.

Scotland

Scotland's right of way network is rather different, and rather less useful. The legal rights of way tend to be ancient pony routes and drove roads, historic passes through the middle of the mountains. They aren't marked on maps, and many are disused and overgrown.

On the other hand, Scotland does have its go-anywhere access law. Great in principle, but leaving completely open the question: yes, but where?

The network of low-level 'core paths' established and maintained by local councils replaces, to some extent, England's right-of-way network. However, there are far fewer of them, and they're mainly aimed at local dog walkers. Given the funding constraints on local authorities – basically, no money – the core paths aren't always signed or maintained and may occasionally be impassable.

Each local authority in Scotland maintains a map of its core path network, and their map can be found online (www.nature.scot/enjoying-outdoors/routes-explore/local-path-networks).

Scotland also has its network of 'Great Trails', 28 of them so far. Some of them may not be all that great – I have never had much fun on the interminable towpath of the Great Glen Way. But all of them are walkable routes (www.scotlandsgreattrails.com).

Northern Ireland

A friend who wrote guidebooks for Crete told me one of the things she liked about the island was the maps, because they were really bad. Poor contour detail, confusing cliffs, misleading path lines. (There's a reason for this. When Crete gets invaded, it's helpful if the enemy soldiers fail to find their way around.) But it means that every walk on Crete will be an exploration: every walk that works, a discovery.

Northern Ireland isn't quite like that. The maps are good. But they mark few footpaths, and there is no system of rights of way. This means that for finding walking routes, you'll be relying on guidebooks and on websites, such as the official Walk NI website (www.walkni.com).

On the internet

A huge amount of information about walking routes is now online. Some of

ABOVE Klados beach, Crete. In rugged country with unreliable maps, every walk's an exploration.

it's from tourist boards, local councils and other authoritative sources. Some is from 'open source' sites that gather information from ordinary walkers and aspire to pay for themselves via advertising. Walkhighlands is one such site, which, despite the name, doesn't restrict itself to Scotland.

A route supplied (without payment) by an ordinary walker will usually be walkable. Sometimes it won't be a particularly good walk. Other times, it'll be excellent.

Rather than patronise any particular website, I simply put the place name plus 'walk' into a search engine. For the purpose of this book I just randomly picked Holcombe Rogus 'cos I liked the name … but given the 18 walks that come straight up on the Visorando website, I'm thinking maybe I ought to head down to Holcombe Rogus and have a poke around. It turns out to be on the eastern edge of Exmoor, which has to help.

And in books

A paid-for guidebook from a proper publisher means you get routes that you can be sure are going to work. And if you're following the route descriptions to find the way, those will have been checked over by an editor. But there is this: the people who write the guidebooks, those authors actually find their way with the map and the app.

BELOW Great for research, but for actually finding the way map, app and compass may be more convienient.

MEASURING YOUR ROUTE, AND NAISMITH'S RULE

I used to pre-measure my walks with a map and a piece of stout button thread, then count up the uphill contour lines. Today, a mapping app on your computer screen does the same thing much quicker. Admittedly, it's far less useful when it comes to refixing any stray buttons.

If the site offers 'Snap-to-Path', that tends to give a distance about 10 per cent longer than if it doesn't. But often, what matters is the total amount of ascent. Here, a site that doesn't offer Snap-to-Path can exaggerate the height gain, as the straight-line sections may dive down and up the slope whereas the actual path contours around it.

Back in 1892, the Scottish mountaineer WW Naismith came up with a formula for working out how slow he was going to be. Calculate 3mph, but then add an hour for every 2,000ft of ascent. Meanwhile, don't take anything off for downhill ground. This is an excellent guide – provided you happen to be an extremely tough mountaineer of the late 19th century. For today, we convert into metric, and adapt for our less effective legs:

1 Count 100m of ascent as 0.8km extra (or, if calculating without a calculator, count it as 1km extra)

2 Now calculate time as:

child, mature walker, heavy backpack	3km/h
reasonably fit walker	3.5km/h
strong, fit walker	4km/h
19th-century Scottish mountaineer	5km/h

This is only a rule of thumb (or, perhaps, of big toe). Tussocks or boulderfields will take extra time, as will long, steep descents, especially at the end of the day. Also add time for photography or picnics and even more time for any geological studies.

When working with today's metric maps, it's pretty awkward to carry on thinking in miles and feet. But if you want to accept that challenge, then count every 1,000ft of up as an extra 1.5 miles, and then reckon 2.5 mph for a strong, fit walker. If you're mixing-and-matching, 100m of uphill contour lines counts as ¾ mile.

On longer trips, it's worth calculating the expected Naismith's Rule times at various points along the walk. This gives early warning whether you'll end up missing your bar meal, or even being benighted.

ABOVE In flat country, even the tiniest hill improves the view. Port Hill above the River Dee is just 20m high.

Finding attractive tracks

So, which are the ways that will be enjoyable to walk along?

The six-word answer is: 'variety, views, and no boring bits'. So study the map for the following features:

CLIFFTOPS These could be above the sea, or in limestone country along the tops of the inland cliffs called scars. Obviously exciting, obviously with grand views. But watch out for paths where the ground above the clifftop is itself steep. Such paths are scary and exposed, fun for some but not for everyone and unsuitable for dogs and small children.

BELOW Coast walk: above Blegberry Beach, North Devon.

ABOVE Ancient woodland is always worth walking through. The Undercliffs, Dorset coast.

RIVERSIDES AND LAKESIDES These have the added advantage that you can switch off the map-reading mind and just follow the edge of the water. Seashore, on the other hand, can be rocks and shingle stones, which are awkward to walk on. Even a sandy beach will be tiring if it goes on too long.

ABOVE Duke of Edinburgh walkers on Limerstone Down. A designated Long Distance Path will almost certainly be walkable and may even have waymarks. This one's part of the Worsley Trail, Isle of Wight.

DOWNLAND OR ANY GRASSY HILLTOP, HOWEVER LOW Even one small hill, raising you for a look out over the countryside, can transform an otherwise ordinary walk.

DENES AND COOMBES These tight little enclosed valleys, often with scrubby woodland, are common in some parts of the country – in Scotland they may be named as cleuchs. They may be formed where a stream erodes through a shallow layer of tough rock into softer ones below. They're especially rewarding in a walk that also includes some open hilltop.

Meanwhile, there are some types of terrain that we'd like to stay off of...

MOORLAND While some of us enjoy the bleakness and the wide, wide views of nothing much, most will find them a bit dreary and often soggy underfoot as well.

FIELD STUDIES Rights of way running stile-to-stile across farmland. Tough to navigate, not much to look at, and often occupied by cows.

ROADS Very quiet country roads can be pleasant, especially on higher ground where they have views. And you do get to keep your feet dry.

Mountain ground

Up in the hills, the route-choosing rules are different. Even in England, the rights of way lines are no longer relevant. Some have been drawn by people who've not even been there: occasionally they even wander off over cliffs. The one way the green dotted lines on the map can matter is in marking where there's going to be a gate through a fence or a wall.

BELOW Field studies: footpath through oilseed rape, Northumberland.

ABOVE Ridge walk on Stob Ghabhar above Rannoch Moor.

Anyway, most mountain ground is open access under the right to roam laws. In Scotland, all of it is.

Paths marked on maps are a useful start point: especially if the map's a Harvey one. But above the 600m contour, the vegetation will be low enough that paths aren't that important. What counts now is the contours.

RIDGES When walking on hills, the natural line is the line along the ridge. It's not only the least steep way on to some summits, it also has views down in two different directions. It's exposed to the wind and weather, which means its plant life will be short-clipped and walkable. And

because everybody else is walking up the ridgelines, there's probably a path. Then, once you've got to the top, there's a farther ridgeline leading to the next hilltop along – this is what hillwalking is all about.

HORSESHOE ROUTES Every valley is separated from the next one by the watershed ridgeline. Link these up all the way around, and you have a horseshoe walk along the ridges. There's your walk, all sorted.

RIGHT Horseshoe walk: Barrow on the Coledale circuit, with Skiddaw behind.

ANCIENT PATHS A path slanting up the hill or going up it in gentle zigzags is not a modern path. In the Highlands, it's an old deer-stalkers pony path; in the Lake District, it's a sled path for bringing down the peat, or maybe made by miners. Once identified, these make grassy and well-graded highways on to the hills. Or else, in the intervening centuries, they've faded away altogether.

ACCESS TRACKS Given the easy going above the 600m mark, the tricky bit may be working out how to get up there. In wilder country, away from established paths and car parks, a walk route may be based on a handy Land Rover track up through the awkward lower ground, and then built upwards from there.

CORRIES These are glacier-carved hollows, normally on the east or northern side of a hill, ringed with crag and often with a little lake. Go right in and appreciate the scenery. Enjoy getting out of the wind for a while. Then enjoy the challenge of how to get up out of the corrie again.

CONTOURING PATHS These run along steep hillslopes at the halfway height. Such paths are rare, but worth seeking out. They offer great views, often better than from a flat hilltop, with steep ground dropping below; and are pleasingly non-strenuous compared with going up the hill and down it again. Up in the mountains, a contouring path will often run both above and below crags, while avoiding the busy ridgelines. When you come across one, these can be the best paths of all.

BELOW Contour path: the Screes Path below the crags on Great Gable.

4

ON NOT GETTING LOST

'*To be lost is to be fully present, and to be fully present
is to be capable of being in uncertainty and mystery.*'
REBECCA SOLNIT, *A FIELD GUIDE TO GETTING LOST* (VIKING, 2005)

For about a million years we found our way by our natural sense of direction – and this was tricky, as humans don't actually have a natural sense of direction. After that, for the last few centuries, we've been making our way with a map. Start off knowing where we are; set off in a known direction with the help of the trusty compass; and keep checking the scenery against what we think the map thinks we ought to be seeing.

And then, once we're really lost, there's the interesting business of looking at whatever's around by way of peaks, rivers, forest edges and, if we're clever, the shapes made by the contour lines – and matching that with things we've spotted on the map. Get it right, and we'll be home in time for supper.

This is an intellectual exercise that's extremely satisfying. In fact,

ABOVE Descending from Carn Dearg towards Loch Ossian, Central Highlands. Bad-weather navigating, when you get it right, is extremely satisfying.

you've downloaded the required map and you've got a back-up battery so you're not going to run out of power.

Finding the way with compass and map

But before getting deep into the mysteries of the 31 satellites and atomic clocks, let's tap into something more ancient and also simpler: the natural forcefield of our planet's own magnetic field.

Your compass comes attached to a chunk of plastic with arrows and little numbers. For the time being, the plastic chunk is just something to hold on to so your fingers don't get in the way. The thing you need to know is:

The red end of the needle is north.

it's fun. But it's a former sort of fun. Like cutting steps in the snow with an ice axe or making signals with semaphore – it's not something we need to do any more.

Later on, in Chapter 16, I'll describe some of the map-and-compass techniques for working out where we are and knowing where to go without a phone. It's a satisfying skill, and occasionally it's useful as well.

However, since the start of the 21st century, this isn't something we need to do any more. For the rest of this section I'm going to assume that you have a mobile phone. And

ABOVE Annan Water. Riverside paths mean navigating is relaxing.

RIGHT Moffat Dale: coming out of the cloud to find out whether you're descending into the wrong glen.

Armed with this knowledge, the compass is already hugely useful, just in terms of 'north-west' and 'slightly east of south'. In addition:

→ The phone tells you where you are; you're in the car park at the start of the walk. But it's not so great at saying which way to go, especially when you only just switched it on. Map says, it's north-east. Compass says north-east is that path through the little green gate.

→ You're heading off Scafell Pike towards the Broad Crag col. The cloud's down and it's snowing. You don't really want to take your glove off, take the phone out of its waterproof case, check the phone, wipe the raindrops off the phone, put the phone away again, then do it all again two minutes later.

Just follow the compass down north-east. It's quick, it's easy, you can keep your gloves on, and the compass doesn't mind getting wet even though you and your phone do.

ABOVE A nice clear path can mislead you into putting away the compass, and then take you to somewhere quite unexpected. Below Ben Alder, Central Highlands.

BELOW Descending from Stob Binnein, Balquhidder. Clear conditions and a well-defined hill ridge make for easy navigation.

Don't stand next to the synchrotron

A Himalayan climber told me this one. On a misty mountain, he found his compass was pointing in exactly the wrong direction. Now, we all know that when this happens it's us who's pointing in the wrong direction, not the compass. However, this man worked for the Atomic Energy Authority. He'd recently been standing next to a high-energy atom smasher thingie called a synchrotron. And his compass had indeed got remagnetised the wrong way round.

An MRI scanner will have the same effect. But so, also, can a tablet computer or even a mobile phone – if it's in the same pocket as the compass. Unfortunately it doesn't just go 'red end of the needle is now SOUTH so there...' It just goes lost and wobbly. So, use separate pockets for phone and compass.

There are also magnetic rocks, made of the same magnetite ore as the original Chinese lodestones. Such rocks are black, and rugged, and on the Isle of Skye – also on Ben More in Mull. You're not on the Isle of Skye or Ben More Mull? It's you who's wrong and not the compass.

Finding the way with a mapping app

A phone without a navigation app is like a lunchbox without a sandwich.

What your mapping app is for
ON THE COMPUTER
1 Have the whole country in your computer, searchable by place name, and switchable between different maps with a click. There's a free-to-use map layer based on OpenStreetMap, and then the OS Landranger and Explorer maps with a paid subscription.

BELOW OS Maps, browser shows a route I clicked out using 'Create Route'.

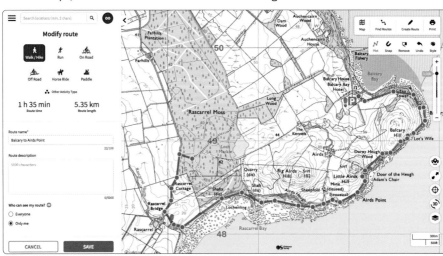

2 A library of existing routes, of variable quality, provided by app users.

3 Click out a route plan of your own: the app will measure the distance and height gain as you go along and may also offer path suggestions.

ON THE SMARTPHONE

1 A tiny piece of map on your phone screen, with your current position marked on to it, and with the same ability to switch between different sorts of mapping.

2 An existing route line of your choice marked on the phone screen, with the option of satnav-type instructions to follow it.

3 A route you've created yourself in advance, similarly set up to follow on the phone screen.

4 A digital compass.

PLANNING OUT YOUR ROUTE: PAPER MAP OR COMPUTER?

A **paper map** shows more of the countryside and is nice to have when consulting with several pals around a table.

A **computer map** doesn't have edges, and switches between different map scales.

Either is fine.

App happy

The best navigation app? The one you already know your way around.

1. Google Maps/Apple Maps

The free app that comes on your phone is excellent for satnav use in your car. It's pretty good for finding your way across Edinburgh – though as it works satnav style, it gets you from the Museum of Scotland to the tram terminal without any experience of actually being in Edinburgh in between.

But: it doesn't have contour lines. And: it won't work if you don't have a phone signal. Most UK hills involve contour lines. And almost none of them involve a mobile phone mast.

2. OpenStreetMap

This is a map layer, rather than an app in itself. It's open source: its information is gathered by people wandering around with their phones on. So it shows paths that aren't on any other map. This makes it very useful – as a map layer. However, its contour detail isn't good enough for it to be one's main route-finding map.

3. Streetmap

The streetmap.co.uk website (browser only, it isn't an app) offers OS Landranger and Explorer mapping for the whole of the UK apart from Northern Ireland. It also has a street map (hence the name) with street names, which is useful in towns. You can search it by place names. You can also determine the postcode, OS grid reference and what3words for any point. And it's free.

Streetmap is a great way of looking at the UK on your computer – especially if you're too mean to pay a map subscription. It doesn't locate you, the user, on to its map; and it doesn't have a phone app.

4. OS Maps

If you live and walk in the UK, then the UK's national mapping agency does everything you need from a UK mapping app. The free version offers what it calls its 'standard' mapping. 'Sub-standard' would be a better name: it's OpenStreetMap with a bit of extra colouring in. Even so, it has better contour lines than Google Maps or Apple Maps.

Otherwise, you pay a yearly subscription for access to OS Landranger and Explorer mapping, on your phone (or phones) and web browser, plus the OSNI maps for Northern Ireland. Along with the maps come all the functions you expect from a decent mapping app: search by place name, show where you are on the map, plan your route on the computer, show that planned route on your phone; plus other stuff you never even thought of, such as lifting your map into a basic sort of 3D viewing, send a little red dot around your route line, or look at the view through your camera and add in the names of the hilltops.

The screenshots here are of the OS Maps app. Other apps will have the same buttons in slightly different places on the screen.

5. Outdooractive

One of those other mapping apps

is called Outdooractive. For about the same subscription level as OS Maps, it offers the same Explorer and Landranger mapping; but being a European company, it offers all of Europe as well. Actually, you get the whole world.

For serious map-lovers it's a bit like football leagues: you get an added level above Premium called Premium Plus. For an additional cost, you get some extra map layers. In the UK, this means Harvey mapping.

As I'm a map-happy sort of guy, I say the more layers the better, especially if one of them is a Harvey map. Also, I'm an outdoor writer, and all the Premium Plus pricing is tax deductible.

At the time of writing, the Hiiker app is the cheapest way to get Harvey maps on to your phone. I haven't used it myself, but it's well reviewed.

Phone for navigation

Before you start using your phone for navigation, you need to take note of two things. First, navigating with your phone is brutal on the battery. If you're also using your phone for taking photos and for keeping track of your WhatsApp messages, then over a full day of walking you'll run out of charge. You'll not only lose your navigation screen, not to mention your WhatsApp feed, but you also won't be able to call for help or rescue.

One solution might be to fire up your phone as infrequently as possible. That way, when you end up lost and down in the wrong valley, you will still have plenty of battery to

ABOVE GPS makes it much easier to find the top end of this ridge of Helvellyn Lower Man.

phone for a taxi. The better alternative is to carry a back-up power pack. They aren't expensive.

Recording your track as you go along is asking the phone to hunt for a GPS reading every 20 paces or so. This is even more brutal on the battery.

On the other hand, switching to airplane mode means your phone isn't currently hunting for a phone signal that isn't there, and this lets the battery last longer. It has the added advantage of cutting you off from your texts and WhatsApp until you get down to the coffee shop. Meanwhile, your GPS signal will still be just fine. Your GPS signal doesn't come from the phone mast, it comes from those 31 American satellites up in the sky.

However, what did just vanish when you switched to airplane mode is your lovely Landranger map. Your mapping, by default, is up in the

Cloud. If you, by contrast, are up in the clouds with no phone signal, you could find yourself with a phone screen as blank as the surroundings.

So you need the relevant mapping saved offline and stored inside your phone in case that happens.

You could download the entire UK at Landranger and Explorer scales. But this would mean the OS could never make any money out of you ever again; meanwhile, you'd use up all your phone's data storage. To protect your phone storage (as well as the OS's own income stream), they only let you download maps into your phone in smallish squares about 40km (25 miles) across.

So while you're still connected to Wi-Fi, find the menu called 'save offline' and download the bits of map you need. To make sure they've arrived, you can switch to airplane mode to cut off the phone signal, switch off the Wi-Fi, and see if the map you need is still in sight. Expand it to full scale to make sure it's all there.

If you've downloaded or saved a specific route, then the bit of map it's on will also get saved offline. So that's useful. And if you forgot, or failed, to 'save offline', then your phone will download the map it needs off the phone signal. Often there will be a phone signal at your walk's start point, so that you can get high on to the hill before finding you forgot to save your mapping offline...

Different mapping apps do things in different ways; but they still do the same things. When you open OS Maps, you'll see a screen like the one shown here. That's unless you were too mean to subscribe to the full maps option: in that case, you'll see a rather less helpful 'Standard' map in shades of olive green.

At the top, there's a search box. Beside it there's a menu button. If you accidentally touch this while the phone's in your pocket, you will be left looking at a sinister black screen with various things you don't want just now. Swipe left to make that go away.

The first of the four buttons on the right has a little red arrow and the letter N: it's pretending to be a teeny-weeny compass. You can orient the phone's map two different ways. You can have north at the top, in which case the little red arrow points upwards all the time – you'll see that I prefer to have north at the top. Or else you can have the map turned round to match the current countryside,

ABOVE OS Maps app on a phone.

in which case that tiny red arrow in its black circle will point to the way north actually is. Touch this button, or sometimes the one below it, to switch from 'north at the top' to 'north where north is in the real world'.

The button below is the really useful one. Touch this, and the map will jump straight to where you actually are. (Or else it won't, if the map hasn't had time to get a fix off the GPS satellites yet.) At that point, an arrow marker will appear on the map itself at your current location. And yes, that's me, standing in the car park at Balcary Bay on the north Solway coast. As you've already worked out, once you've started moving, the point of the arrow shows the direction you're currently moving in.

To make the map bigger or smaller, you pinch in or out, in just the way you expect. As you do this, the map will spontaneously switch to a different scale: Landranger will suddenly replace itself with Explorer. But to shift to a different sort of map – the olive-green 'standard' map, or a satellite view showing the woods and mudflats, you hit the useful little layers button at the bottom.

So what of that third button down? Well, every app wants to be some sort of Social Media, and the map apps are no different. That third button will access all the pre-laid routes lovingly uploaded by the OS Maps 'Community'. My start point at Balcary Bay already has 27 routes starting from it.

ABOVE OS Maps app, following a pre-loaded route.

Following a pre-set route

Now let's suppose you've been browsing through the pre-laid routes generated by other users of this mapping app, and found one you like the look of. Or you may have travelled forward to Chapter 15 and created your own route line in advance.

Once you've travelled to the walk start, and brought the route itself up on the screen, here's what you'll see.

At bottom left is 'download map' (if you haven't yet downloaded the map) or 'remove map' (if you have). Provided that you've still got phone signal, you can download the route and its bit of the map onto your phone. Better still, do that with your Wi-Fi

before you leave home. Now you don't need to worry about losing your phone signal; you can switch to airplane mode to save your battery.

To keep things simple, you just keep an eye on the red 'here I am' marker as you go along. On the screen above, there was a distracting side path and now we've ended up with nothing but water on all sides. The screen shows that, yes indeed, we're slightly north of the desired route line, on that little promontory (see page 74). Heading a short way south-west will get us back on track. Guesswork, or a glance at the compass, will show us south-west.

Route followed!

Or let the phone take control

To make things complicated, you can hit that large, inviting 'start route' button. This accesses all sorts of useful information, none of which you actually want. Spoken instructions as you go along, which you can't hear unless you shut out the world with some headphones. Alerts when you're 10m off the route line because whoever laid it out decided to walk slightly farther up the field. Constant updates on just how slow you're going, and just how many miles are still left in your outing.

In this case, you could be looking at something

like this screenshot. This is you actively following a route using the OutdoorActive app. Almost none of the screen is actually showing you where you are. However, it gives plenty of detail on which way to go.

The big advantage here is that you walk the route looking at the screen rather than the scenery. So next time you walk the same way, it'll still be quite fresh and new. But looking at the landscape and the map has to be better than steering by satnav. Doesn't it?

ABOVE Just off the Southern Upland Way path beside Loch Trool.

LEFT OutdoorActive app: route navigation near Portpatrick, Dumfries & Galloway.

Devouring the hamburger: the rest of the menus

All of which leaves us with the 'menu' or 'hamburger' button (the three little lines) at top left. Touch it to reach the black screen shown.

The first thing to work out here is: how the heck to get back to the map? Because at some point as you walk along, when you really, really need to know where you are, you'll find your finger touched the hamburger and you've been switched into the menu screen.

OK, you're currently sitting in a nice warm room with unfrozen fingers and no rain falling on you from any direction, and it's obvious that you just need to hit 'close' or, alternatively, to swipe left. Or, possibly, right.

This screen also has a button to record your route as you walk along it. You can then retrieve your track later for gloating purposes. You'll also be able to display it on your computer to show your friends the exact point where you ran away sideways because of the bull in the field.

You'll have also spotted that this is the screen where you can download chunks of the map onto your phone, so they'll be there when the phone signal isn't.

RIGHT OS Locate app.

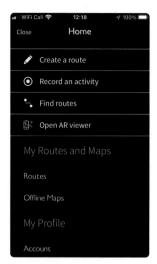

ABOVE OS Maps app menu page.

Other appropriate apps

OS Locate

This free app gives you Ordnance Survey grid reference, accurate to the nearest 100m, and independent of any phone signal. If you don't have a mapping app, you can use this to pinpoint your position on your paper map – just so long as you know how to use the OS grid reference.

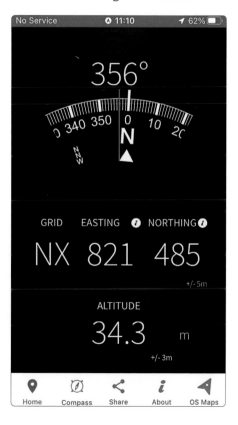

(There's a guide on the edge of your map and in Chapter 16 of this book.) More usefully, Mountain Rescue does know how to use the OS grid reference. If you read this out to them, including the two letters at the beginning, they'll know exactly where you are.

It also includes a digital compass. This gives your direction accurate to a fraction of a degree. However, it quite often gives it to you wrong – especially if you only just switched your phone on, or are in a wooded area, or underneath a crag.

A weather forecast app

BBC, Met Office and that Norwegian one called Yr are all good. Take your pick.

Moon phase

This is handy if you think you might be hiking in the dark. Your weather app will give you sunrise and sunset times.

BAA avalanche forecasts

This is essential if you think you might be hiking in the snow. Less useful if if you are not.

British Red Cross first aid app

This talks you through how to try to deal with a casualty. It's not as good as a training course but a lot better than blind panic. Even finding the right buttons in the app is so much harder when you're dehydrated, cold, tired, anxious and trying to keep your phone dry. Let alone hyperthermia and hypothermia and working out which is which... So this is a good one to dip into in those impatient moments waiting for your friends to get their boots on. You refresh your mind on 'casualty unconscious but breathing' while they get their laces knotted just the way they like them. That's a win all round, I'd say.

BELOW West ridge of Schiehallion. On a misted ridgeline it's easy to find the way up, a bit trickier to come down.

Emergency SMS

It's not an app, but you can register your phone for emergency text messaging at www.emergencysms. net. This will let you reach Mountain Rescue (or other emergency services) by text when there isn't enough signal for a voice call.

ABOVE Paths beside streams make easier navigation. 34th Nottingham (High School) Scout Group. (Used with permission of the Scout Group)

BELOW Heading to Ettrick Pen. Rounded, grassy hills such as the Southern Uplands are great for getting lost on.

On getting lost

Getting lost: it's going to happen. Maybe not right away – maybe not for your first 10 or 20 times on the hills. For those first 10 or 20 times, you've waited for a clear, sunny weather forecast, and you've kept track of where you are, and you've ticked off the stream crossings and the summits and the tricky saddle points. But after the 10th time, or maybe the 20th, you know a thing or two about this maps malarkey. And maybe the weather forecast's got some little grey clouds in it, but you want to go up Great Gable.

Great Gable is great, just like the

ABOVE Woodland paths need careful navigation, especially when they don't match the map. Mabie Forest, Dumfriesshire.

guidebook said it would be. But up at the top of it there's a waft of fluffy white cloud, just like they get up there on Everest. Inside the cloud it's all clammy and romantic, rocks and boulders looming like sleepy trolls, rainwater dripping off all the little overhangs. And it's easy! You just follow your nose past some cairns, and here's the top of Great Gable with its little rocky outcrop and its plaque commemorating the fellwalkers of the First World War.

You're heading for the route down towards Beck Head. So now you turn right, 'cos that's what the map tells you to do. The stony plateau doesn't show any paths; but look, you're passing a cairn. But then you notice another cairn a few metres away on the left. And another one on the right... Great Gable has cairns everywhere, which

is just as helpful as having no cairns at all.

So you go back to the summit and start again, and this time you use the compass to get the correct direction. A few minutes later you're at the corner of the plateau. The stones and rocks are a bit trodden on, so this does look like the right way. And the mapping on your phone thinks so too. But it's rather steep, lots of little head-high crags, and jammed boulders. You work your way downhill, on the rather slippery rocks.

And somehow – it's actually a rule of Nature – the cloud on this side of the hill goes down a lot lower than it did when you were coming up...

Eventually, with greater experience, finding the way on hills gets to be almost instinctive. A couple of decades back, I headed on to the Glyder range

LOST BUT NOT LEAST

When you do get lost, stay calm and do the following:

→ Is there a sheltered spot behind a boulder or a stone wall? Head for it. But don't walk on getting more and more lost while you're looking for it.

→ Don't split up the party to look for the right way down. Just don't do it! Please! Better one group of lost hillwalkers consoling each other than six separate lonely lost hillwalkers.

→ Put on some more clothes, have a drink, have a snack. Cold, dehydrated minds don't think so well.

→ Take a good look at the map and work out where you think you are, and where else you might perhaps be. Then take a quick look at the smartphone to see if you're right. (You probably don't want to take a long, slow look at the phone, not while it's raining like this.)

→ Still can't work out how to continue your planned route? Then what does the map say about the slopes around you. Among the eight possible directions, there's going to be one that gets you down into the valley without any crags or very steep slopes or raging torrents. It might even be a valley that doesn't involve a £70 taxi ride to get back to your youth hostel.

→ Finally, congratulate yourself. You've had an educational experience worth hundreds of pages of guidebook instruction. You've learned how to get lost.

BELOW Even in busy Lakeland, a stony plateau won't show the path. Descending from Great Gable towards Windy Gap.

in Snowdonia (Eryri) on a damp summer day. Even on a dull day, Llyn Idwal is a lovely place. *Llyn* means lake, and this one, half a mile long, is backed on three sides by high, craggy mountains. The rain brings out the patterning of the various volcanic rocks that make the path. At the lake's head, the way zigzags up beside the black, basalt chasm of the Devil's Kitchen.

At the plateau above, another pool of grey water was whipped into little waves by the wind. Here, it's just turn left, and follow the rough path up into the cloud, and soon the weird rock towers mark the summit of Glyder Fawr, the big Glyder. The next bit is a little tricky. The stony plateau doesn't show the path, and the continuing ridgeline is wide and flat. Expecting this, I'd already set the arrow on my compass into the necessary direction, just north of east.

As the ridge dips, it has grass as well as stones, and the path gets clearer. And as it rises again, it's just a matter of heading directly uphill to reach the familiar pile of huge, rounded boulders that's the summit of Glyder Fach, the smaller Glyder.

The next stage, I knew, was going to need a little attention. Getting up a hill is basically a matter of going

LEFT Devil's Kitchen, Cwm Idwal.

BELOW Glyder Fach from Glyder Fawr.

ABOVE Esk Hause, looking towards Scafell Pike. The wide saddle feeds down into three separate valleys. Ending in the wrong one is not uncommon.

uphill. Getting down off it isn't quite so simple. Fortunately, the top of Glyder Fach is a place I've been many times before. I clamber off the rockpile and continue north-east, the compass bearing already set in advance. In less than a minute, the rockpile is lost in the grey murk behind me. A couple of minutes more, and the Cantilever rockpile emerges from the grey mist ahead. The Cantilever is a narrow rock suspended at one end like a diving board. And like a diving board, it usually has three or four people bouncing up and down on the unsuspended end. I pass to its left, following the tops of the steep drops leading down into grey cloud. Cloud that I know is obscuring a fabulous view down on to the A5. And in another couple of minutes, the next familiar landmark: the cluster of splintery rocks that's the top of the Bristly Ridge.

If you want to follow this on the map on page 82, the line of Bristly Ridge is straight down north along the Number 66 grid line.

The rocks of Bristly Ridge descend to the wide and important saddle at the base of the next hill, which is Tryfan. Bristly Ridge is a splendid scrambling route, quite steep and with a few airy moments. The rock is sound and rough, and there are plenty of handholds and footholds. But in rain and wind I wasn't fancying those airy moments. So I headed to the easier way, the wide gully running down beside the ridge on its right-hand side. There's a big, zigzag path, or rather multiple paths, their top marked by a sprawling cairn.

The cairn is slightly down from the top of the slope, and in the mist I passed above it without seeing it. Once I realised this, I turned left, down the slope, to meet the zigzagged path now somewhere below me. At once I found a small sheep trod and followed it down for a while. But the main path down here is a big, eroded one,

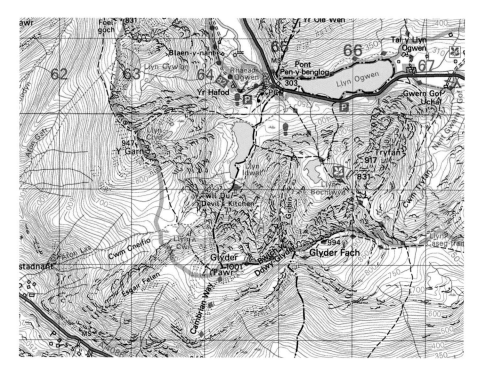

all loose stones and gravel. As I still hadn't found that main path I started slanting left towards it.

The slope was quite steep, but not steep enough to be worrying. The downhill direction was a bit wrong, more north-west than north-east, maybe I needed to head back to the left a bit more. It was raining, and my hands were cold. I really didn't want to get out my map, and my glasses, and put on my glasses, and verify this stuff, which I knew anyway. So I carried on downhill. I still didn't find the big zigzag path.

OK, I could head back up and find the sprawling cairn and start again from there. But I'd been going downhill for quarter of an hour now, and I really didn't want to go back up. I carried on downhill.

I still didn't find the big zigzag path.

This was in the days before GPS mapping on the mobile phone. I did have an early GPS device, which I carried to record eight-digit grid references for the readers of my guidebooks. As a competent map-and-compass man, I certainly didn't need to use the thing for finding my own way with.

I took out my GPS device. I asked it for my current grid reference. I took out my map, and my spectacles, and worked out where the grid reference was at. Just as I had it figured out, the low cloud rose enough to save me the trouble.

Readers paying very close attention may have worked it out already. But it isn't so easy for wet and tired walkers, however competent we believe ourselves to be with our compasses and maps. When I'd passed the instantly recognisable rocks at the top of Bristly Ridge – well – I hadn't. I'd passed some other rocks instead. When I'd failed to see the sprawling cairn at the top of the path because it was just down the slope in the mist – I'd actually failed to see it because it wasn't there at all. I'd turned downhill on the nearer, left-hand side of Bristly Ridge instead of the farther, right-hand side.

It wasn't too serious. I just needed to contour to the right below the foot of Bristly, to the wide saddle I'd been aiming for and Tryfan rising behind it. Not great, for a guidebook writer: but I was the only one who'd ever know. It wasn't as if I'd be writing it down in a book, for all the world to see. I mean, that would be embarrassing, wouldn't it?

BELOW GPS receiver from 1993, Science Museum, London. Today, this magnificent piece of electronics sits inside a tiny corner of your mobile phone.

This is a pretty clear example of getting lost, on a hill, in the mist. It can't do any harm to go a little deeper into the various mistakes made. And it could even do some good in inducing a proper sense of humility in the hillwalker involved, in this case, me. But to spare myself at least a couple of blushes, let's look first at:

A couple of things I did right:

→ I had a picture in my mind of the general layout of the hill. I was aware that the steep slope dropping to my left (north-west) led down to Llyn Bochlwyd and the A5.
→ I had a mental picture of the landmarks I was expecting to pass: the Cantilever, the sprawling cairn, the eroded path below it.

The most obvious things I did wrong:

→ Not stopping to get out the spectacles, wipe them, put them on, and look at the map. This would have shown that a steep slope leading down north-west would be to the left, not to the right, of the Bristly Ridge. If I'd stuck around on the plateau for 15 years or so – then the development of the smartphone mapping app would have shown me exactly where I was. That being, not far enough along.
→ I'd expected to see a sprawling cairn. The sprawling cairn didn't happen. The cairn is there and I just missed it: no, this is not the correct conclusion. If the cairn isn't there, that's almost certainly because the cairn is there, but there isn't here.

Again, the cloud is down on the tops. This time I'm on Lamachan Hill, in the southern part of the Galloway Hills. I've a friend with me, a chap called Ian, and we're heading for Curleywee.

Lamachan is a hill I know very well indeed – I didn't just read the guidebook: I wrote the thing. Coming up from Mulldonoch to its flat summit, you then turn to the left. You head down the gently rounded slope, and in a couple of hundred metres you're on the ridge leading down towards Curleywee, a place that's even nicer than its name. On the way to that ridge, you'll pick up a line of old iron fence posts.

I haven't seen Ian for a year or so, not since that great long-distance race across Wales. As we reach the summit plateau and the ground levels off the chat becomes interesting and lively. We turn left, I check my compass, and we set off down the gentle slope.

After a couple of minutes, we're a bit off the line. Dimly, in the mist, I can make out the ridge crest a little up to our left. I adjust the course accordingly. Somehow, the ridgeline doesn't quite materialise, so I edge around to the left a little more.

After another couple of minutes I know we've failed to find the ridgeline. Well, not we: I'm the guide here, it's me who's failed to find it. I break off the chat and take out the compass. It shows exactly the correct

BELOW Lamachan Hill from Curleywee.

WHO'S WRONG: ME OR MY COMPASS?

➜ Just check the compass. Especially if leaving a summit, just check the compass. And then check it again.

➜ The compass is correct. It's you who's pointing in the wrong direction.

In the absence of any high-energy synchroton to remagnetise your compass, can a compass get it wrong?

If you put a compass in the same pocket as your phone and it got remagnetised, you'll know it's happened. The compass will be pointing aimlessly in no particular direction, rather like the lost person it's trying to guide.

Magnetic gabbro rocks occur on the Cuillin mountains of the Island of Skye (and possibly also on Mull). You can get around this by holding the compass high up away from the rocks and taking three separate readings several metres apart. Magnetic rocks have been reported at various other locations but are almost certainly confused walkers rather than confused compasses.

So, no, it's not the compass. It's me...

direction. No, hang on a mo. Red end of the needle is north and all that, the compass shows exactly the incorrect direction. We should be heading north-east for the next ridgeline, but the compass is pointing south-west.

Has the compass got remagnetised the wrong way round? Given that I'm not a nuclear physicist I haven't been standing next to any high-energy atom-smashing machines. So no, the compass hasn't got remagnetised.

I apologise. Ian is very understanding; he's done the same thing himself. We turn around and head back the way we've just been coming. As we leave the summit for the second time, I keep the compass in my hand, not my pocket.

RIGHT Map and guidebook on Wainwright's Coast to Coast path.

5

LOOKING AFTER THE MOUNTAIN

Hills are good for us and our well-being. But the same thing isn't true the other way round. You don't walk far in the Lake District, Peak District or Snowdonia without seeing that we do a certain amount of harm.

Litter is the easy bit. It's not hard to just not drop the stuff. But here's a tip – instead of the low-level irritation of looking at the litter dropped by other people, you can substitute a warm little glow of self-righteousness. Simply pick up one piece of litter and carry it away for recycling.

When there isn't litter already, people are less likely to leave any of their own. And where there is some, they'll drop more. Along the UK's squalid road verges it'd be completely pointless to pick up just one piece of litter. But over the hill country and moorlands, while roughly one person in 20 may be a litterer, roughly one person in ten is a picker-up of it.

ABOVE Path team descending from Ben Venue, Trossachs.

ABOVE Sphagnum moss.

RIGHT Pitched path above Sty Head on Great Gable.

And one person in ten picking up one item a day means that one item a day is all the litter there is.

What nobody's going to pick up is used tissues and toilet paper. But here's another tip – if you are caught out and find yourself digging that discreet little pit at a decent 30m from the nearest watercourse – instead of bog paper, use the bog itself. Sphagnum moss was used as wound dressings in the First World War and replaces toilet tissue in all the most expensive wellness spas. Or if it doesn't, then the expensive spas are missing a trick.

Path masters

Worn-out footpaths are our other impact. Some old paths in Somerset are worn down metres deep into the countryside. A century ago, the path down Great Gable was 7m wide and said to be visible from outer space, except fortunately there weren't any astronauts up there yet to look down in shock at Sty Head.

Cars and effect

As you look down from Snowdon or the Langdale Pikes, among the woods and meadows sunlight sparkles and gleams – is that a little tarn or lochan? Well, no, it's not. It's a rather large car park. The hills are free; but, on the valley floor below, the roads are clogged up, and the car parks are full. At Pen-y-Pass below Snowdon, or up the Great Langdale valley, during the main summer season you simply won't get in.

One day, Snowdonia and the Lake District will be pedestrianised, with

FOOTPATHS: SIX WAYS WE CAN DO A BIT LESS DAMAGE

1 Avoid walking on the grass edges of a footpath. Walk in the stony middle or leave the path altogether.

2 Is it a path? Is it a stream? Feet plus flowing water are more effective eroders than either on their own. Path engineering is mostly about keeping water off it. So please stay on the zigzags and don't shortcut them. Those shortcut lines make ideal waterways.

3 On rebuilt paths, stone culverts carry away the water. Step over these, as walking around them creates a channel for path water to flow on down the path.

4 It's reasonable, once in a hill day, to clean stones out of one culvert.

5 Don't lift stones out of paths to make into cairns. Most cairns are unnecessary anyway.

6 Just now and then, give some money to path-repair people, such as Fix the Fells in the Lake District (www.fixthefells.co.uk), or Save Mountain Paths in Scotland (savemountainpaths.scot).

BELOW Walking alongside an eroded path is about to create a second eroded path. Carrock Fell, northern Lake District.

ABOVE Borrowdale open-top bus passing Derwent Water.

BELOW Quick culvert cleanout, Lingmoor Fell, Little Langdale.

park-and-ride at the national park boundary and little green shuttle buses shuttling up and down until two hours after sunset. However, it may be a long wait for that little green bus – given that, so far as I know, the only person in Britain actually agitating for this is me. (And while I'm being a bolshie agitator – our national parks are no place for annoying drones buzzing overhead.)

Yes, the hills are free. However, that doesn't include those car parks! Again, there is a way to avoid the annoyance of having to pay up every time you set off on a walk. Just regard it as your contribution to maintaining the footpaths – which is what it gets spent on. And replace that moment of irritation with a glow of generous benefaction.

This is harder to do when what they want is £9 paid entirely in one-pound coins, however.

6

CHILDREN AND/OR DOGS

Children on hills

My Dad planned to enrol me into the Scottish Mountaineering Club, as his own father had once enrolled him. So he kept records of all my early ascents. Which lets me determine that, when I first conquered Pew Tor (320m) on the western edge of Dartmoor, I was a big one year and ten months old.

Pew Tor is a place of magic. It's actually a cluster of little tors, where you can run around and lose sight of your Mummy in no time at all. There are piles of granite, shaped like really big cow pats, and as rough as your Daddy's chin. One of them has a mighty chasm or ravine that you stride right across to reach the highest point. And that high point is a basin, a stone dip where you lie below the rock rim with nothing to see but sky – until you peep over the edge to see if Mummy's still looking for you. And the chasm's

ABOVE Pew Tor.

just as great at ground level, where you stomp along the ravine floor on little crystals fallen from the rock.

But another of the mini-tors goes even better. There's a gap in it, a tunnel, where, if you're little enough, you can creep around the corner and come out on the other side of it.

I was little enough.

Once, on the moorland beside the little leat, the artificial stream running across the hillside, I found a shiny thing, a disc of pale metal, like one of those metal objects they tell you to never, ever pick up because it might explode and kill you. So I picked it up. And it was a yo-yo, a whirly disc toy on a string, not working too well because of the string being so wet.

But there's one subtle detail of Pew Tor that I didn't work out at the time: the distance from roadside to summit. This comes in at just 0.4km (0.25 miles), with 60m of ascent, at an average gradient of 15%.

Small people need small hills. But they also need slightly larger meals... You'd think I'd remember that when taking my own children up their first real hill. But halfway up Helm Crag, daughter aged eight-going-on-nine comes to a stop, exhausted and not having any fun at all.

After a pause, I think to ask what she'd had for breakfast. 'The usual ... half a Weetabix.' Two muesli bars later, and daughter's ready to again confront the stern realities of Helm Crag.

Helm Crag is, indeed, one of the great hills for little people. It's not quite so small as Pew Tor, perhaps, but just as rocky on top. At the Grasmere end, the 'Old Woman Playing the Organ' is a picnic perch that makes

BELOW Children can get tired quite suddenly.

the lake we've come up from seem a long, long way down indeed. All along the ridge there's the jumble that's the top of the eastern landslip. And at the other end, the Howitzer rock, a sweet but serious Grade 1 scramble, with a big drop down the back of it. To scramble, or not to scramble, that is the question for every parent. No? Well, maybe not.

When you're taking someone up a hill or along a windy clifftop, there's a lot to worry about. Will they get cold, hungry or demoralised? Will your bad planning lead to a boring or unpleasant walk? Will your bad planning lead to getting lost? Oh no, is that a raincloud coming? But when the someone else is a child, you need to worry about all that at least twice as much.

Here are some top tips:

→ Take lots of food, drink and spare clothes. And then take some more.
→ If there's a river, at least one child will fall into it and go home wearing flip-flops and Daddy's fleece jacket.
→ Recent crawlers can astonish you with their power-to-weight ratio: making mere grown-ups seem like a cumbersome and overweight sort of scrambler. Some will even climb before they start to walk...
→ Many children love to scramble on the rocks. Any rocks. Including ones with big drops under or crashing waves of the sea. As parents, we're worrying about keeping them safe, while at the same time wanting them to be happy and adventurous outdoors. The trick is to be sensible

– but not too sensible. A sensible ratio is one supervising adult for each child.
→ It's never too soon to start with the exercising-own-judgement and learning-from-own (non-lethal) mistakes. My younger sister lets her little darlings choose their own gear – and, if necessary, carries something more sensible hidden in the rucksack.
→ And if you do get everything right, the small person will enjoy it all twice as much as any boring old grown-up.

Adventuring again

In the much-loved Enid Blyton books, written in the 1940s, the four children (plus Timmy the dog) go exploring tidal sea coves, sailing in small boats without wearing lifejackets, and spending nights on uninhabited islands. What were their parents thinking about? In the stories of Noel Streatfeild, and the same in the Harry Potter series, the author's start point is to kill off the parents before Chapter One begins. With the responsible adults out of the way, the young people can start having proper adventures.

Attitudes to children and adventure have changed. When I was ten, my Dad took me up Jack's Rake on Pavey Ark. The rake is a Grade 1 scramble, serious in the grade, slanting up through vertical climbing crags. The big drops are right beside you on the left-hand side; big cliffs rise above you on the right. Once you've started, you can't go back.

I thought it was wonderful. Why

TODDLER ON TOP

Most toddlers love going for a walk in one of those backpack carriers. It's great getting that high-level grown-up viewpoint without the accompanying hassle of mortgages, tax returns, etc. For the grown-up underneath it's like having a rather heavy rucksack, but with a little foot sticking out on either side. And a 10kg (22lb) daughter or son is a great training aid for your next big expedition. But when they're up behind you it's tricky keeping track of whether they're warm and content, so it's good to have another adult along. My daughter used to sing along, while rubbing bananas into my hair: this is a clue that everything's OK up there.

BELOW Backpack baby.

can't all mountains be like Jack's Rake on Pavey Ark?

And my Dad? My Dad went through the Second World War, and his climbing style was what they called 'bold', meaning it had a proper risk of serious injury and death. I took my own ten-year-old up a much less serious scramble, Halls Fell on Blencathra. I would not, myself, have taken her up Jack's Rake.

Of course we want to offer our children excitement and adventure. Of course we also want to protect them from all possible harm. Previous generations were more adventurous than we are today, and some parents are more adventurous than others. But there are risks, too, in being overprotective.

Dogs

I'm not a dog person. My knowledge of dogs is seeing them bounding towards me along the path, a wolf-like grin on their lips, while somewhere behind them someone shouts 'He's very friendly really...'

Like children, dogs can have a huge amount of fun in the open countryside. Like children, a dog can also be a constant worry.

A well-trained dog walks to heel even in the presence of sheep; stops or returns when called even in the presence of deer or ptarmigan, doesn't need to bark at me just for the offence of being there. A dog like that is a delightful hill companion. They enjoy themselves almost as much as a child can. And watching them bounding across rough ground, ears flopping in the breeze ... my cat Biba just doesn't do that.

If you do have a dog and want to take it walking, these are the things to be aware of:

HILL LAMBING (mid-April to mid-June; earlier in the lowlands) A pregnant ewe that gets chased by a dog can miscarry or even die. And the watching farmer can't tell that your dog is just rambling around having fun and isn't about to start hunting down lambs. So considerate walkers will keep even well-behaved dogs on leads or avoid the sheep and lambs altogether.

GROUND NESTING BIRDS (April to June) While sheep and lambs are pretty obvious, you probably aren't

BELOW Children are natural scramblers. Parents are naturally anxious.

aware of birds like curlews (seriously endangered these days) and lapwings. Without even noticing, a dog can scare them off the nest; the eggs cool down; no chicks this year.

COWS (especially ones with calves) These beasts just don't like dogs. And if you're tied to the dog, they'll go for you at the same time. One dog owner slips the lead through the collar and back again. Then she can just let go of one end and pull it through, so that the dog can run away safely.

Repel an advancing cow by pointing a walking pole directly towards it. Suddenly opening a map can also be quite intimidating.

FOOD AND DRINK Dogs can be hyperactive on the hill. And being smaller, they need proportionally more food and water to keep them going. Just the same as children, except of course no chocolate.

COSY CLOTHING Small creatures get colder quicker. (Basically, their insides are closer to the surface.) In cold, windy rain, sleet or snow, smaller or short-haired dogs may need a protective jacket emblazoned with some jazzy outdoor logo.

ABOVE A dog trained enough to be trustworthy off the lead will be a happy dog.

LEFT Dog warning sign in the Brecon Beacons.

PAWS Dogs that mostly walk on grass have soft paws. It takes time to harden them up for gravel and rocky surfaces. According to the Mountaineering Scotland website, gabbro and quartzite are the worst. But human climber Gwen Moffat used to climb gabbro barefoot, and dogs can do the same if toughened up gradually.

ADDERS Because dogs approach the world nose-first, they're more likely than people to get bitten by an adder. If bitten, the advice is to carry them off the hill (if small enough) and get them to a vet – adder bites become very painful after an hour or two.

DOG POO The Mountaineering Scotland website says that in open hill ground, it's OK to flick the dog poo away from the path or anywhere people might want to sit down, and let it decompose naturally. Elsewhere, you will of course pick it up and put it in a dog poo bin, rather than suspending it from a tree branch.

TICKS As the owner of a hill-going dog, you're going to spend quite a lot of time picking off ticks. Dogs can get Lyme disease the same as humans. Dogs (but not humans) can get two-in-one flea and tick medicine every month, which makes the ticks die and drop off.

SNOW Something called Musher's Secret will make your dog feel like a husky, and it will also stop snow from balling up on their paws. Yes, it's available from the Snowpaw Store. (Aren't dog merchandisers just so sweet.) And for long-haired dogs, rub baby oil on their legs, belly and tail. Honest! The big burly folk at Mountaineering Scotland say so.

MOUNTAIN RESCUE If your dog is ill or injured, it's OK to call Mountain Rescue. They work with search and rescue dogs and tend to be dog lovers, too.

BELOW Happy scrambler: Betty the Jack Russell on Blencathra.

7

GETTING SERIOUS: SCRAMBLING

Going high with the Pumpkin Person

Scrambling on Blencathra, the big hill on the northern edge of the Lake District, is the single most risky mountain activity – much more serious than roped climbs. It's the most fun you can have in Keswick in a public place. It's messy, and damp, and on a drizzly day it can make your hair frizz up in a nasty way. It's a great day out for kids who don't like horrid hills – but does this also apply to grown-ups?

These tricky questions come up when a family member, recently retired to cultivate his pumpkins, decided to do Blencathra. Was it a good idea, which way to go, and do I want to come too?

The third of the questions was the easy one. Taking into account the

ABOVE Halls Fell (Grade 1) on Blencathra.

weather and how long it had been since I was last on Blencathra and the state of the world economy – yes, I do. There's never a day when I don't want to go up Blencathra. The second is only a little bit difficult. There are 22 different routes up Blencathra, but for one who's only going to do it once, the choice reduces to two: Sharp Edge or the rather easier Halls Fell ridge.

As for the first one – would it be fun? We'd find the answer to that when we got there.

Time passed and another email whooshed into the inbox. 'We are both somewhat sedentary and certainly nowhere near your level of fitness being both retired now, but we are both keen to give it a bash – probably not via Sharp Edge though.' Shucks! Someone's been showing them pictures of Sharp Edge.

I hit reply. 'OK, there's Halls Fell, straightforward but pleasantly scrambly. T and J [my kids] did it when

11 and 9, and I did it when about 6, so multiplying those ages together and taking the square root it's altogether suitable for retired gentlemen taking time off from their vegetable garden.'

Halls Fell is genuinely rocky, and careful camera angles can make it seem almost alpine. But it's also got little paths, and big handholds, and the sides aren't steep enough to be truly scary. It goes on being not-truly-scary for about 300m of height gain, and it arrives like a real ridge should at the very tip-top point of the mountain. All the way up, there are ever wider views of the Vale of Keswick, and the Helvellyn ridgeline, and every single one of the central fells.

Well, there would be, except the cloud's down.

We set off briskly. But we slow down as we get on the steep, stony lower ridgeline of Halls Fell. Soon, we hit the mist: but not long after that comes the first of the rocks. Halls Fell's towers

BELOW Looking down Halls Fell Ridge.

SCRAMBLING STRATAGEMS

→ The best thing when scrambling is to go for something you're not sure you can do, and then do it. This is a joy of a very special sort. The worst thing when scrambling is to go for something you're not sure you can do, and you can't.

→ One person's straightforward scramble is another person's terrifying climb. So start with something you're sure you can do, and move on up from there.

→ For confidence, and also for photography: take a friend. Or be taken by one.

→ And for anything more than the popular scrambling classics, take the guidebook, too.

→ Try not to be terrified of things that haven't happened yet. Let's go up and have a look, and if we don't like it, we can come back down.

→ Scrambles on good, clean rock aren't much harder in the rain. But they get a lot harder when it's wet and also windy. And scrambling is like horse racing. All bets are off when there's ice and snow on the course.

→ If you're nervous, it's tempting to go off down the side on that gravelly little path. But it's better not to. The firm rocks of the crest are usually easier, and also safer, than the loose gravel of the path.

→ Rock makes a better handhold than heather. But if you have to grab heather, grab it by the roots.

→ 'We've come so far; we've got to keep going.' This is a poor strategy even if you're only investing your pension pot into Bitcoin. For scrambling: 'We've come so far, what a huge amount of judgement and moral integrity we're displaying by turning back now.' And yes, I really ought to apply the same principle to my pension investments.

and pinnacles, which aren't large in any meaningful way, expand and grow romantic with scraps of cloud tearing between their not-very-mighty excrescences.

And then the cloud tears apart in holes and we emerge on top of it. Well I'd read the weather forecast; I knew that was going to happen.

At this point, we confirm that scrambling is subjective. Human beings can climb El Capitan in the Yosemite Valley if we want to, vertical rocks with some of the holds easily big enough for a fingertip. Meanwhile, Halls Fell can be a nice rocky bit for a six-year-old – but it can still disconcert a retired gentlemen, with somewhat dodgy knees, who now reveals a problem with vertigo.

At this moment, helpfully, a small dog occurs. A Jack Russell scampers up the ridgeline. Betty the dog is clearly having a whale of a time. And somehow, it's hard to be scared in the presence of someone who's

LEFT Grade 2 scrambling on Aonach Eagach, Glen Coe.

way down. We followed the top of Scales Fell, then took the grassy slope to a gloomy and cloud-locked Scales Tarn. Down beside the waterfalls, and that contouring path along the high side of Glenderamackin to the sudden col above Mousthwaite Comb.

Blencathra by Halls Fell: it's one of Lakeland's best. Even if you aren't a small dog called Betty.

Wild scrambles

The classic scramble will follow an obvious line,

only 24cm (9½in) high.

'Sorry, but the top's only 20m above us now.' They didn't believe me – but that's Blencathra. The ridgeline tops off like a lift arriving at the penthouse floor. We strolled the crest line to Gategill Fell Top, with the cloud lapping against the ridge side like walking along a jetty of the sea. Up in this magic world of blue and white it was just us, and some distant Scafells poking their dark heads through the cloud-sea, and a couple of dozen others who'd also read the small print in the weather forecast.

There may be two really good ways up Blencathra, but there's only one

with rock worn clean by many feet. But there are also scrambles that are 'go anywhere on this whole hillside'. These tend to be less technical, but with the route choice up to you, pretty wildflowers on the handholds, and nobody else about.

Gill scrambles

Scrambling up the bed of a tumbling mountain stream, sometimes in the water, sometimes through deep moss and slime, always among damp but dramatic situations. This is a special form of fun enjoyed mainly in the Lake District. Romantics spell the Norse word gill as 'ghyll'.

SCRAMBLING GRADES

Grade 1 Rocks will be clean, and firm, and well attached to the mountain. The route will normally be obvious. More difficult moves, if any, will be above a broad ledge or somewhere safe to land on. There won't be serious exposure (exposure is the technical expression for 'argh-huge-scary-drops-below'). Confident, reasonably agile walkers in good weather can tackle the Grade 1s; the classic ones are very popular.

Grade 2 This grade may involve more difficult moves in exposed situations, and some skill and judgement in route choice. Confident scramblers will tackle Grade 2, in good weather, without a climbing rope.

Grade 3 More difficult moves in seriously exposed situations, route-finding difficulties, possibly with loose or vegetated rock. All but the most confident and experienced scramblers will use a climbing rope.

Scrambling grades are set *on* stone but not set *in* stone: for example, Sgùrr nan Gillean on Skye, by the so-called Tourist Route, gets graded anywhere between Grade 1 and Grade 3 – on the easiest route line, the rock moves are technically easy, but with big, serious drops below. Route choice, weather and how seriously you take big drops will all affect the subjective grading.

RIGHT Gill scrambling: slimy but romantic.

SCRAMBLING SUGGESTIONS

EASIER GRADE 1

Snowdonia
The Glyder Gribin,
   above Cwm Idwal
Yorkshire Dales
Gordale Scar
Lake District
Halls Fell, Blencathra
Striding Edge,
   Helvellyn
Scotland
Càrn Mòr Dearg Arête,
   Ben Nevis
Fiacaill Ridge of Coire
   an t-Sneachda,
   Cairn Gorm

GRADE 1

Snowdonia
Tryfan North Ridge
   and Bristly Ridge to
   Glyder Fach
Crib Goch and Crib y
   Ddysgl, Snowdon
Lake District
Helm Crag
Sharp Edge, Blencathra
Jack's Rake, Pavey Ark
Scotland
Am Fasarinen, Liathach,
   Wester Ross
Ledge Route (Ben Nevis)

GRADE 1 (WILD)

Lake District
Cockley Pike to Ill
   Crag, Scafell
   Pike (Eskdale)
Scotland
Avon Slabs to Ben
   Macdui, Cairngorms

GRADE 2

Lake District
Old West (Pillar Rock)
Scotland
The Cobbler summit
   tower, Loch Lomond
Aonach Eagach, Glen
   Coe
Forcan Arête, the
   Saddle, Glen Shiel
Skye Cuillin (everywhere)

BELOW The so-called
Tourist Route, the
easiest way up Sgùrr
nan Gillean, Skye.

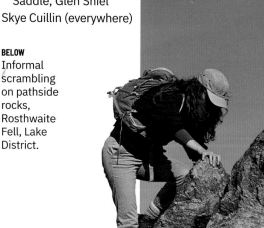

BELOW
Informal
scrambling
on pathside
rocks,
Rosthwaite
Fell, Lake
District.

BELOW Damp rock, but no wind: a scrambler chooses an exciting off-route line on Crib y Ddysgl, Snowdon.

THE SCRAMBLING GUIDEBOOKS

➜ Snowdonia: Steve Ashton and revisers, *Scrambles in Snowdonia* (Cicerone Press)

➜ Lake District: John Fleetwood, *Scrambles in the Lake District – South and Scrambles in the Lake District – North* (Cicerone Press)

➜ Ben Nevis and Glen Coe: Noel Williams, *Scrambles in Lochaber* (out of print but the scrambles are timeless)

➜ Skye: Noel Williams, *Skye Scrambles* (Scottish Mountaineering Club Guide)

➜ North Highlands: Iain Thow, *Highland Scrambles North* (Scottish Mountaineering Club Guide)

➜ Cairngorms and South Highlands: Iain Thow, *Highland Scrambles South* (Scottish Mountaineering Club Guide)

BELOW Sharp Edge, Grade 1: the more demanding scramble on Blencathra.

Walk 2

BLENCATHRA BY HALLS FELL

WALK 2: **Hall's Fell, Blencathra**
START/END: **Threlkeld village**
DISTANCE: **9.5km (6 miles)**
ASCENT: **750m**
APPROX. TIME: **4 hours**
HIGHEST POINT: **Blencathra, 868m**
TERRAIN: **Hill paths, sometimes steep: scrambling Grade 1 (easier in the grade)**
OPTIONS: **Many possible descent paths**

PARKING: **Above Threlkeld (NY318255; nearest postcode CA12 4SA)**
CAR-FREE: **Frequent Penrith–Keswick buses X4, X5**
TOILETS: **Threlkeld**
FOOD, DRINK **Horse & Farrier, Threlkeld: traditional Lakeland inn with good food**

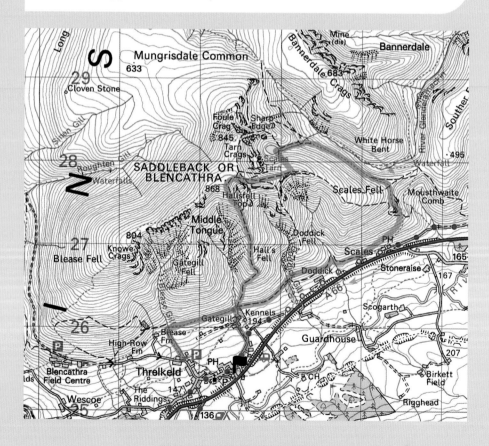

WALK 2: BLENCATHRA BY HALLS FELL

ABOVE On Halls Fell.

Bus travellers: from the east end of Threlkeld village, take the street uphill to a rough track running up to the left. It becomes a path, with a stream in a gorge alongside. At the top of enclosed fields, turn right across the stream to the foot of the Halls Fell ridge. Motorists: from the car park above Threlkeld, take a path directly uphill to the foot of the open fell. Turn right, above a wall, to pass high above the village. After 1km (0.6 miles) of level walking (a useful warm-up for what's ahead), cross Gategill Beck (stream) to the foot of the Halls Fell ridge.

Immediately across the stream, the steep path slants up to the left.

After a pretty stiff ascent (nearly 400m of height gain) the ridge levels off and becomes narrow. Now the scrambling starts. Follow little bits of path and well-worn rocks up the crest of the ridgeline, all the way to the sudden arrival at Blencathra summit.

From here, you can take a gentle wander down the ridge south-west for 1.5km (1 mile) to its end at Blease Fell (an uninteresting path descends to Threlkeld from here) then back to the main summit.

Follow the wide path east, over the plateau rim. It drops in engineered zigzags to where the ridgeline levels. Here, a steep path down to the left could take you to Scales Tarn, but it's more scenic to stay on the main path, next to the abyss that drops to your right into the Vale of Keswick. The path descends another set of zigzags: at the foot of this you could turn down to the right for a rough but beautiful descent of the Doddick Fell, Hall Fell's little sister. But my suggestion is to turn left down moderately steep grass to Scales Tarn outflow.

> As you descend, the ridgeline opposite, high above Scales Tarn, is Sharp Edge. It's another classic scrambling route, steep-sided and exposed, and quite a bit harder and scarier than Hall's Fell.

The path descends beside the tarn's outflow stream, then turns right to contour, delightfully, along the steep slope high above the infant River Glenderamackin. The path arrives on the foot of the Scales Fell ridgeline –

you were on the top part of it above Scales Tarn.

A path runs up and down the ridgeline from a major saddle just below you but go straight across that on to a smaller path ahead. This one edges around the brink of Mousthwaite Comb ('comb' is the Lake District word for a hollow or corrie). Then the path drops to pass above the White Horse Inn at Scales village.

Follow the path along the foot of the fell above the fell wall. After 400m (¼ mile) it turns down into the hollow of Scales Beck, with a scramble out again up bare, well-used rocks. In another 400m (¼ mile), fork right on a path that rises gradually to a wall corner and continues above the wall. After fording the beck of Doddick Gill you reach Gategill Beck back near the start of the walk.

BELOW Descending Scales Fell towards the Vale of Eden, evening.

8

GETTING SERIOUS: WINTER WALKING

'Dreaming of a White Christmas.'
'Walking in a winter Wonderland.'
Even Frosty the Snowman with his
two eyes made of coal. On the high
tops, winter is the best time of all.
Except, of course, when it isn't...

Winter can mean plodding uphill
in wet snow, looking at snow clouds
from the inside. It can mean gale
force winds and driving sleet, and
you're happy to be at home beside
the crackling fire dreaming of a white
Christmas just so long as you don't

have to be out there underneath it.

But winter also means crisp
winter sunshine. Miles and miles of
mountains retinted in gothic black
and white and all prettied up with
icicles. Winter is the special comfort
brought on by two layers of fleece
clothing. Winter is when the buses
stop running – but the car parks are
nice and empty. It's when there's

ABOVE Winter walking on the north
Solway coast.

No snow go

ABOVE White Christmas Day above Nithsdale, Dumfriesshire.

BELOW Why walk in winter? The answer: a snow-free January evening on Beinn Ime, above Loch Lomond.

Even without snow, a nice day in winter is one of the nicest days there is. Waterfalls become a 50:50 mix of falling water and crusted ice, with dangling icicles on either side. I've been to two weddings recently, and I've noticed they do something fancy with the photos: they blacken all the shadows for a stark and arty look, while desaturating the colours to pastel tones. It's fashionable just now, but Lakeland in winter have been applying these photo filters since the end of the Ice Age. Winter sunlight gives that harsh 'noir' look. All-day frost gives pastel green on the fields and turns Buttermere to an appropriate buttery colour. It's an effect that's as much 'high style' as High Stile.

Such no-snow winter conditions are a pleasure that, with global warming, are getting easier and easier to find. Even in Scotland, hills over 900m can be found all bare and brown. And winter without snow can mean no more than checking the weather forecast, checking the time of sunset,

nowhere open to stay the night in; but the places that are open, you don't need to book. Winter covers up the eroded footpaths and sends away almost all of the other people.

and taking plenty of warm clothes and a torch.

It can also mean serious, proper snow, where you maybe don't yet feel confident about the skills of the ice axe, and being absolutely sure there won't be any avalanches, and what if the weather forecast's really, really wrong? But isn't that just the day for that low-level ramble around the lake, the one you never get around to in summertime because it's not proper hillwalking and anyway it's ever so busy.

Then one day, you've learned to trust the weather forecast, and got a set of fleece and windproofs that you trust as well, plus a hat that won't blow off in that unexpected blizzard – and you've been keeping an eye on the Weatherline Lakeland fell top conditions report (see below), and you've decided you aren't going to look silly wielding one of those ice axe thingies. Note that ice axe thingy stuff is covered in Chapter 17.

BELOW Climbers Traverse path.

Let it snow

Tuesday's forecast said 15cm of new snow, and Tuesday evening's fell top conditions report confirmed it. So on Wednesday I set out for Great Langdale. I took an ice axe, just in case. But soft new snow, with nothing old and frozen underneath it? – I wouldn't have any use for my crampons.

Langdale was just lovely in the rosy pink of dawn. Even lovelier as the daylight brightened over the snowfields, with the craggy Langdale Pikes an intricate pattern of black. And high on the side of Bow Fell, there's the exciting Climbers Traverse path.

Except, there isn't. The overnight snow has covered it up. What I've got is a steep white slope, all covered in loose, floppy snow. Well, the ice axe sticks through that all right. Work across the snow slope, with Langdale a long way down below the right-hand boot sole. High above my left shoulder, the Great Slab stretches upwards like a handy ski-jump for trolls; and kicking aside the snow, the crampons grip comfortingly in the hard-frozen turf.

Except, of course, they don't. Because I didn't bring them. So I turn back and take a less adventurous way on to Bow Fell. It's slow, slow going – not because of the deep new snow; previous people have trodden that down nicely – no, it's because I have to keep stopping and taking photos down the snowy valley below.

Bow Fell is splendid, and you can stand there until your toes are well chilblained before you've named every single Lakeland summit spun out around like a computer-generated magic kingdom. But even better

ABOVE Bleak mid-winter on Swarth Fell, north Pennines.

than counting round the Scafells and Borrowdale is to get down to the Three Tarns and start counting out the Crinkle Crags. Just how many of them are there, and how many snowdrifts will I struggle through to get to them? It can be a long, long way along to Long Top.

By the time I get to Red Tarn, the sun's getting low. And now the comfortable, well-trodden path runs down to the Old Dungeon Ghyll Hotel. But...

But up ahead, there's Pike of Blisco. And it's going to be so grand, leaning my back against the stone-cone cairn, as the sunset turns Swirl How to a black shape against yellow and turquoise, and tints the Langdale Pikes in a delicate pink that's as girly-licious as any Disney lunchbox.

And then I'm wondering, in a pleasantly tired-out way, how the heck I'm going to get down off the Pike of Blisco before it gets dark.

Well I'm not. But downhill snow slopes go surprisingly quick even when I can only half see them. And that rocky section on the path, I can just about fumble down it without turning on the torch and spoiling my night vision. And there's the bar window of the Old Dungeon Ghyll Hotel shining into the night to guide me down...

Until I reach the black shadow that's the Little Langdale road seen by starlight. And the black tarmac's got a glaze of black ice, so over I go – bump! – with a bruise on my backside that can only be repaired by the magic touch of a half pint of Jennings ale taken by firelight.

So whether it's below the snow – or full-on Ice is Nice – may your days be merry and bright.

And may all your Christmases be white.

A bit of snow-how

Where to go

It has to be Lakeland, Snowdonia, or the more approachable Scottish mountains such as Ben Lomond. Even if there is some snow cover in the Pennines or Southern Uplands, their unpathed snowfields are heavy going and they're remoter than you want in the middle of winter in that sharp little snow shower.

When to go

In some seasons, the best or indeed the only snow can be in November or even in May. The time to go is … when the weather forecast says so.

What to watch

The weather forecast will tell you, several days in advance, when the clouds are going to be high and the winds low. Specialist mountain forecasts are:

ABOVE Winter conditions on Ben Lawers, Southern Highlands.

→ Mountain weather information service at www.mwis.org.uk.
→ Met Office mountain forecast at www.metoffice.gov.uk and search 'specialist forecasts'.
→ There's a daily report on snow conditions on the Lake District Weatherline website at www.lakedistrictweatherline.co.uk. Yes, those two chaps walk up Helvellyn every single day, all through the winter. Just for us.
→ For Scotland, the avalanche reports at www.sais.gov.uk are essential viewing – or there's a 'Be Avalanche Aware' app. They also give an account of current snow conditions.

When does it start getting serious?

A few inches of soft, newly fallen snow merely slow you down a bit, while making the entire landscape look lovely. It's when the snow has thawed and frozen again, and thawed again and frozen again, that it turns into the halfway-icy stuff known at *névé*. (That's French, pronounced 'nevay'.) For people who know how to cope with this, involving ice axes and the spiky sort of shoes called crampons, such refrozen snow is the finest sort of walking there is – so see the later chapter about that.

When it's sensible to be sensible

→ Assume there could be a harsh little snow shower: do you have enough warm clothes, and can you get down the mountain from here using just your compass because the map's going to blow away and the phone's gone cold?

→ If there's been a lot of new snow, you might have to think about avalanches – see Chapter 17 for more on More Serious Snow.

→ If you come across hard, old snow – and it's steep enough to slide down, and you haven't sorted out your ice axe and crampon technique – then it's time to find a way around or go back down.

RIGHT Looking down Langdale from the Band, Bow Fell.

SEVEN WORDS FOR SNOW

Névé Snow that's thawed and refrozen several times, so it's hard enough to walk on top of. Excellent stuff. On steeper slopes you may be able to kick steps but probably will need crampons as well as an ice axe.

Hoar frost ('ice') A very pretty formation of frost crystals condensing out of the air on the downwind side of stones and fence posts. When it's thick enough to cover the whole mountain, climbers call it 'ice' and clamber up it with ice axes.

Verglas is known to motorists as black ice. Cold rain falling on to hard-frozen ground leaves a coating of hard ice over everything. Nasty! Especially on the North Face of the Eiger.

Wind slab Snow on the lee side of a hill that's been compacted by the wind. It can make comfortable walking. But on steeper slopes, if it has a layer of softer snow underneath, it can crack away in an avalanche.

Powder Dry, cold snow that's never thawed. Excellent for skiing. Less good for trying to walk in.

Spindrift Flying snow lifted up by the wind. This can reduce visibility at ground level. Especially if you've got your eyes closed because you weren't wearing any goggles.

Cornice At the top edge of a downwind slope or cliff face, snow piles outwards in an overhanging ledge. If you're on top of a cornice, you may fall through it, and if you're underneath, it may fall down on you.

9

WHEN THINGS GO WRONG

Fellwalking is not a high-risk sport. In fact, given the health benefits, you're probably safer walking up a hill than you would be sitting at home eating a cream cake. However, as the years go by, you might come across someone needing help in the hills, or even get into difficulties yourself.

If this does ever happen, it helps to be prepared. It also helps to think things through a bit before they happen.

The weather is on the Mountain Weather Information Service (MWIS) website (www.mwis.org.uk). Please bear in mind that while the Met Office and the MWIS are astonishingly accurate, they can still sometimes get it wrong.

The gear: I take one layer of clothing more than the worst I think I'm going to need, and on serious hills a torch and an emergency survival bag as well.

ABOVE Snowy Cairngorms.

Not sure of your knowledge and skills? That's a matter of educating yourself slowly. Plan for a walk that will test those skills, but not to destruction – and be ready to turn back if it is more testing than expected.

In the olden days, mountain rescue was simply a matter of hillwalkers and mountaineers helping one another out. My first two mountain rescues were when I was a teenager, and they were both pretty undramatic. On a school trip to the Cairngorms in winter, the teachers were told that someone had failed to make it out of the mountains. I was assigned to a group setting out at daybreak to check one of the low-level bothies. However, the missing man was found safe and well in a pub at closing time. The teachers were stood down, and I passed through my first rescue effort without even waking up... And the second one was similar. A neighbour summoned us to the foot of Liathach to help bring down a casualty. About 50 people gathered from the youth hostel and the campsite. When word went round that the casualty was limping down with the help of his own party, we went home and had our tea.

BE ADVENTURE SMART

These are the three questions the Mountain Rescue team asks us to ask ourselves:

1 Do I know what the weather will be like?
2 Do I have the right gear?
3 Do I have the knowledge and skills for the day?

BELOW Winter evening above Ennerdale: exciting, or unsettling, depending on how well you know your navigation and your gear.

Mountain Rescue today is more organised. Indeed, it's fully professional in every sense apart from the technicality of not getting paid any money. But the tradition is still the same: climbers and hillwalkers helping out other hillwalkers and climbers. And it doesn't stop with the Mountain Rescue. Everybody on the hill has a duty of care towards everybody else. A person lying down on the ridge of the Old Man of Coniston with someone standing beside them looking worried? A quiet, 'Is everything OK?' and yes, they're waiting for the helicopter, but they may welcome a reassuring chat and the loan of a survival bag. Never mind that my wife's down in the Coppermines youth hostel, watching the Mountain Rescue Land Rover zoom up the track with its lights flashing and thinking, 'Oh dear, Ronald's messed up there at last...'

A duty of care and concern – but that doesn't mean a right to tell people what to do when you think they're doing it wrong. Just now and then someone's tried to order me off the hill for wearing what they call 'trainers' but are actually fellrunning shoes. And that's a bit obnoxious. But, 'You do know it'll be dark in an hour?' when I'm heading uphill with what looks like a daysack (but is actually a bivvy bag and lightweight sleeping bag) – that's courteous behaviour, so thank you.

Awkward moments for those left at home

A later rescue I was involved in was equally undramatic – but it does illustrate the value of thinking things through beforehand. Philip's partner phoned me up one evening. 'Philip's on a big trek across Scotland, he was supposed to arrive at the top of Glen Coe this evening but he hasn't phoned. Should we call Mountain Rescue?'

Phil's last contact was a WhatsApp photo from the top of Ben Starav, sometime yesterday. There is, though, a route plan. A hugely ambitious route plan involving four of those very steep and craggy Munros at the back of Glen Coe. Not finishing that lot by sunset isn't so surprising. Then again, Philip could be lying at the foot of one of those very steep craggy slopes with a broken leg. But on the third hand, if we call out Mountain Rescue when he didn't need rescuing, Philip's going to be really, really cross.

In the end, we thought we'd just talk it through with the Mountain Rescue guys.

They thought yes, that was a jolly ambitious bit of hillwalking. So what they'd do, they'd send one of their Land Rovers up the track along Glen Kinglass, to the south of the hills, and another one up the road to the Kings House. The Land Rover sent up to the Kings House found Philip strolling along the West Highland Way. It turned out that the mobile phone mast on the edge of Rannoch Moor wasn't working that day.

And yes, Philip was really, really cross.

So leave a route plan with someone sensible. That doesn't mean you absolutely have to stick to that plan: Mountain Rescue know about people who take a sensible shortcut, or ambitiously go for something extra. But, somewhat less obvious: do, on that plan, include your phone-in time, and how long after it they're allowed to start worrying. If I'm carrying a plastic bag that I could survive the night in, 'when to worry' is breakfast time the next day.

And then, when you're lying with a broken leg at the bottom of that steep and craggy Munro, you'll know exactly when your sensible friend's going to be picking up the phone, and when, two hours after that, to start listening out for the helicopter. It can be a comfort of sorts.

Hiking over the hills and the wild places: it's about exercising not just your legs, but your judgement. That's half the point of it, in a world where we're increasingly regulated and told what to do. Exercising your judgement means sometimes getting it wrong. It sometimes even means getting it

wrong in a silly and embarrassing way. Like the people we saw on the nasty slope of Crib y Ddysgl one night.

It was the hottest night of a very hot summer. We were on the summit of Snowdon (Yr Wyddfa) getting ready to go to sleep, when we saw two torches shining from somewhere above the Pig Track. It's little crags and runnels of slippery scree, that slope of Crib y Ddysgl: a bad place to be in the dark. So it wasn't too surprising when the torches started shouting for help.

'SOS,' they shouted, from the dark spaces of Glaslyn down below. So we fired up the phone and called up Mountain Rescue.

GENERAL VITAL ADVICE

→ Read up about emergency first aid.
→ Download the OS Locate app and register your phone for Emergency SMS (www.emergencysms.net).
→ Plan the route, but also the escape routes off it.
→ Save some phone battery for emergencies.
→ On serious hills, carry a torch and survival bag (especially in winter).
→ Leave word of where you're planning on going.
→ Don't be too embarrassed to turn back!

An hour later, we got to enjoy a special lightshow: the helicopter flashing red, and the search beam across the rockfaces, and the tiny black figures dangling in the searchlight. The helicopter swooped away over the ridge, its lamps soon lost in the general glare of Bangor. And a couple of hours after that, an even more spectacular display, as the sun rose slowly above a sea of mist, with the black triangle of Crib Goch like a shark cruising through some bloodstained custard.

When I got home, I emailed the team to say sorry. It was an unnecessary call-out, for sure. But the people down there were shouting for help, and they could have been injured. I hope they got a good talking-to in the car park.

'You're right,' said the rescue person. 'They should have just sat tight until sunrise. But the thing is, they weren't sufficiently experienced to realise this.'

So yes; when it comes to getting things wrong in a silly and embarrassing way, the Mountain Rescue people know all about that. They are fellwalkers, and the ones who aren't fellwalkers are climbers or cavers or paragliders. Every one of them has, at some point in their life, got things wrong in a silly and embarrassing way.

Because, to be honest, we all have. Haven't we?

BELOW Winter on the Howgill Fells.

WHERE TO GO

ENGLAND

The sport of going for walks in the countryside was invented in England. Right back in the 1820s, Jane Austen's heroines were mud-staining their skirts on the field paths, and even attaining the 235m summit of Raddon Hills on the edge of Dartmoor.

Even today, every small town is ringed with dog-walking paths. And almost every Englander lives within a two-hour bus ride of some sort of moorland or mini-mountain. Toytown-sized mountain ranges like the Quantocks or the Mendips or the Malverns that rise above the M6 motorway. Cosy uplands like the Cotswolds, with a thatched pub every couple of miles, each with a micro-brewery in a shed around the back. From the centre of Sheffield, you can walk up through city parkland on to the moors; Manchester is developing its own perimeter path, 300km (186 miles) of it; from London's East End, you can walk right out along the River Lea into Epping Forest.

If I was describing everywhere to go for a walk in England – that would be all of England. So if you fancy going somewhere that isn't described below, just go for it and get out there. Look, I haven't even covered all ten of England's national parks.

Peak District

The Peak District could have been placed by the gods of geology as a charming, not too demanding, hilly bit fitted into the tiny gap between Manchester, Huddersfield, Stoke-on-Trent and Sheffield. In fact, it's the other way round – the industrial towns of 18th-century England formed around the waterwheel sites at the southern edge of the Pennine range.

But enough of this history lesson. Some people like white chocolate; some people like dark. But everybody

ABOVE Limestone pavement at Malham Cove, Yorkshire Dales.

likes chocolate. And the same is true of the Peak District.

One reason everybody likes the Peak District is its position: right on the edge of Sheffield, and at the same time right on the edge of Manchester. But the other reason is the way it comes in those two completely different flavours. The white, and the dark. The sweet, and the harsh. The green and grassy limestone, and the peaty grit.

But let's get one thing clear: the place is named after a Saxon tribe called the Pecsaetan. The Peak District has absolutely nothing to do with peaks. In the Dark Peak, the high-up places like Bleaklow and Kinder Scout

SHORT BREAK
Church Stretton

Like England itself, southern Shropshire is astonishingly varied, with five of the 11 geological periods within walking distance of this one town. Over a long weekend, you can cover the knobby volcanic Caer Caradoc, the stream-carved 'batches' cutting into the Long Mynd, and the reef limestone of Wenlock Edge.

Getting there: Welsh Marches rail line from Chester to South Wales
What's there: YHA bunkhouse, busy town with shops and accommodation
Getting out: Long Mynd, with its little valleys west of the town.

Caer Caradoc, Ragleth and other small hills east of the town.

Wenlock Edge at Craven Arms, one stop down the railway
Moving on: YHA Bridges just the other side of the Long Mynd

BELOW Stiperstones, Shropshire Hills.

are absolutely flat. The one time I managed to find the summit of Kinder Scout, it was a small peat pool with a fence post in the middle. The White Peak does have several pointy places, but they're all so low down that in the Scottish Highlands they'd count as the valley floor.

This makes the Peak District ideal for any hillwalker who's still not sure whether they like walking up hills.

In the south, the limestone of the **WHITE PEAK** means green, bumpy countryside, with lots of wildflowers; and every mile or two a deeply cut little river valley, sometimes without even a river in it. The valley sides are creamy-white limestone crags and slopes of grey pebbles, and then you come across a cave.

The hugely popular walk here is lower Dovedale, with its stepping stones and diversion up the little hill called Thorpe Cloud – even Lizzie Bennet, heroine of *Pride and Prejudice*, visited Dovedale around 1812. A less busy dale walk from Hartington is Walk 3 below. West of Buxton, the White Peak also has a clump of charming hills just topping the 500m mark. The Roaches is the rocky one. Shutlingsloe was excitedly

SHORT BREAK Edale

Edale is a Peak District honeypot, very busy in holiday periods. With good reason! It's a great place for sampling both Dark Peak and White Peak. Getting there by train avoids parking problems, and staying there lets you start up ahead of the crowds. Even better is a short break in the quieter times of autumn or winter.

Getting there: By rail from Sheffield or Manchester
What's there: Youth hostel, two independent hostels, campsites, pubs
Getting out: Kinder Scout (Walk 4)
  Mam Tor and Lose Hill.
  Train to Chinley, back over Lord's Seat.
  Train to Hope, back by Castleton

LEFT On the Roaches, White Peak.

described in one walking magazine as the 'Staffordshire Matterhorn'. This is not entirely appropriate, as it's in Cheshire. But it does closely resemble the Matterhorn in every way, apart from being a rather small grassy hill rather than a rocky, icy mountain 4,478m high.

The **DARK PEAK**, from the Edale valley northwards, is different. Like the dark sort of chocolate, it's for those who like their treats with a hint of bitter aftertaste and coloured in sombre tones. The rocks here are the millstone grit, laid down by the estuary of a huge river that wandered over middle England for 12 million years or so. Its high, moorland country features brown peat in heaps and soggy hollows. The usable paths tend to be formed of stone slabs laid on top of the bog. All this is sprinkled with little

rocky outcrops, stolen from the Yorkshire Sculpture Park and left out in the rain for a few thousand years.

But around the edges are the Edges – long, low gritstone crags, loved by rock climbers and with grand walking along their tops. The flat plateau of Kinder Scout has a walkable pathway for 24km (15 miles), all around its rim. Part of this forms our second Peak District route, Walk 4.

The Peak District is pretty good to get around without a car. There are half a dozen youth hostels and several independent bunkhouses to stay in, and good bus services throughout the national park. You can even walk up to Stanage Edge in the Dark Peak, right from the centre of Sheffield, along the River Sheaf. But the prized transport link is the Hope Valley railway, joining Manchester and Sheffield through the Hope and Edale valleys.

ABOVE Anvil Stone on Bleaklow, Dark Peak.

BELOW Castle Naze, White Peak.

WHITE PEAK: HARTINGTON VALLEYS

Hartington is a pretty town in pale grey stone with a pay-and-display car park, two pubs and at least one ice-cream van. The walk demonstrates the principle that the best of the Peak is the valleys: a triangular trip down one of them and up another. it also features stepping stones and two caves.

Head through the town eastwards, but at once turn right into an uphill lane to pass the youth hostel. Immediately after it, take a signposted field path forking right. Cross two fields with narrow gap stiles between, to join a stony track.

Follow the track to join a road at Dale End, then take a signposted path on the right. It runs into a little dry valley, Biggin Dale. This gradually gets deeper, with scree and small outcrops. After 1km (0.6 miles), the path bends left to a junction of valleys. It's a fairly straightforward bit of compass work to determine which one to continue along! (Or see at the end.)

Continue along the floor of the dry valley, on a path that's sometimes very stony. After another 1.5km (1 mile), a rickety stile on the left gives access to a mine hole cave, which runs in for about 25m before water on the floor turns most of us back to the green light of the open air.

In another 500m (0.3 miles), the dry valley emerges to Wolfscote Dale and the River Dove, with dramatic small limestone cliffs above. The route will continue upstream, but first head left, downstream on a wide, smooth path for 200m. Here, a path forks up left to a cave chamber, while the path

LEFT Cave opposite Drabber Tor, Wolfscote Dale.

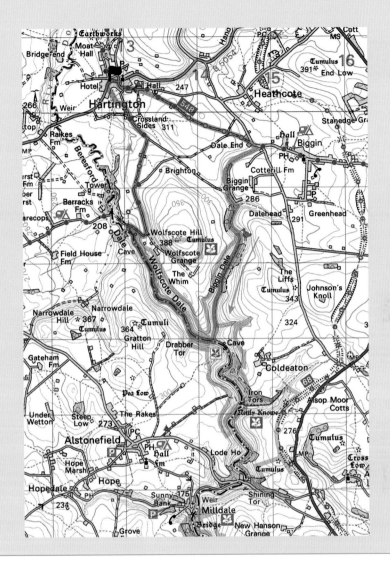

WALK 3 Hartington Valleys

START/END **Hartington centre (SK128604; car park postcode SK17 0BE)**

DISTANCE **10km (6 miles)**

ASCENT **200m**

APPROX. TIME **3 hours 30 minutes**

HIGHEST POINT **Highfield Lane, 317m**

TERRAIN **Wide paths, occasionally stony**

OPTION **Ahead along River Dove at the walk end, avoiding the final short ascent**

PARKING **Mill Lane, which runs south-west out of the village**

CAR-FREE **Buses from Ashbourne and Buxton**

TOILETS **Hartington**

PUBS & CAFES **Two in the village centre**

SO WHERE'S THE RIVER GONE?

This valley has been carved by a fair-sized river. So where's all the water gone? The quick answer is that limestone dissolves in water, so the river has managed to make itself a new passageway underground. When such a stream then makes itself another passage even further underground it leaves the dry caves and passageways beloved by cavers – including the two caves later on in this walk.

During the end of the Ice Age, about 20,000 years ago, great lakes of meltwater were trapped behind lumps of left-over ice. These broke through to make huge temporary torrents. These meltwater streams, grey-white with ice particles and trundling huge boulders along their beds, carved out the deep-cut valleys now dry or occupied by placid trout streams, such as the River Dove.

ahead leads to a scenic footbridge and stepping stones. (The side path across the bridge/stepping stones climbs very steeply out of the valley towards a nearby village with a pub.)

Return upstream, on the wide path to the right of the River Dove, below some little crags. After nearly 2km (about 1 mile), another cave chamber is above the path. This one has a passageway

BELOW Stepping stones, Wolfscote Dale.

ABOVE Drabber Tor, Wolfscote Dale.

just to the right of the entrance, through which small people aged around 12 can emerge to the hillside 5m away.

Immediately upstream, a gate leads to a track with a footbridge over the river. There's an option here to continue ahead along the riverside for another 400m (¼ mile), for a wide field path on into Hartington. But for a view out over the countryside after the enclosed valleys, fork up right on the track (signed as a cycle path), then turn up right again on a grassy track. This slants up to a farm lane on the slopes of Wolfscote Hill. (A permissive path formerly ran up and over its summit but has now lapsed.)

Turn left down the road, with wide views over green, bumpy limestone country. Where the lane rises and bends right, bear off left through a gap stile to join a farm track. Follow this ahead, soon with views down to Hartington, to a road near the Whim Brewery. Keep ahead past farm buildings, to a signed

footpath on the left just before a field barn. Follow this barely visible path north-west through gap stiles and down to a bottom-left corner under a large sycamore.

Here, a step stile leads to a short track down to the roadside opposite the pay-and-display car park.

That junction in Biggin Dale? The correct valley runs south-west, which is to say, the right turn signposted for Wolfscote Dale.

DARK PEAK: KINDER SCOUT

WALK 4 **Kinder Edge**
START/END **Grindsbrook Booth, Edale (SK122859; postcode S33 7ZD)**
DISTANCE **13km (8 miles)**
ASCENT **650m**
APPROX. TIME **5 hours**
HIGHEST POINT **Wool Packs, 610m**
TERRAIN **Rugged paths, with a scrambly moment at Grinds Brook**
OPTIONS **Various descent paths off**
Kinder Edge for a shorter or longer walk
PARKING **Edale village (full at busy times but overflow parking often available)**
CAR-FREE **Trains from Manchester/ Sheffield to Edale**
TOILETS **Edale village**
PUBS & CAFES **The Old Nags Head, start point of the Pennine Way**

ABOVE Path up Crowden Clough.

The rim of Kinder Scout has grand views over Edale and lots of little rocks to clamber about on. Best of all, the walk doesn't visit the 7 sq km (2.5 sq miles) of peat bog that's Kinder Scout's summit.

On the left below the Old Nags Head, a stone-paved sunken path starts the Pennine Way. Emerge to contour around open fields, already with great views across to the Great Ridge that's the south side of Edale. After 2km (1.2 miles), the path slants down to Upper Booth.

Cross Crowden Brook on a stone bridge, then turn up a small, bumpy path under trees to the left of the stream. Follow this upstream, with a footbridge after 500m (0.3 miles), on to rough open hillside, a vee notch running up towards the plateau high above. The Crowden Tower is prominent on the skyline, and the path slants up the left-hand (west) side of the valley to pass below it. This is steep and eroded, a tough ascent gaining 100m of height, before the path doubles back left to Crowden Tower, a rocky low tor above cliffy drops.

It's well worth continuing along the path beyond for 500m (0.3 miles) into

the cluster of small, sculptural outcrops called the Wool Packs. Adventurous parents note that these are just great for hide and seek or posing on top of for photos to scare Grandpa with.

There are lots of ways down off the Kinder Plateau. Eastwards, there are four or five points of descent, including the well-marked path by Ringing Roger. Westwards, you could continue past the Pym's Chair rock formation, practise your map navigation by trying to find the trig point on Kinder Low, and descend by the well-constructed and busy Jacob's Ladder steps of the Pennine Way. You could even continue around the plateau to Kinder Downfall for the tempting right of way (but no path) back across the plateau. This offers the interesting navigation challenge of the true summit at Crowden Head, 632m – and is an excellent way of finding out for yourself that a public right-of-way line on a map isn't always a path on the ground.

Return along the wide path back past Crowden Tower to join the path along the plateau rim. After 1km (0.6 miles), the path bends right, south-east. At a rock outcrop like two up-pointing fingers you could keep ahead for a short return to Edale over Grindslow Knoll, but the plateau-edge path turns left (north-east), soon heading in around an incised stream. The crossing of the stream involves a rocky step that some dogs may find awkward (they can divert farther upstream through the heather) but people can overcome by sitting on it and then jumping down the few inches to the rock platform below.

The rim path continues east, below the 604m spot height called Hartshorn. Arriving above the east wall of Grindsbrook Clough, a large, sprawling cairn below marks yet another descent route, via Ringing Roger. But the rim path continues past a couple more cairns, and around the head of Ollerbrook Clough.

Here, fork right on a path that slants down a hollowed-out groove, sign of a once popular path in past centuries but currently little used. At Rowland Cote Moor, pass left along the wall to its corner, for a path running down to the left of the wall. At a gap in this, cross a stile and go down grassland to the right

ABOVE Footbridge at Grindsbrook Booth.

BELOW Upper Tor, above Grindsbrook Clough.

of the wall. The slope gets pretty steep but there's the grassy groove of an old zigzag path.

As the slope eases above the valley floor, there's a small gate on your left, for a path leading down to a farm track. Turn right through a gate and head down the right-hand side of the field below to a stile on the right. Cross this to join a track passing below a handsome stone farm to arrive in Ollerbrook Booth.

You could fork down left for a track descending to the lane above Edale. Or keep ahead, level, on a farm track. Where it bends uphill, keep left on a path running down to a narrow stone bridge into Grindsbrook Booth and the Old Nags Head Inn.

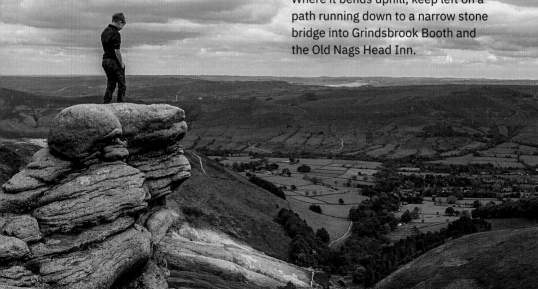

Lake District

And note, I do not refer to the 'English' Lake District. The RAF is the original air force; Royal Mail is the first ever postal service and doesn't need the UK's name on it. And the country of Cumberland and Westmorland is the original and only Lake District, of which all the rest are Johnny-come-lately imitations.

It's hard to believe that, a mere quarter-millennium ago, people looked at all this and didn't like it. Indeed, they were disgusted by the useless and ugly precipices, the scruffy oak woods. Either that or they were scared it was all going to fall down on their heads. It was here in Lakeland, around the year 1780, that it suddenly became cool to stand around in the rain, looking at scenery that included some stones and rocks.

Today, 30 million visitors a year agree with this proposition. The hills here may be small by international standards but they are splendidly craggy, carved by glaciers and then by the rain into ten thousand picturesque knobs and hollows. The Herdwick sheep, with some assistance from the Swaledale ones, have cropped them down to a smooth, lawn-like finish. The streams carve out a hundred romantic little chasms, ancient oak woods grow along the valley floor, stone walls pattern the fellsides, cottage gardens glow with roses and geraniums. And above all – or rather, below all – the dozen lovely lakes sparkle in the sunshine or hiss gently under the grey and silky rain.

As you get to know it, it just gets better. Down at valley level, you'll find thousands of miles of enchanting walks along the lake shores, under the ancient oak trees, beside the cheerful little streams. Up on the fellsides, the paths are well used and clear; and while some have been worn

ABOVE Evening on Harrison Stickle, Lake District.

down to rubble by millions of feet, many have been neatly repaired with stone cobbles. Fell-top views often include the gleaming mudflats of Morecambe Bay or else the sea itself, not to mention a couple of the lakes. The volcanic rocks are rough but firm, grippy underfoot even in the rain, warm like friendly old elephants in the summer sun. (The mudstone ones north of Derwent Water aren't quite so extremely accommodating.)

The tangle of valleys makes the Lake District seem bigger than it is; it's actually just twice the area of Greater Manchester. Given that on summer weekends most of Greater Manchester relocates to the Lake District, it can get crowded. Twenty-first century social media hasn't helped here. People look at Instagram and see something called Cat Bells and it's extremely pretty and so they head up Cat Bells. While they're up there they take some pictures and post them on Instagram... In Walk 1, I've specially suggested a first-walk-sized walk that isn't Cat Bells.

Yes, the Lake District can get quite crowded at times. And at other times, it can get very crowded indeed. Those times being summer weekends, and the whole of July and August through the English school holidays.

Fortunately, we don't need to bother working out which are the good bits. Of the Lake District's 2,400 sq km (900 sq miles), every one is a good bit. You could spend a lifetime pottering about in the Lake District, and many people do. Gentle lakeside rambles, exciting crag-top scrambles, relaxing ridgelines, challenging day-long expeditions, multiday treks from village to village via green, secret passes – I could write every chapter

of this book and just make it about Lakeland. And to some extent I have: a Lakeland backpack route is in the backpacking chapter, the Cumbria Way gets a spot in the section on Long-distance Paths, half a dozen Lakeland scrambles are included under Scrambling.

So instead of listing the reasons for going to the Lakes, it's simpler just to list the reasons not to. If you like your hills big, remote and challenging, then you'll head to Scotland. If you're after bleak and empty moorland stretching to the skyline, then you'll head for mid-Wales, or the non-National-Park parts of the Pennines. If you like limestone, you'll probably not be satisfied with the bits of it that sneaked into Lakeland's southern corner, and you'll be off into Yorkshire. And if you like seacliffs, then it's Wales again, or south-west England.

But if you like your hills craggy but comfortable; if you like your valleys green and scenic with little white-walled villages; if, indeed, what you like is lakes; where else would you go but Lakeland? And the only question will be: can we, to some extent, get away from the crowds?

BELOW Summit rocks of Slight Side above Eskdale, Lake District.

Borrowdale

Arguably the most beautiful valley in Lakeland? Well that's arguably true about all of them. Fully equipped with oak woods, lake and river; surrounded by two of England's highest hills and a splendid selection of smaller ones including the overtrodden Cat Bells; four little stone villages, six tearooms and a dozen pubs; and a first-rate bus service up and down the valley, over to Buttermere, and out to Keswick. Borrowdale: hard to beat it.

Getting there: West Coast Main Line to Penrith, frequent buses to Keswick, frequent buses into the valley

What's there: Youth hostel, Derwentwater Independent Hostel, Rosthwaite camping barn, campsites, pubs

Getting out: Mountains: Dale Head, Great Gable, Glaramara, Scafell Pike, Great End, Esk Pike, perhaps don't bother with Ullscarf

Crossings: Honister Rambler bus to Buttermere and back through the hills

Smaller hills: Castle Crag, Great Crag, Grange Fell, Walla Crag ... oh, and Cat Bells

Lower walks: Honister Rambler to Honister Hause and walk back; walk to Keswick and bus back; around Derwent Water; Watendlath and Langstrath

BELOW On Glaramara above Borrowdale.

LESS BUSY LAKELAND

Off-season weekdays: April, May, June and September are the nicest months anyway.

Late evening: Most people leave the fell tops around 3pm in time for the tearooms. In high summer, it stays light up there until 10pm. That's seven hours of solitude, if you want them. Stay up overnight and you've got the place to yourself through to 10am the next day.

Really rainy days: I did once walk from Scafell to Helvellyn and only met one other person. Well, it was Midwinter's Day, and rainy, with the cloud down to the valleys. But with good waterproofs, and good navigation skills, there's a surprising amount of fun to be had when it's bad. Oh, and you also need a decent drying room at day's end.

Wintertime: In January and February, there are no worries about booking a table for your bar meal. The bar itself is closed. The fells are almost empty. And snowy or no, a winter's day with the clear, cold air, the golden sunshine – it makes mere summertime seem almost uninteresting.

Less frequented hills: You'll get quieter summits north of the main fells at the Back o' Skiddaw; or along the eastern fringes, accessed from the A6. But there is a reason. These are the grassy-boggy hills without the craggy charm we look for in the Lakes.

THE BUSY BITS

Great Langdale: This is great, but not in the high season, at least unless you come in on the bus. It's the easiest to reach from the motorway, and by 9am on a sunny Saturday every parking place will already be being parked on.

Ambleside, Grasmere or Windermere: Avoid these unless you need to spend some outdoor time in some outdoor shops. Keswick is more like a real place. But elsewhere are slightly quieter small towns and villages such as Coniston, Cockermouth, Ulverston, Gosforth or Pooley Bridge.

BELOW On Gowbarrow Fell, above Ullswater: winter in the Lake District can offer wonderful light, as well as easier car parking and bar meals.

GREAT GABLE

Scafell Pike is not a bad summit. Not bad at all. It would be a really enjoyable ascent if it weren't for being the highest in England. Highest in England means a crowded (or possibly already full-up) car park; a busy and heavily trodden path, much of it rebuilt in pitched stonework; a noisy summit at which to eat your sandwiches; and the only pathside litter you're likely to see in all of Lakeland.

For a hill that's every bit as fine, and a mere 79m lower, my suggestion is Great Gable. Like Scafell Pike, you can get at Gable from several different valleys: Ennerdale, Wasdale, even Buttermere. Unlike Scafell Pike, there's an option to start from a high pass at Honister Hause. But one of the best is from Borrowdale. It's the route that offers a mix of steep ground and easy terrain; some big waterfalls; a hidden hanging valley halfway up the mountain; and a tarn to stop beside at teatime. The route also offers two adventurous options, on small and airy paths, for the bonus peak of Base Brown and an add-on extra waterfall.

And OK, Great Gable summit is another busy place. But 100m away at the plateau edge there's a cairn that isn't the summit one, with an even better view, and a little cliff to lean your back on. Yes, the clue is in the name. Great Gable.

ABOVE Great Gable and Green Gable.

BELOW Path to Sty Head, below Great Gable.

SCAFELL AND ITS PIKES

Sometimes they say 'I'm off up Everest' – when they're actually off up to Everest Base Camp. 'We're off up Scafell' is rather less of an offence against geography and altitude. That said, Scafell and Scafell Pike, are different peaks.

Up until about 1810, the great brooding lump of Scafell was the high point of England. The lesser summits lying to the west of it were the Pikes of Scafell, or Scafell Pikes. By 1818, when Dorothy Wordsworth made the first recorded ascent, the topmost Pike was known to be the high point of the hill. Even so, Dorothy apologised to her readers for not continuing to what she still considered the main mountain.

For as with K2 and Everest, Mount Kenya against Kilimanjaro, the second highest is actually a whole lot more challenging. Scafell Pike is a fine mountain, especially when approached out of Borrowdale or its wild southern side above Eskdale. But look at Scafell from Mickledore, the Alpine-style pass between the two. And you realise that Scafell is in a different league, the most impressive crag-ringed thing in England.

In case you're interested, there are three routes on to Scafell from Mickledore. The direct way is a short but exposed rock climb called Broad Stand, an accident hotspot very familiar to the Wasdale Mountain Rescue team. Down on the Wasdale side there's a stony gully slanting up through the heart of the crags: this is the scrambly Lord's Rake route. The walkers' way involves rather a long descent towards Eskdale, for a bouldery gully leading up to the hidden jewel that is Foxes Tarn.

BELOW Sour Milk Gill, Borrowdale.

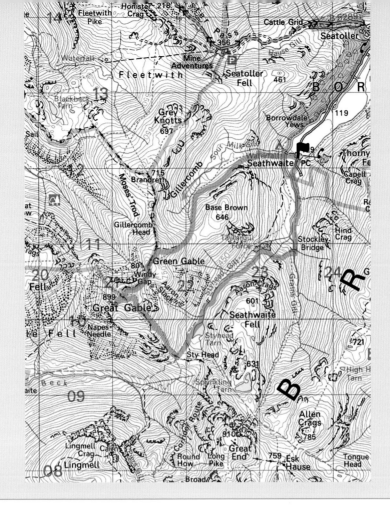

WALK 5 **Great Gable from Borrowdale**
START/END **Seathwaite, Borrowdale**
  (NY235122; postcode CA12 5XJ)
DISTANCE **9km (5.6 miles)**
ASCENT **850m**
APPROX. TIME **4 hours 30 minutes**
HIGHEST POINT **Great Gable, 899m**
TERRAIN **Hill paths, steep at the start,
  steep and stony on to Great Gable**
OPTIONS **Two adventurous options
  available on small, airy and slightly
  scrambly paths**

PARKING **Verge parking and
  inexpensive farm parking at
  Seathwaite; expensive National
  Trust car park at Seatoller**
CAR-FREE **Good bus service
  Keswick–Seatoller**
TOILETS **At Seathwaite**
PUBS & CAFES **The Langstrath Country
  Inn at Stonethwaite, excellent
  restaurant, booking needed most
  of the time**

From Seathwaite Farm, take a walled path through an arch to a footbridge over the River Derwent. (Or from Seatoller, take the lane south towards Seathwaite then a path to the right of the river.) A well-built path zigzags up slopes to the left of Sour Milk Gill and its waterfalls, all the way to the entrance to Gillercomb hanging valley.

Adventurous variant: The left-hand 'gatepost' of the valley is the steep, cragged end of Base Brown. Head straight up towards the first low cliffs. Above a boulder the size of a garden shed, a path contours off to the left below the cliffs, to run around the steep, east-facing slope. After 200m, the path turns back up to the right, slanting up and then turning directly uphill to the ridge crest above the crags. (This path appears on OS Explorer maps, and on OpenStreetMap layers on phone apps.)

The path runs up to the cairn and flat plateau of Base Brown, then gently downhill to the saddle at the head of Gillercomb.

The path runs up the hidden little hanging valley and climbs to the wide saddle at its head. Here, it turns right, with the 'adventurous' path from Base Brown joining again. The combined

BELOW Great Gable from Green Gable.

path, with cairns, runs up to gentler slopes and bends left to the summit of Green Gable, with a close-up view of Great Gable and its northern crag.

A stony path leads down to the narrow pass, Windy Gap. (Here, a rather steep and stony path down to the left is an escape route back to Seathwaite.)

Ahead, the path up Great Gable is steep and stony, with a section on bare rock. Then a line of cairns leads to the rock outcrop at Gable summit, recognisable by its brass memorial plaque. Descend south-west for 100m to Westmoreland Cairn, a quieter and more sheltered lunch spot, whose fantastic views down to the Napes Buttresses and Wasdale are considered the best in all Lakeland.

Return to the summit, and head down east past a large cairn. The path gets clearer, turning south then

becoming a pitched path all the way down south-east to the metal stretcher box at Sty Head Pass.

Turn left on a wide path running along the left (north-west) shore of Styhead Tarn and along its outflow stream to a footbridge.

Here, the more adventurous route keeps ahead to the left of the stream, to reach a little hanging wood of larch. The path edges along above a fence (to stop you falling into the waterfall below, especially if you're a valuable sheep) then contours across a steep slope alongside the high waterfall, Taylor Gill Force.

The path runs on to rockier ground, with some scrambling down with big holds to a gate below crags. The path becomes intermittent along slopes down the valley above the Grains Gill stream.

After 500m (0.3 miles), walls enclose a former plantation still with a few scattered birch trees in it: head for a single low pine tree at the top edge of this, where there's a ladder stile. The path now works down to the riverside opposite Seathwaite Farm.

Across the footbridge, the wide path heads downstream then bends away to the right, to the very pretty stone-built Stockley Bridge over Grains Gill. Turn down left to Seathwaite Farm.

Cleveland Coast

Known as the 'Dinosaur Coast', because 'Jurassic Coast' was already claimed elsewhere, Yorkshire offers tall cliffs of sandstone and ironstone, fossil hunting on the shingle beaches, delightful villages and towns such as Robin Hood's Bay and Staithes, Whitby and Scarborough. You can link the two ends of a clifftop walk by bus, or else by a long sweep inland over the North York Moors.

BELOW Sunset at Staithes, Cleveland coast.

Getting there: Railway to Saltburn, Whitby, Scarborough, and bus links along the coast

What's there: Youth hostels at Whitby Abbey, Scarborough and Robin Hood's Bay; Cleveland Way luggage transfer services along the coastal path. You can also use the North Yorkshire Moors Railway south from Whitby for valley and moorland walks.

Getting out: Chalk cliffs of Flamborough Head

Coastal walking on Cleveland Way between Filey and Redcar, about five day-stages

The fearsome Lyke Wake Walk, 64km (40 miles) across the moors from Ravenscar to Osmotherley

Yorkshire Dales

Yorkshire is not like the Lakes. Instead of huge vertical crags, crags are flat on the ground in the form of limestone pavement. Instead of lakes and mountains, there are wide, green dales with gently winding rivers. Instead of pay-and-display at £8.50 (just make sure you've got the coins!), you can park for free. And on an early summer evening when the Lakeland pubs had every table reserved, the one in Ingleton hadn't bothered to open the kitchen.

No, Yorkshire is not at all like the the Lake District.

Instead, imagine yourself on the lid of a typical English tin of biscuits. A little sandy coloured village under hillsides as green as mushy peas, field walls of golden stone matching the miniature crags breaking out above in an utterly unthreatening way. Cows knee deep in the stream, a waterfall in the foreground, and below the church spire, men in white standing around playing cricket.

This picture is incorrect. Nowadays, the cricket team wears a colourful outfit in imitation of the Australians; and the people inside it are just as likely to be women.

RIGHT Hardraw Force, Wensleydale.

Otherwise, the biscuit tin lid has got it spot on.

And they're quite right to name the place after its valleys. The best walking can be the low bits like Swaledale or Dentdale or Wharfedale. Along the riverbanks counting off the waterfalls, through the pretty villages laid out so suitably for the lid of the biscuit tin; then halfway up the valley side along a little limestone scar, one of the cliffs that interrupt the flat planes of the landscape.

Meanwhile, much of the high ground is wide and empty moorland, criss-crossed with grouse-shooters' tracks, where a rain-blackened signpost drips in the mist. Much of the high ground – but not all of it. In the south of the national park, south-flowing glaciers have carved

out pointier peaks, including the Yorkshire Three of Whernside, Ingleborough and Pen-y-ghent. And every now and then you come across a patch of grey-gleaming limestone pavement, or a stream that plunges down a hole into airy, dark spaces below. And did I mention the waterfalls?

Every dale is different. Wensleydale is the one with the waterfalls, from the wide but low river steps at Aysgarth to the fantastic freefall at Hardraw Force. Malham is the really busy one, with its spectacular crags. The other busy bit, Ribblesdale, with its Three Peaks, is for hillwalking, supposing you came to the Dales for the sake of the summits.

And so far north in the national park that they're not actually in Yorkshire at all, the Howgill Fells are a different sort of stone and a different sort of walking. Steep-sided and grassy, they're grand for long days out along the high ridgelines. They're easy to get into, from Sedbergh in the south. For car travellers, the northern valleys are long and lonely. Just avoid the western rim, where you're looking down on the noisy M6 motorway.

So yes, the Yorkshire Dales are England's finest upland walking that isn't the Lake District. And 'isn't' is the important word. Just a hop away across the M6 motorway, the Dales, with their caves and little crags, their wildflower meadows, their windswept moorlands, are different from Lakeland in every way. Except one. The business of being an extremely pretty place to go for a walk.

ABOVE Howgill Fells – in Cumbria, but also in the Yorkshire Dales National Park.

BELOW Path to Janet's Foss near Malham, Yorkshire Dales.

WEEK AWAY Settle

Settle's a charming small town, overlooked by limestone crags, with not one but two railway stations for getting to it – one of them on the famous Settle–Carlisle line. It's within walking distance of overcrowded Malham, so you can visit the Cove and Gordale Scar happy that you'll be spending the evening somewhere quieter.

BELOW Settle.

Getting there: By rail to Settle or Giggleswick

What's there: Plenty of pubs and B&Bs. The youth hostel is over at Malham

Getting out: Short walk to Stainforth Force and Victoria Cave

Long day across to Malham Cove, Gordale Scar and Malham Tarn

Train to Horton for Pen-y-ghent; back by Stainforth

Bus to Austwick and back by Giggleswick Scar

Relocate: To Ingleton (by bus) for the Waterfall Walk; Ingleborough; Whernside; Gragareth

INGLEBOROUGH

It's typical of Yorkshire walking that the very flat summit is far from the most exciting point on the walk. Just after the underground scenery of Ingleborough Cave, there's the dry gorge of Trow Gill between converging crags. At the walk's end, there's the hide-and-seek boulderfield of the Norber Erratics. But most impressive of all, there's the otherworldly landscape of Moughton Scars. If you saw it in a movie, you'd say they should have tried a bit to make it look like an actual plausible place.

That said, the summit plateau of Ingleborough isn't bad at all either.

If you start at 9am, you'll be reaching the show cave at 10am, just as it opens. Follow signs for Ingleborough Cave past the church, then uphill to the left of Clapham Beck. A metal arch ahead is for the nature trail to the cave. Or, 100m farther on, a track on the right

ABOVE Ingleborough summit plateau.

WALK 6 **Ingleborough**
START/END **Clapham, West Yorkshire (SD745692; postcode LA2 8EG)**
DISTANCE **21km (13 miles)**
ASCENT **800m**
APPROX. TIME **7 hours 30 minutes**
HIGHEST POINT **Ingleborough, 724m**
TERRAIN **Hill paths; rocky going over Moughton Scars**
OPTIONS **Shortcut from Sulber Gate by Pennine Bridleway: saves** 3km (2 miles) and avoids the challenging Moughton Scars
PARKING **National Park pay-and-display, Clapham village**
CAR-FREE **Clapham station 2km (1.2 miles); or buses from Settle**
TOILETS **Clapham car park**
PUBS & CAFES **Pub and cafe in Clapham (and recommended Game Cock Inn, Austwick); light snacks at Ingleborough Cave**

to Clapdale avoids the paid-for nature trail with its lake and ancient woodland. The two routes rejoin just before the entrance to Ingleborough Cave.

The cave costs around £10 and is impressive. There are stalactites and stalagmites, a little stream with pools and bridges, and flowstone formations with amusing names like Queen Victoria's Bloomers and Grandfather and Grandmother's False Teeth. The concrete walkway runs in for about 500m (0.3 miles), though it feels farther. There's one 20m section where adults will have to crouch.

ABOVE Trow Gill.

To the right of the cave, the wide path continues up the dry riverbed into the spectacular gorge Trow Gill. The path continues beside a wall, then over a stile on to open moor. The path up Little Ingleborough is obvious ahead but ignore all left forks until you've followed the main path up to Gaping Gill.

Here, the Fell Beck disappears into a gap in the ground, with no hint of the huge cavern opening underneath. (Don't try to peer over the edge, you won't see anything unless you actually fall in, when you'll have 4.5 seconds to examine the cavern before hitting the floor.)

Cross the stream just up from the chasm and keep ahead to join the well-used path up to Little Ingleborough. After a relaxing level section, the path climbs the final rise on to Ingleborough plateau. Cross it westwards to Ingleborough's cross-shaped shelter.

Turn back across the pathless plateau, just north of east, to its north-east corner. Just before the corner itself, the best path starts just below the left-hand, north-facing rim, slanting

ABOVE Ingleborough Cave.

BELOW Moughton Scars plateau.

down through the slab of riverbed gritstone that forms the top of the plateau. As the slope eases, bear right on a path that slants down the south-facing slope of Lord's Seat. The path drops across grassy moorland, then enters limestone pavement.

The path is sunken below the limestone surface. Then it dips to a path crossing with a four-way signpost.

Turn right on the grass track signed as the Pennine Bridleway to Clapham. It runs south-west to a gate (Sulber Gate) with a ladder stile. Through this, turn left to a small and little-used gate in the wall. (Even if you're now shortcutting out by the Pennine Bridleway, take a look through this gate anyway.) Now you're looking down over a low scarp on to a square mile of crumpled limestone, leading up to the unnamed trig point above Studrigg Scar (marked 427m).

People who know how to read can still get thrown by the instructions on YDNPA's pay-and-display machine down in Clapham. And people who think we know maps find we don't after all, on this grid square covered in crag markings, almost contour-free apart from the limestone scars, and they are so steep their contour lines are all →

on top of each other. Even when you've worked out where they are on the map, you can't tell which is the top and which is the bottom. On OS Explorer, the yellow-coloured 'access land' corresponds with the limestone plateau. On Harvey, the plateau is white and grey, and it's the valley below that's yellowish 'enclosed farmland'. On Landranger, the plateau's the ground without contour lines.

A small path runs down through the first limestone scar on to the flat plateau below. A faint path leads ahead for about 100m before bearing right, south, through the limestone pavement. You may fail to find it – in which case just keep south to find the plateau edge overlooking Crummack Dale. Here, the path dips towards a wall stile just below (Beggar's Stile). Don't cross this but turn up left on a faint path along the top of the drops above Crummack Dale.

Pass a cairn and continue along the scarp top overlooking Crummack Dale for 1km (0.6 miles), until a wall runs across ahead. Turn left alongside this, until it drops into a little incised valley. You could follow the wall down, over scree and bracken, but it's more comfortable to continue left, east, along the scarp top, to pass another cairn and reach the little valley's head. Here, an old cart track heads down into it, to a gate in the wall that crosses its exit.

On the way down the Whetstone Hole valley, the ground abruptly becomes heathery. We've descended off the limestone into much, much older Silurian mudstones. These slaty-looking, grey-brown rocks can be seen in the worn bed of the cart track, and soon appear in the drystone walls.

These ocean floor sediments got tilted to more than 45 degrees by the England–Scotland collision, before being carried thousands of miles northwards on the moving continent. Finally, just 337 million years ago, they were worn down flat by the arriving limestone sea.

So, these lower rocks are at →

a quite different angle from the flat-lying limestone above. This 'angular unconformity' suggests the huge gap in time that we've just walked down over. Halfway up the Studrigg Scar, on the left-hand valley wall, the two different rocks can be spotted lying one above the other. We'll meet the unconformity close up in another couple of miles.

The old, walled trackway runs down Crummack Dale below the limestone scars. After 2km (1.2 miles), turn right over a stone slab footbridge beside a ford, for a track rising across the valley. At the T-junction, turn left down the unsurfaced road. After 500m (0.3 miles), it becomes surfaced, passing a farm track on the left.

As the road bends left, look out for a wall stile up right, signposted for Norber. Head uphill to the left of a wall, with views over the wide valley. (Ahead is a conspicuous cliff, Robin Proctor's Scar: you'll shortly be passing along the foot of this.) At the field top, the path runs along a terrace in the small cliff Nappa Scar. At the end of the cliff, bear right up a small field to a step

BELOW Descending through the gritstone layer off Ingleborough plateau.

BELOW Norber Erratics: Ordovician mudstone on Carboniferous limestone.

stile. Above is the ground scattered with dark-coloured boulders, the Norber Erratics.

On Nappa Scar, you're right alongside the unconformity, the cliff at shoulder height is limestone, knee level is the Norber Formation, of Ordovician siltstone/limestone. The unconformity itself is a pebbly jumble that, 334 million years ago, formed the bed of the newly arriving Carboniferous sea.

A few steps later, you're among the scattered Norber Boulders of the same grey-brown, thin-layered rock. But here they're lying *on top of* the much younger limestone. Long-ago cricket-playing giants? The waters of Noah's flood? Today, we see these 'erratic' (or wandering) boulders as evidence of the great glacier that flowed down Crummack Dale and over this shoulder of the hill. To see the erratics actually perched right on the limestone you'll need to head uphill by 50m or so. It's a place →

to linger. After their birth on the ocean floor, being shoved around by moving continents, unearthed by erosion only to be buried under the limestone of a different sea, unearthed by erosion for the second time, and a little uphill trip by glacier, the boulders now have great views over the valley below.

The faint path contours west through the jumble of boulders, aiming for the base of Robin Proctor's Scar. You should pass a path signpost 'Clapham' ahead, then walk below the scar cliff above a wall. Through a small gate, the wall bends downhill, but now slant away from it down the field. Ascend gently across a final patch of limestone pavement to a gate and nearby stile on to a gravel track, Thwaite Lane.

Turn right, with a T-junction after 1km (0.6 miles). Turn left for Clapham, with a steep, stony descent and a dark tunnel to pass through, to arrive beside Clapham church.

England's coastlines

Seaside is in some ways quite like mountainside. The scenery is still pleasingly dotted with rocks. The coast path with its constant ups and downs is every bit as strenuous as heading up to some summit. The clifftops have the same harsh winds and weather, with the same wide, hazy-blue views, even if that blue haze is the North Sea rather than the suburban countryside of the Vale of York. The main difference is stopping every few miles for an ice cream and some sunbathing on the beach.

England has an awful lot of coastline. Shingle and sand dunes make for somewhat dreary walking, along the multi-coloured plastic litter of the high tide line. But wherever there's a cliffy bit, there's likely to be a likeable bit of walking. And most of the best bits have coastal paths, with a slow project to fill in the gaps along the less interesting sections.

For starters, there's the 1,000km (630 miles) of coastline crossed by the South West Coast Path: the shorelines of Dorset and some of Somerset, both coasts of Devon, and all of Cornwall. Great walking, every bit of it: you may decide where to go on the basis of the beach to relax on afterwards.

The Jurassic Coast of Dorset and south Devon is very busy in high summer. In spring and autumn, winter

ABOVE Clovelly harbour, North Devon.
BELOW Lizard Head, Cornwall.

The 'Three Peaks of Somerset', Selworthy Beacon, Dunkery Beacon and Periton Hill, rise around this small seaside town. There's high striding above the sea, deeply green woodland hollows, and the wide spaces on the edge of Exmoor.

Getting there: Bus from Minehead at the end of a long, slow railway line

What's there: First (or final) stop on the South West Coast Path, plenty of walker-friendly B&Bs, youth hostel at Minehead

Getting about: Bus to Minehead, back on the coast path over Selworthy Beacon.

Horner Wood to Dunkery Beacon.

Coast path west to County Gate, back by bus or by higher 'Coleridge Way' route.

Quantock Hills just down the road

---

even, it has a much wilder feel; also, it's easier to find somewhere to park the car. Then again, when well-known beaches are busy, there's satisfaction in finding sea-washed sand and solitude an hour's walk from any car park. The Dorset coast has downland above the sea, often giving a higher-level return after a clifftop excursion. The same is true of the Exmoor coast.

With such wonderful country inland, it wouldn't be fair if the Cumbrian coast were also a cracker. And it isn't, though there's a grand few miles of sandstone at St Bees Head. Northumberland has a much better coastline. And where the South Downs National Park meets the sea, at Beachy Head near Brighton, is a grand place to walk on the chalk.

JURASSIC FANTASTIC, DURDLE DOOR TO OSMINGTON

In high summer, the beach at Durdle Door is full of holidaymaking humans, beach towels edge to edge all the way along the sand. But in the springtime, when the sea's slaty grey and chilly winds nip in off the English Channel, there's only a couple of people in fleece outerwear watching the seagulls, and the famous coast path stretching like a pale, chalky ribbon through the yellow grasses.

Along this part of the Dorset coast, the clifftop path goes energetically up and down, as dry valleys carved into the chalklands reach down towards the sea. But a mile or so inland, level downland offers even bigger views. Combine the two for a huge selection of out-and-back walks, going as far away as you want.

Which, in this case, means the Smuggler's Inn at Osmington Mills. The coast path was built as a bit of anti-smuggling infrastructure. The Smuggler's Inn really was the place where they persuaded the exciseman to hide up the chimney while they brought the brandy ashore in the nearby bay. And on the return walk, for the bold, there's the airy zigzag path up the cliff face, the secret way used by the smugglers themselves and described in the Victorian adventure story *Moonfleet*.

BELOW Durdle Door.

WALK 7 Durdle Door to Osmington
START/END **Lulworth Cove, Dorset coast (SY823799; postcode BH20 5RH)**
DISTANCE **19km (12 miles)**
ASCENT **750m**
APPROX. TIME **7 hours**
HIGHEST POINT **Chaldon Down, 160m**
TERRAIN **Good paths and tracks: pebbly foreshore and narrow, exposed zigzags on the Smugglers' Path to White Nothe**
OPTIONS **Car parks above South Down Farm or at Ringstead, or start from Osmington village, for shorter walks taking in the Smugglers' Path; turn back at White Nothe for a shorter walk from Lulworth**
CAR-FREE **Jurassic Coaster Bus from Poole and Weymouth to Lulworth Cove and Osmington**
TOILETS **Lulworth Cove**
PUBS & CAFES **Bar meals and outside tables at the Smuggler's Inn at Osmington Mills**

The Zigzag started off as a fair enough chalk path, but in a few paces narrowed down till it was but a whiter thread against the grey-white cliff face, crossing a hundred feet direct above our heads... I do not believe that there were half a dozen men in England who would have ventured up that path. The ledge was little more than a foot wide, and ever so little a lean of the body would dash me on the rocks below.

J MEADE FALKNER, *MOONFLEET* (1898)

From the top of the large car park at Lulworth Cove, the wide, chalky track of the coast path slants up to pass above St Oswald's Bay and down to lower clifftops above Durdle Door arch. Follow the clifftops down to Scratchy Bottom, then take a gate on the right to slant away from the sea, up the grassy slope to a fence gate at its top. Turn up right to join a grassy track running along the downland high above the sea.

After passing below one concrete column ('Beacon' on the OS maps) and above another one, turn down left

beside a fence, to rejoin the coast
path along the clifftops. As you pass
the coastguard cottages at White
Nothe, you can divert to the clifftop,
where a low stone marker is the top of
the Smugglers' Path: look down it and
assess whether you want to use it on
the return journey. It's actually not quite
so alarming as it looks when seen
from above.

In another 1.2km (¾ mile), above
Holworth House, turn inland on to a
small track, bending left and rising to
a car park with tremendous sea views.
Here, turn downhill to South Down Farm
and turn left to reach a field path down
a grassy spur line. Follow the tarmac
track ahead (the toll road to Ringstead)
then turn left on a woodland path. After
a ford, join the track ahead to the road
above Osmington Mills. Turn down this
to the Smuggler's Inn.

Stirring tales of the smuggling times
are on a printout kept behind the bar.

ABOVE Chalk coastline towards Durdle Door.

The coast path back towards
Lulworth starts just above the inn.
In a few steps, a side path leads down
to the beach, where you can examine
shelly fossils and the spheroidal
'dogger' stones, limestone concretions
from when the sandy limestone rock
was forming.

At Ringstead, turn briefly inland.
The coast path continues on a track to
the right. After a trackside house, for
the Smugglers' Path you turn down to
the foreshore. Pass below the oily shale
slopes of Burning Cliff: you could find
ammonite traces in the beach boulders.
After 1km (0.6 miles), a wooden ladder
leads up into the wooded undercliff,
a lumpy ledge formed by landslips
below the main cliffs.

A tiny path weaves through the
scrubby undergrowth. Then it zigzags
up the grassy slopes

RIGHT Dogger concretions, Osmington Mills.

BELOW Smugglers' Path to White Nothe.

with chalk cliffs above it and soon below it as well, to reach the clifftop at White Nothe.

Turn back along the coast path, contouring around the steep slope of West Bottom then forking down right past the lower of the two stone beacons. The path climbs and descends along the high clifftops, back to Durdle Door. Follow the outward route back to Lulworth Cove.

At the top end of the car park you can head to the clifftops of Dungy Head, a superb and almost secret viewpoint, especially at sunset. →

Or from the small visitor centre in the village, the clifftops there are the sea-arch hollow containing the Lulworth Crumple, where the earth movements that are currently raising the Alps at the other end of Europe are happening right in front of your eyes.

WALES

England, with its honey-coloured Cotswold cottages, its leafy lanes, its lazy rivers: maybe it's a bit too comfortable and cosy. In which case, its wilder brother country lurks in the west. Wales – with its gnarled old oak woods, black mountains, and slate grey lakes. Wales, which even the Romans never really conquered. Wales, where the landscape's so tough they named three of Earth's geological periods after it.

Conveniently situated right up alongside England, Wales attracts huge numbers of climbers, cavers and canoeists as well as the tougher sorts of cyclists. And if you aren't lucky enough to already live there, it may well be your first destination for the more rugged uphill expedition, the less cosy sort of coast.

Away from the cities and former coalfields of the south, almost all of Wales is wild country. And the moorlands of mid-Wales can be very bleak indeed. But the bureaucrats have got it right this time. The three national parks are the place to start.

ABOVE Castell y Gwynt, Glyder Fach.

BELOW Feral goat enjoys the rough volcanic rocks of Tryfan.

WELSH HILL WORDS APPROXIMATED FOR ENGLISH SPEAKERS

CONSONANTS

C	always hard, as 'Cambria'
Ch	as in Scots 'Loch'
Dd	hard 'th' sound, as in 'breathe'
F	as English V, 'van'
Ff	as English F, 'fan'
Gh	guttural, as in English 'argh'
L	as English, 'lake'
Ll	compound, 'chl' as in Loch Lomond
W	when operating as a consonant, as English 'worm'

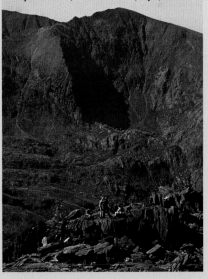

BELOW Garnedd Ugain from Glyder Fawr, Snowdonia (Eryri).

VOWELS

Au	close to English y at word end, 'cry, multiply'
U	closer to English I, 'bit'
W	when operating as vowel, as English oo, 'boom'
Y	as English U, 'bum'

Aber	Foot of (stream or river)
Afon	River
Bach/fach	Small
Bannau	Beacons, peaks
Bwlch	Pass or col, saddle
Carnedd	Cairn, pile of stones, or stonepile type hill
Cefn	Rounded ridge (literally, 'back')
Coch/goch	Red
Craig/graig	Crag
Crib	Hen's comb: sharp ridge
Cwm	Valley, corrie
Du, ddu	Black
Fan	Peak (singular form of *bannau*)
Fawr, mawr	Large; greater of two hills
Foel, moel	A hump-shaped hill
Glas	Blue, blue-grey
Isaf	Lower
Llyn	Lake
Mynydd	High moorland
Ogof	Cave
Pistyll	Waterfall
Rhaedr	Waterfall
Sgwd	Waterfall (yes, Welsh has three words for waterfall)
Uchaf	Upper (often paired with *isaf*)
Y, yr	The, of the

Snowdonia (Eryri)

Snowdonia, named in Welsh as Eryri, is the most concentrated chunk of mountain ground south of Glen Coe. Its heartland, north of the Vale of Ffestiniog, feels like the same craggy ground as England's Lake District crammed into half the size. The hills here are slightly higher: 15 of them over the 914.4m (3,000ft) mark as against England's four. But mostly, they're really, really rocky. A rugged mountain path turns into a clamber over boulders or an airy ridgeline. So if you want to admire the magnificent crags from underneath, rather than grabbing them in your hands as you go by or falling off the tops of them, you'll need to choose routes with a bit of care.

You may also need to choose your dates. Mountains like Tryfan and Glyder Fach are not only jammed closely together, they're also conveniently close to Manchester. Accommodation can be fully booked up right through the summer, and car parks are often full up as well. If you're prepared to book ahead, or arrive in the off season, there are six youth hostels and many inns and independent bunkhouses, all with hills rising straight from the doorstep. And all linked together with the useful Sherpa Bus service.

Four separate ranges are squashed into this little patch of ground. In the north are the Carnedds (or Carneddau – but check the box for the pronunciation). Wild and generally grassy up near the sea, they get craggier and craggier as you head south. Across the A5 is the magnificent Glyder group. Scrambly ridges or bouldery paths get you up Tryfan, whose summit is a vertical boulder you won't find it simple to stand up on. Glyder Fach and Glyder Fawr offer more rocky ridges and a bleak, stony plateau dotted with weird,

OPPOSITE Ten ways up Snowdon (see page 162).

BELOW Snowdon from Moel Siabod.

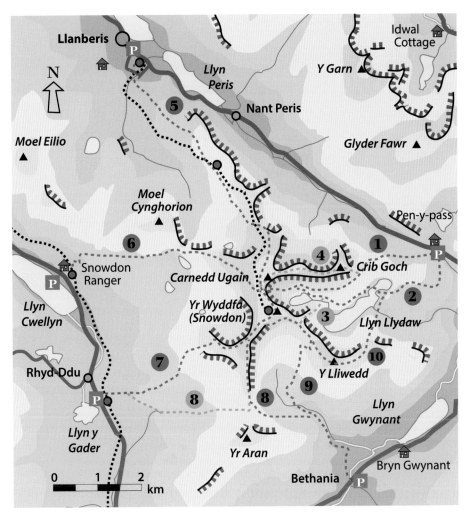

sculptural rockpiles – all reached from the craggy depths of Cwm Idwal.

In the west, the group starting at Moel Hebog offers more crags and ridges with a rather quieter ambiance. While in the south-east, the line of hills above Blaenau Ffestiniog has the Moelwyns and Cnicht at one end, Moel Siabod at the other, and some rather bleak rocks and bogland in between.

At the centre of all this rises Snowdon itself – named in Welsh as Yr Wyddfa. Not just the highest, but also the finest mountain in this fine mountain country. And yes, Snowdon is a busy hill. A very busy hill – not least because it's embellished, or defaced, with a mountain railway all the way up from Llanberis and a concrete cafe just below the summit.

On summer days you'll have to queue for the summit of Snowdon. And that's assuming you even got into the car park at the bottom. The main one at Pen-y-Pass fills up at breakfast time: you could book in advance – or,

CARNEDDS OR CARNEDDAU?

Carnedd means a cairn or big heap of stones, and the Welsh-language plural is Carneddau; similarly Glyders (Fach and Fawr) become Glyderau. Many prefer to use Welsh-language plurals even when speaking English: they should note that Carneddau is (approximately) pronounced *car-nethi*, with the last syllable like the word 'thy' rather than 'thigh'. The Welsh name for Snowdon is Yr Wyddfa (roughly, Ur Wuthe-va), and of Snowdonia is Eryri (Err-uroo).

better, take the bus from Llanberis.

And yet, despite all this, Snowdon remains supreme. On either of the routes from Pen-y-Pass, you may be traipsing in a queue of fellow tourists – but what you're traipsing through is a crag-ringed hollow sheltering two dark and slaty mountain lakes. High over your head is a steep-sided, spiky-topped ridgeline over Crib Goch that's one of the best scrambling routes in Britain. Meanwhile, all around the back are seven more ways of going up Snowdon, featuring oak wood hollows, waterfalls, more grim crags, more little lakes, and even more airy ridges. Best of all, the entire mountain is ringed by the Sherpa Bus service and the Welsh Mountain Railway through Rhyd-Ddu. So you can mix one way up with another way down for about

TEN WAYS UP SNOWDON (NOT COUNTING THE TRAIN)

See map (page 161).

1 **The Pig Track** Scenic and fairly short, a classic ascent route.
2 **The Miners' Track** Almost as good as the Pig, with Llydaw lakeshore but a longer final ascent.
3 **Gribin Ridge** A short scramble (Grade 1).
4 **Crib Goch and Garnedd Ugain** Grade 1 scrambling along a rocky, pinnacled ridge on excellent rock.
5 **Llanberis Path** The long but gentle ascent makes this Snowdon's easiest route
6 **Snowdon Ranger Path** A less-frequented route along the top edge of the dramatic climber's crag known as Cloggy.
7 **Rhyd-Ddu Path** The sharp ridgeline of Llechog has the airy feel of Crib Goch, but on a path.

OPPOSITE TOP Pig Track above Pen-y-Pass.
BELOW Y Lliwedd summit.

50 different combination expeditions.

Spoilt for choice on Snowdon? Well, if you're tough and confident, get into the car park early for the Snowdon Horseshoe: going up by the scrambling ridgeline over Crib Goch, coming down again over Y Lliwedd. For the rest of us: chose a quieter time of year and take the park-and-ride from Llanberis up to Pen-y-Pass. The Pig Track through Bwlch y Moch gives a surprise entry into the great central hollow. Once at the top, after refreshments at the cafe, there's the long but gentle descent of the north-west ridgeline to Llanberis. Or, for the extremely energetic, the long ramble onwards over Moel Cynghorion and Moel Eilio. Or, for the extremely tired, just buy a ticket and hop on the Snowdon Mountain Railway.

Being so close to big cities, Snowdonia could clearly do with being bigger itself. Which must be why, when they were designating

8 South Ridge from Bethania
Used by the Cambrian Way, with waterfalls, a sheltered hollow and a high spur line. A quieter route with real mountain atmosphere.

9 Watkin Path A sheltered route with an awkward scree finish.

10 Y Lliwedd Over a fine side-summit on the return half of the Snowdon Horseshoe.

PIG OR PYG?

Over the last century, the Pig Track out of Pen-y-Pass has suffered a linguistic transformation into the Pyg. This is possibly because of starting at the Pen-y-Gwryd Hotel (although it doesn't) or just being altogether more Welsh. Well, *pyg* is Welsh for tarmac, and with the heavy use it gets the path might even end up that way. The original spelling? It passes through Bwlch y Moch, the pass of the pigs.

the national park back in 1951, they stretched it so far to the south – more than doubling the size of the original Eryri or Snowdonia. This pulls in two extra mountain areas. North of Barmouth, the Rhinogs (or Rhinogydd) are low but very, very rugged, made of heather and tough, grey gritstone. Moel Ysgyfarnogod takes even longer to cross than it does to say its name. Cwm Bychan, right in the middle, offers the Roman Steps pathway up to the craggy ground. Rhinog Fawr and Rhinog Fach are big heaps of boulders peppered with little lakes. On a clear day, there are great sea views, supposing you can take your eyes off the awkward stuff underfoot.

South of Barmouth, the magnificent mountain Cadair Idris isn't much smaller than Snowdon itself. Its 14km (9 miles) of east–west ridgeline can be explored by various routes out of Dolgellau.

Between the mountain ridgelines, Snowdonia's deep, steep-sided valleys have main roads running through them. This is handy for bus-riders, but it makes Snowdonia not so special when it comes to valley-bottom rambling. For milder days out, on ground that's not so grimly forbidding, you could look southwards to the smaller national park at the other end of the country.

WEEK AWAY
Capel Curig

The scattered but ancient village has been the entry point to the mountains for several centuries. Today, the Sherpa Bus links to start points for most of the mountains.

Getting there: By rail to Betws-y-Coed, then frequent Sherpa Bus
What's there: Two ancient inns, an independent hostel, and the National Outdoor Centre at Plas-y-Brenin. There are cafes and the famous Joe Brown outdoor shop
Getting out: Moel Siabod, above the village (Walk 8).

Bus to Llyn Ogwen head, to cross Tryfan and return by the long eastward ridge over Cefn y Capel.

Bus to Llyn Ogwen head, for Llyn Ogwen and Glyder Fach, returning by the old track south of the A5.

Bus to Llyn Ogwen foot for Carnedd Dafydd and Llewelyn, again returning on the old track.

Short but vigorous crossing of Crimpiau, north-east of the village

BELOW Moel Siabod above Capel Curig.

MOEL SIABOD

Go up Snowdon? It's where everybody else is going and yes, they've got the right idea. But for a quieter day out, and one that involves a bit of boulder work that almost counts as climbing, I'm suggesting Moel Siabod above Capel Curig. It also offers some ancient oak wood, a riverside path and a spot of industrial archaeology alongside the old quarry pit, as well as a moorland lake with some bits of bog around it.

A moment on the soggy stuff only helps you to appreciate the wonderful roughness of the boulders above: a huge intrusion of volcanic rocks marvelled over by Charles Darwin

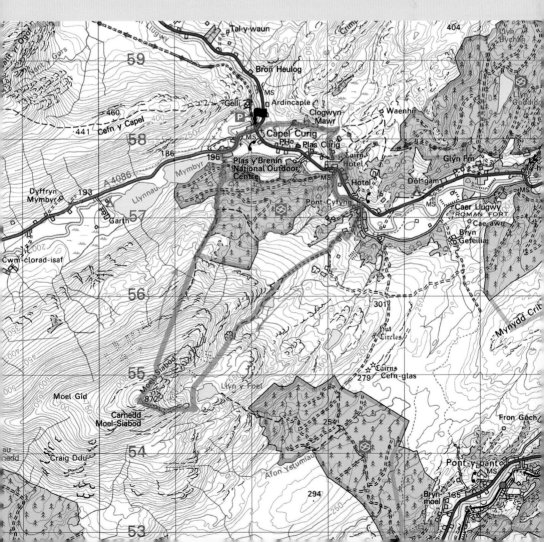

WALK 8 Moel Siabod
START/END Capel Curig (SH720581;
    postcode LL24 0EN)
DISTANCE 12km (7.5 miles)
ASCENT 900m
APPROX. TIME 5 hours 30 minutes
HIGHEST POINT Moel Siabod, 872m
TERRAIN Rough paths; bouldery
    scrambling (less than Grade 1)

PARKING Above Joe Brown's shop,
    may fill up at holiday times
CAR-FREE Sherpa Bus from the rest
    of Snowdonia and Betws-y-Coed
TOILETS Car park, Capel Curig
PUBS & CAFES The end of the route
    passes, or passes through, the
    cafe bar at Plas y Brenin

back in 1831 – let's not suppose it was the peaty bit around Llyn y Foel that made him flee Wales for the shipboard comforts of the *Beagle* later in the same year.

Up at the summit, there's the great view into the heart of Snowdon. Or else there isn't, letting you congratulate yourself on a slightly lower mountain that's not currently wrapped inside a cloud.

Maps have the hill as Carnedd Moel Siabod. Carnedd is a stony hill and Moel a humpy one; mostly,

however, it's just known as Moel.

From Joe Brown's shop, cross the A5 to a ladder stile marked for the Snowdonia Slate Trail. A faint path heads east up the field to its top-left corner. Now clear, the path continues behind the knoll Y Pincin, through a gnarly oak wood, and across open moor towards a stout footbridge. Just before this bridge, turn back sharp right onto a much fainter path. It runs down to the right of a wood, to meet a residential track.

Turn down right for 250m. Where it

BELOW Small quarry lake on the way to Moel Siabod.

ABOVE Scrambling on the Daear Ddu Ridge, Moel Siabod.

a footbridge over Afon Llugwy opposite Cobdens Hotel.

Head into the wood and turn left on a bigger path, soon alongside the river. It emerges from the woods and joins a driveway out to a small tarmac road at Pont Cyfyng.

Turn right, away from the river, and fork right up a tarmac driveway. As the lane emerges from woodland it takes a sharp right, and here a footpath keeps ahead through the bracken. It bends up to rejoin what is now a rough track that heads uphill.

After a holiday cottage, the track, now grassy, runs up towards Moel Siabod. It passes through two gates to head along below the left-hand slope of the mountain. After passing along a small lake, the stony path runs uphill to the right of a quarry spoil heap, to a deep, scenic quarry hole with a pool. The path passes up left of this, and continues uphill, south-west. It is now rough and could be mistaken for the

bends right, you could follow it down to the A5 again. But it's better to take the gate and stile on the left for a rough track up a field. After 100m, at a waymark post (unless the cows have knocked it over), turn off right, contouring across the field and down to a hidden gate into another wood.

The good path winds down to reach the A5. Turn right and walk for 200m to

BELOW On Moel Siabod summit, view west.

stream it sometimes becomes. After 400m (¼ mile), it crosses a slight col, where you look down into the hollow of Llyn y Foel.

There are various intermittent paths keeping to the right of the flatter and wetter ground next to the lake, to reach the foot of Moel Siabod's gently angled but rocky east ridge.

Who Daears wins

The ridge is Daear Ddu on Explorer maps, allowing the obvious but still effective pun. Its crest offers blocky scrambling, on slightly pimply rounded rock.

> The intrusion itself is huge, forming both walls of the corrie above Llyn y Foel. This meant that it cooled really slowly, enough to crystallise as microgabbro. The crystal texture is what makes it so grippy underfoot.

A small path winds up the ridge crest, with several passages of scrambling in short, easy-angled grooves with no exposure. More challenging lines, on good clean rock and some exposure, are up to the right, overlooking the drops to Llyn y Foel. After a tiny shoulder high on the mountain, the spur line becomes grassy and stony, soon leading to Moel Siabod's stone-built trig point.

A stone-built shelter ring is just north of the summit. Pass to the right of it, to head down north-east. The ridgeline is fairly definite, with a steep crag drop on its right. About 300m from the summit, the ridge levels off before a slight craggy rise ahead. At this levelling, you must ease down to the left. Once you've found the top of it, a clear path slants down the hill flank, north-north-east, passing through a fence. As the slope widens out, the path heads for the top-left corner of an area of plantations and clear-fell. A sharp dip leads to a gate into the former plantation.

The path, now clear but rugged, runs down through open rowan woods and plantation remnants. Where it reaches a crossing track, turn left for a few steps across a stream, then downhill again on the continuation path. This soon reaches a track at the slope foot. Cross this, to a footbridge below Plas y Brenin. The path passes up to the left of the outdoor centre, but you can go through gates to the bar/cafe there.

At the road above, turn right. There's no pavement and it's an A road; but it's not far to the crossroads in Capel Curig.

ABOVE Leaving Pen y Fan summit towards Corn Du. Wide, easy and well-used paths.

The great scarp: Brecon Beacons (Bannau Brycheiniog)

Snowdonia is jaggy. Brecon isn't jaggy, it's flat. Snowdon's volcanic and craggy. Brecon is flat-lying sandstone. Snowdonia is covered in stones, and heather, chewed at by wild goats. Brecon is gently grassy, with ponies. Snowdonia is one of the UK's very best places for mountain walking. Brecon is also one of the UK's very best places for mountain walking.

A great north-facing escarpment runs for 70km (45 miles) across the southern part of Wales. It's named as four separate ranges: the Black Mountains (with an s on the end), the Brecon Beacons proper above Brecon, the Fforest Fawr and the Black Mountain (without an s, in Welsh the Mynydd Ddu). But basically it's all one ridge. Short spurs run down northwards, enclosing high-level lakes. Long ones run down to the south, offering full-day mountain horseshoe routes. And the A470 road runs right through one of the high passes, offering a short half-day up Pen y Fan.

Pen y Fan is the high point, and at 886m it's only a pebble or two lower than Cadair Idris and the Welsh 3,000-footers (914m) up in Snowdonia. I have to say it doesn't feel like it. The walking here is altogether less demanding. Paths are wide, smooth, and sandy. In the popular parts around Pen y Fan, the steep bits have been rebuilt with cobbles and tidy stone steps. Only the huge views northwards remind you that you're on one of the UK's major ranges.

I've never warmed to the Black Mountains, the bit at the eastern end. Maybe it's because this is where I spent teenage years learning my maps by getting lost on the wide and soggy ridgelines. But the valleys between are green and wooded with little rivers, and the northern corner of the high escarpment, where it butts up against England, is named as Lord Hereford's Knob – so what's not to like?

The true Brecon Beacons, the 15km (9 mile) stretch featuring Pen y Fan, is the most soaring and spectacular part of the ridgeline. But given the short ascent out of Storey Arms, it's also the busiest. Westwards, the Fforest Fawr and the Mynydd Du or Black Mountain are the quiet end of it all, and the cliffy edge below the Black Mountain has two lovely lakes.

Oddly, it's the bottom bits of Brecon where the rugged walks are. Among the wooded river valleys of the southern edge you see the warning signs: 'These paths are narrow, unsurfaced and slippery...' No such warnings in Snowdonia, where slippery, narrow, unsurfaced paths are all the paths there are. But the warnings are more needed here if you've come from the smooth-topped summits down to the rocky riverbanks, steep-sided valleys, and trails that can even have you walking behind the waterfalls.

The Waterfall Country, at the southern edge of the Fforest Fawr, is where you can visit nine of the splashy items in one long walk. In summer, it's so busy there's a park-and-ride from the small town of Glyn Neath.

BELOW Passing behind Sgwd yr Eira on the Waterfalls Walk.

PEN Y FAN HORSESHOE

The walk from Storey Arms on the A470 up to Pen y Fan isn't just extremely busy. It's also rather short (8km/5 miles and 500m ascent, about 4 hours). You can make it more exciting, and also quieter, by heading up over Y Gyrn for more of the north-facing edge. But if you've the time and energy, a circuit from the south gives far more of that northern edge line, and much more peaceful walking apart from the short stretch over the two highest tops. Plus you're more likely to come across the numerous ponies.

Blaen-y-Glyn is just as high up as Storey Arms. This walk does have a fair amount of up in it, but the high start means it comes in bits all through the walk. And the paths are mostly smooth and easy. So you could even say the route feels less strenuous than it actually is.

At the foot of the car park, head up a well-made path to the right of the stream, then up open hillside on to the steep nose of Craig y Fan Ddu. The wide, smooth path runs along the top of steep drops to the right. It crosses

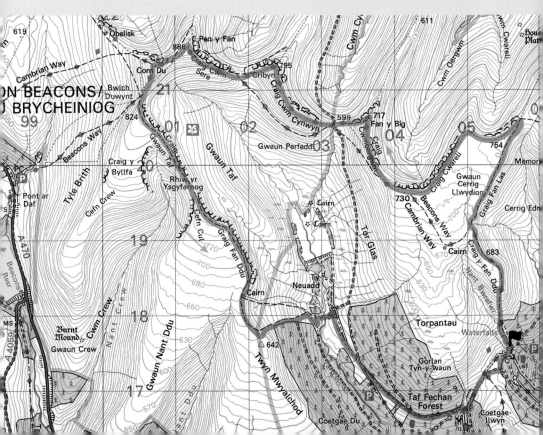

WALK 9 **Taf Fechan Horseshoe to Pen y Fan**
START/END **Blaen-y-Glyn upper car park (SO056175; postcode CF48 2UT)**
DISTANCE **20km (12.5 miles)**
ASCENT **1,000m**
APPROX. TIME **8 hours**
HIGHEST POINT **Pen y Fan, 886m**
TERRAIN **Good hill paths, steeper sections mostly stone-surfaced**
OPTIONS **Turn back on the old road before Fan y Bîg: 13.5km (8.5 miles) with 500m ascent – about 5 hours**
PARKING **At start, also in upper Taf Fechan valley**
CAR-FREE **Buses run from Merthyr Tydfil to Pontsticill, 5km (3 miles) from the walk. The Welsh Mountain Railway, from the edge of Merthyr Tydfil, starts too late in the day and ends too early to be useful for this walk**
TOILETS **Portaloos at start**

a slabby stream (which can be dry in summer) then runs north-east along the plateau edge of Gwaun Cerrig Llwydion, still with steep drops on the right.

Follow the path to a wide saddle with a sudden view down the steep scarp towards the River Usk and Brecon. Here, turn back sharp left along the scarp top. The path, occasionally rough, runs around the head of two deep hollows, with views ahead to Pen y Fan.

At the back of the second hollow, Cwm Oergwm, the path drops north-west to a col. Here, the main path contours left but take a less obvious one up the crest ahead, still next to the drops into the cwm, to arrive at Fan y Bîg.

This feels like the corner of everything, the cairn perched high above the Brecon lowlands. There's nowhere to go but back in the arrival direction, but this time bearing right, south-west, still with those big drops to the right. At once, you pass the Diving Board, a projecting sandstone slab for photo-posers to pose on. Then the path leads steeply down, well rebuilt in the spring of 2016 and nicely grassed in since. On the way down, a contouring

BELOW On Craig y Fan Ddu.

path joins from the left, the bypass path noted earlier. Then the path reaches a major pass with a dirt path or narrow track passing through it.

> This is Bwlch ar y Fan, the 'gap on the peaks'. The track through it is the former road between Brecon and the Taf Fechan, marked as 'road used as public path', and appearing on at least one internet journey planner as a usable route for drivers. More usefully, it's a shorter return to Blaen-y-Glyn, avoiding the busy high points of the walk ahead. Simply turn back down left, raking down the slope above the head of Taf Fechan, to rejoin the main route on the track above the valley floor.

The path slanting up leftwards bypasses Cribyn, so keep straight uphill on a steep but well-built path. At Cribyn summit on its high corner, again turn back left, down into another deep saddle for the big path up Pen y Fan.

It's lucky the summit triangle is so wide and flat, given the number of people picnicking or simply standing about up here. The wide, sprawly cairn has a National Trust marker on top.

The wide, smooth path runs down north to a narrow col. Here, one wide path contours ahead to bypass Corn Du, the other heads up to its summit. Turning south-west at the top, there's a rocky corner with slabby bare rock steps down to the next saddle, Bwlch Duwynt. (Here, the main path to Storey Arms strikes down right, taking most of the crowds with it.)

Now a much smaller path runs ahead along the brink of a steep and slightly craggy slope dropping left to the head of Taf Fechan valley. It follows this edge for 2km (1.2 miles) – note that the Upper Taf Fechan Reservoir marked on some maps has been drained and no longer exists.

After 2km (1.2 miles), you reach a slabby stream crossing with a sprawly cairn. Here, the map shows a path dropping left down a stony groove, very steep and uncomfortable – don't take this one. Instead, carry on along the scarp top for another 500m (0.3 miles) to the second of the paths marked on OS maps, directly above a forest corner. Here, the main path turns down left,

BELOW The Diving Board, Fan y Bîg summit, Pen y Fan behind.

Head up to a tarmac track heading right, down valley. At a wooden 'Taff Trail' signpost, a wide path joins from above: this is the 'old road', the shortcut route descending from Bwlch ar y Fan.

with only a faint one continuing ahead. (If you reach a trig point on the wide ridge crest, you need to turn back north for 200m.)

This descent path has been heavily and effectively repaired, but at the very top the stone slab steps have loose stones and gravel over. It descends to the left of the plantation, then down grassy moorland, to a gate into a belt of trees. Through this, the path winds down to a stout footbridge, then up to some ruined reservoir buildings.

At this X-junction, the tarmac track slants downhill but take the wide path contouring ahead, a former railway line. The railway path runs through several small gates, with views across the valley and the reservoir farther down it. It becomes a forest track, soon reaching a road.

Turn left up the road. At its top, a side track right leads to a gate before a mobile phone mast. Turn left down a rough path to a signpost at the track end for the car park.

Welsh coast

A coastal path covering the entire country? Not a possible plan, I thought when the Welsh Government proposed it back in 2006. But it was, and they did it in a mere six years – less time, almost, than it takes to walk the thing's 1,400km (870 miles).

It helped that the Welsh Parliament had only that year been reformed after a 600-year break, and wanted to show the English it could do things. What also helped was that important bits of it already existed. There were paths in place around Ynys Môn, the Isle of Anglesey, as well as the Llŷn peninsula that sticks out south-west from Snowdonia, and the whole coast of Pembrokeshire. And those paths were popular.

The process is also aided by events of 350 million years ago, when Africa crashed into Europe and Wales found itself in the crumple zone. Western Wales is made of ancient rocks that have been raised, folded and broken

ABOVE St Non's Bay, Pembrokeshire Coast Path.

BELOW Devil's Bridge at Worm's Head, Gower.

in this huge movement of the earth. This ends up as a wild and jagged coastline with a small grassy path along the clifftop, a fearsome salty wind off the Atlantic, and little bays where in September the baby seals lie around among the stones like leftover bags of cement.

'Oh for a horse with wings,' cries Imogen in Shakespeare's *Cymbeline*, 'to fly me to Milford Haven!', though I've misquoted her slightly. The lively, cross-dressing princess has got the right idea, although she's a bit off on the detail. Milford Haven is actually the one bit to skip on the magnificent Pembrokeshire coast. The 300km (186 miles) of it form a national trail around Britain's second thinnest national park. That's short enough to walk in a fortnight – especially if you sensibly skip Milford Haven.

OK, the national park that's thinner than the Pembrokeshire Coast is the Norfolk Broads. There's some good walking there as well, but it's very flat.

St David's

This charming city, the smallest in Wales, has not only a 12th-century cathedral but also a palace. The saint could almost have founded it for the purpose of walking bits of the Pembrokeshire coast.

Getting there: A long but scenic train ride from Swansea, then bus from Haverfordwest

What's there: Youth hostel at St David's Head 3km (2 miles) from the city; hotels, B&Bs and self-catering; cafes and all useful shops including outdoor gear

Getting out: Bus/walk to St Justinian for summer ferry to Ramsey Island

'Puffin Shuttle' bus to Marloes for Skomer Island

Choose your own coastal chunk with direct buses from/to Newgale, Solva, St Justinian, and the Strumble Shuttle along the coast road to Fishguard

BELOW St David's Cathedral.

SCOTLAND

Southern Uplands and other lower-level walking

The Highlands, as the name suggests, are great for high-level hikes; but a low-level walk leaves you low in spirits with a bog seeping into your boots and spruce prickles down the back of the neck. Perhaps there'll be a newly built timber extraction track to spoil your walk or scrambling through a stream in spate.

Scotland's open access laws don't actually help here. Open access almost everywhere means Scotland's countryside doesn't have a network of designated paths – nothing like the widespread rights-of-way in England and Wales.

For lower walking, then, the best idea will be to go to one of the places with its own network of waymarked walks. For instance, Kinlochleven: a 3km (2 mile) stroll, or a 20km (12 mile) all-day ramble, right from the bus stop or the porch of your hostel. The ancient pinewoods around Aviemore, at the edges of the Cairngorms, are also fine walking: perhaps even more so when the wind whips the branches, the cloud dashes by a few metres over your head, and real waves lap the shoreline of Loch an Eilein with its island castle.

But when thinking low-level, there's also the Southern Uplands. Hills rising not much above the 500m

ABOVE Loch an Eilein Castle in the Caledonian forest near Aviemore.

mark stretch across from Galloway in the south-west all the way to the Cheviots in the east. Smaller, and much less challenging, than the mountains of the Highlands, they're a good place to practise your map reading and maybe get lost a few times, with no real danger of falling over a cliff as a result. To help your learning experience, most of the hilltops are deserted, except for the sheep.

Pitlochry

Pitlochry, in what used to be called Highland Perthshire, isn't just the Scottish capital of the tartan tearoom. It also has a wide and wooded network of well-made paths around Loch Faskally and up the great River Garry to Killiecrankie. Above the town there's a great wee hill, Ben Vrackie – 841m being, in the context of Highland Perthshire, a pretty minimal hill. Just upstream at Blair Atholl you can head on to the big, lumpy summits of Atholl. And if at the end of an energetic day you're feeling just like a nice cup of tea and a bit of shortbread – you're in the right place for that as well.

Getting there: Frequent trains and coaches from Edinburgh. The walks are straight from the town, no car needed

What's there: A grand Hydro Hotel, a humble youth hostel, and everything in between. Also distillery, Festival Theatre, and Blair Castle up the river

Getting out: Riverside walk to Killiecrankie and back down along the other bank.

Ben Vrackie, with possible descent to Killiecrankie.

Beinn a' Ghlò and Atholl Munros from Blair Atholl.

Rob Roy Way long-distance path to Loch Lomond

ABOVE Killiecrankie riverside path.

SCOTLAND'S SMALL BITERS

MIDGES

These nasty little insects have nasty little wings that fly at 2km/h (1.2mph). So if you're still walking, you're safe. Or if you're on a slightly breezy hilltop, you're safe. But if you're camping out, then you'll need midge repellent. And a midge net as well. Oh yes you will.

ABOVE An effective little tick-picker.

TICKS

Ticks are horrible little things with eight legs that clamp their jaws into you and suck your blood. And they clamp into your dog even more. A few of the ticks carry Lyme disease, which is a serious illness if untreated. Watch out for a spreading rash around a tick bite, a rapidly growing circle 10cm or even 20cm across. This is harder to see if your skin is black or brown, it may just look like a bruise. If in doubt go to a doctor anyway. Ticks can be pulled off with fingernails, but the handy little tick remover does a neater job.

What to expect if you do decide to raise your game in the Southern Uplands? Miles and miles of rounded, grassy hilltops, with peewits and skylarks overhead and views (on a really clear autumn day) right across the Lowlands to Ben Lomond or Ben Lawers. Below the wide ridgelines, the valleys are deep, steep-sided and green. There's probably a pele tower, a small fortress left over from when the people charging across these hills

BELOW Loch Enoch, Galloway Hills.

were on their way to steal someone else's cows.

After five or six hours across the beige-coloured grasses and occasional peaty bit, having passed several sheep and possibly a fox, you're looking down into the next of the green, deep glens, with its own gleaming silver river and another pele tower.

Just one word of warning. Away at the western end of the range is a patch of hill ground that's rather less sheepish and soothing. I guess I do need to give a mention to the Galloway Highlands, the hill group north of Newton Stewart – given that they might, just might, be Scotland's third national park. Also because, untrodden and ignored as it is, it's my local hill group and a special favourite of mine.

No rounded grasslands here. Galloway is a place of wild goats, granite slabs and silver lochans. Galloway's grey crags gleam under the rain; harsh peaty paths lead into

SHORT BREAK
Peebles

Borders Region used to market itself is 'Scotland's Top Short Break Destination'. The handsome Border township of Peebles lives up to the slogan, with a network of low-level walks and easy access to the long ridgelines of the Manor Hills. Hill paths here were once used by raiding cattle thieves, and later by the drovers.

Getting there: By bus from Edinburgh
What's there: B&Bs, some of which will also accommodate your horse
Getting out: Over the low Cademuir Hill with its impressive hill forts, back by River Tweed with its impressive Neidpath Castle.

John Buchan Way (22km/14 miles) to Traquair.

Glen Sax horseshoe over Dun Rig (742m).

Very long Manor Water circuit to Dollar Law (817m)

BELOW Looking at the Manor Hills from the small Cademuir Hill near Peebles.

ABOVE Beinn a' Ghlò, a group of three Munro summits in the south-east Highlands.

wide acres of nothing much at all. It's a long way to get to Galloway, there's hardly any places to stay, and most of the walkable ways in are through plantations of gloomy spruce. Oh, and the midges are quite bad too. No, I'm not just a grumpy bloke who wants to keep the Galloway Hills people-free just for me...

The Munros

They who have a Why to their life, endure almost any How
– Friedrich Nietzsche

German philosopher Friedrich Nietzsche did his hiking around the shores of Lake Silvaplana in Switzerland. You can put up with almost anything – low cloud, wet feet, interminable bogs – so long as it's part of a project. Nobody said the project has to make any sense...

There are 282 hills in Scotland over 914.4m (3,000ft) high. The sport of going up every one of them was invented in 1891. Today, most people going up hills in the Highlands are going up the Munros.

The project is persuasive. Almost every one of the 282 is a worthwhile summit (the exceptions might be the A9 hills, the Monadhliath mountains and Beinn na Lap). Chasing after the whole lot will give a rich and varied experience: from the pointy peaks of the west to the great granite plateau of the Cairngorms; the far-flung summits of Sutherland, and the boat ride to the Isle of Mull; serious scrambling on Skye, plus the day dangling on the climbing rope at the Inaccessible Pinnacle.

Best of all, the ticking off of the list might even persuade you there's some ultimate point to all this walking up hills and back down them again.

➜ Two hundred and eighty two sounds like a lot. But often you cross two, four or even more in a single walk. Up 914.4m is tough, and down is even tougher; the nice bit is the linky ridges from Munro to Munro.

ON NOT GOING UP BEN NEVIS

Ben Nevis is, for many people, their first Scottish mountain. And it does have one plus point in this respect. If you enjoy Ben Nevis, straight up from sea level at the edge of Fort William – well, every one of the remaining 281 Munro summits is even nicer than that.

Ben Nevis by the Pony Path – and even after they've renamed it as the Mountain Trail – is still one of the grimmest things in hillwalking. Up and up, on a line of jammed boulders, for four hours or even five. The magnificent crags to the north, do you see them? You do not. The interestingly varied chalets and caravans of lower Glen Nevis, do you see those? Yes you do, a nice full-on view, all the way until you finally arrive inside the summit cloud and drizzle.

But if up is not much fun, just wait till you hit down. Or rather, down hits you, on the toe tips, over 10,000 uncomfy footsteps. The sun goes down, and the shadows gather in the glen, and the lights go out in the bar of the Nevis Inn.

Just one consolation. As the busiest hill path in Scotland, it's a friendly and sociable day out, with plenty of fellow sufferers to share a good moan.

It's no great secret that there's a better way up Ben N. For Munro folk, the Carn Mor Dearg Arête also gets you Carn Mor Dearg, Britain's sixth highest hill unless I counted them up wrong. It also gets you a mountain mile of jammed granite, a line across the sky like a vapour trail made of solid stone. The scrambling from boulder to boulder is easy enough for most people: not usually counted as even Grade 1 for difficulty. This is just as well. You don't want to be too distracted from the

→ The popularity of the Munros means they're actually easier than hills of 914.0m (2,999ft) and below. There'll be a recognised car park, and a clear, possibly eroded, path. Munros guidebooks (there are several) list the car parks and the shortest ways up on those standard baggers' paths.

→ As your skills and experience improve, there are fabulous days to be had by seeking out the longer routes around the back: the untrodden ridgeline, the hidden corrie and the quiet riverside. The trodden path of the standard baggers' route can then be used for coming down again.

→ Public transport in the Highlands is patchy and getting patchier. A serious Munro project pretty much always requires a car – perhaps hired at the railhead of Inverness or Fort William. But for the strong and confident, there is the option of long backpacking trips of a week or more, over many Munro summits, with nights in a tent, bothy, bunkhouse or one of the Highland inns.

mighty Ben Nevis north face, its cliffs and towers and buttresses, spread just behind your handhold.

So it does make sense to leave Ben Nevis until you've built up the confidence for that serious, and seriously magnificent, rocky ridgeline. In the meantime, for your start-up Munro, how about the rather more rewarding, and considerably less tiring, Ben Lomond. And for a serious, high-mountain ascent that still isn't Ben Nevis, Walk 16 offers two tops and an airy ridgeline high above Kinlochleven.

BELOW The great north face of Ben Nevis, unseen by most walkers.

Loch Lomond and the Trossachs National Park

With so much richness on offer, where to start? Surprisingly, this one has a straight and simple answer: Loch Lomond and the Trossachs. At the southern edge of the Highlands, these hills are easier to get to: the West Highland Railway and the Citylink coach from Glasgow go right through the middle. There are places to stay, even if the ones on the West Highland Way get booked up through the summer. The national park's 21 Munro summits are craggy and interesting, with just a couple of dull ones to lend weight to the mix. (Which two are those? You'll find out as you go along.) At the same time, none is seriously difficult; the rocky-topped Cobbler is, endearingly, just too low to be a Munro.

And to start off, how about the most southerly, and most straightforward, of them all?

A FIRST MUNRO: BEN LOMOND

Ben Lomond is almost on the outskirts of Glasgow – if you happen to be here on a winter's night, you'll see the hill lit up in neon orange by the cities of the south. It also has one of Scotland's most famous songs about it. These two, together, make it a busy hill. Two further factors make it even busier still.

First, it's surprisingly easy: a wide, clear path running at a fairly gentle angle all the way up. And most important of all, with shapely mountains all around, the great loch all along its foot, and views stretching all the way to Ben Nevis, it really is a very lovely place.

Though not, as I said, a place of great solitude.

Along the summit ridge there are drops on the right that are exciting or scary, depending on your temperament and tastes. And at the summit itself, there's an option to try out something more adventurous, or at least to take a peep, down Ben Lomond's north-west ridge. The path is rather steep and rather rocky, and the ridge sides drop down and down to the moorlands below. But here's the clever bit: the steepest, rockiest bit is right at the top. So if the top feels OK, you can take it all the way down. And if it doesn't, you can turn back down the busy main path you came up by.

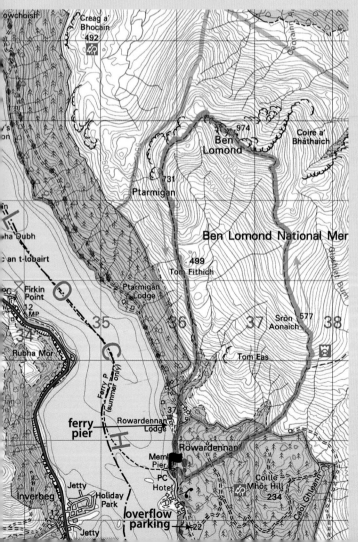

ABOVE Ben Lomond seen across its loch.

WALK 10 **Ben Lomond**
START/END **Rowardennan, Loch Lomond (NS359986 postcode G63 0AR)**
DISTANCE **11km (7 miles)**
ASCENT **1,050m**
APPROX. TIME **5 hours 30 minutes**
HIGHEST POINT **Ben Lomond, 974m**
TERRAIN **Wide, well-maintained hill path: maintained but rugged path for the descent**
OPTION **Shorter and easier return by ascent route**
PARKING **Large car park, plus overflow parking 800m (½ mile) south**
CAR-FREE **Train or coach Glasgow–Tarbet (Loch Lomond) for waterbus April–October to Rowardennan. Overnight stop at a youth hostel, Rowardennan Hotel or a bunkhouse**
TOILETS **Rowardennan car park**
EAT AND DRINK **Rowardennan Hotel, alongside lots of West Highland Way walkers**

Confident walkers will take this in the reverse direction, when the gentler main path becomes a pleasant and easy descent route.

From the overflow parking, take the left-hand of two forest tracks gently uphill to a bend to the right. Here, turn left, signposted for Ben Lomond, on a side track through →

birch and buddleia. In 500m (0.3 miles) there's another signpost as the main path crosses the track.

From Rowardennan, pass through the middle of the information/toilet block to the wide Ben Lomond Path.

The path runs up through birch woods planted at the beginning of the century, and still young enough to allow views up Loch Lomond. It emerges to open hill and ascends north on to the near-level shoulder called Sron Aonaich (the shoulder of the ridge, though the Gaelic *sron* literally means 'nose'). Finally, it ascends more steeply on to Ben Lomond's short summit ridge. Just above the path you could follow the ridgeline itself, with craggy drops behind it.

The main path then goes up over rock slabs to Ben Lomond's flat, rocky summit.

The rugged path down the north-west ridge starts immediately behind the concrete trig point, and zigzags down, with steep drops on either side. After a couple of more level shoulders, the ridge drops to a flat area of moorland. Just above that point, the path slants down left, and crosses a wide saddle.

Now the path passes along a series of bumpy tops, skirting left of the first of them and crossing the next one, the Ptarmigan. It bends left to the top of a broad ridge descending south-east. After a few hundred metres it eases down on the right-hand flank, high above Loch Lomond, and passes through a gate in a deer fence.

The song 'The Bonnie Banks o' Loch Lomond' mentions the 'steep, steep side of Ben Lomond', and the path slants down this, finally bending down through woodland to a track at the hill foot. Follow this to the left, past the youth hostel's entrance track. A path on the right takes you along the loch shore, past a ring-shaped memorial sculpture, to the disued pier at the car park.

BEN LOMOND'S PATH

Today's path that's 1–2m wide replaces a former 15m-wide scar, the worst in Scotland and visible from the Moon. Maintaining it in its current state takes 280 person days – equivalent to a single National Trust for Scotland ranger working every weekday of the year plus a couple of Saturdays. The NTS's first request to helpful people, even ahead of making a cash donation, is not walking on the verges of the path, encouraging it to creep ever wider.

BELOW Summit ridge of Ben Lomond.

More Munros

And the other 281? They range (pun intended) from the lumpy, rocky, high-rainfall summits of the western Highlands to the rounded, heathery slopes above the Angus Glens. All over the Central Highlands, great east–west ridgelines carry four or five or even eight Munro summits: huge, and hugely enjoyable, hill days. The Mamores range, sampled in Walk 16, is just one of these. Meanwhile the eight peaks that comprise the Black Cuillin of Skye almost all involve rocky scrambling: one of them, Sgùrr Dearg, is a proper rock climb.

Being a mountain biker is a bit of a help for the stony tracks leading in to the bottoms. None actually requires an overnight camp in the wilderness, not even A' Mhaighdean, but it can make things easier.

And this is the glory of Munro bagging. The way it takes you to the rest of the hills: not just beautiful Bidean but big boring Beinn Heasgarnich, not just jagged Sgùrr nan Gillean but along the long river and up the grassy slope to An Sgarsoch.

The Top Ten are Liathach and An Teallach in Wester Ross, Sgùrr nan Gillean on Skye, Cairn Toul and Ben Macdui in the Cairngorms, Ben Nevis by any route not the Mountain Trail, Buachaille Etive Mor and Bidean nam Bian at Glen Coe, Ben Lui above the West Highland Way and (just for the view) Ben Lomond. But you aren't the sort of person who eats the cherry fondants first. You aren't, are you? Because in the super-sized chocolate box of Scotland, there are so many other tasty treats.

Here's a selection of some of the other morsels in store:

ABOVE Ladhar Bheinn, Knoydart, the most westerly mainland Munro.

BUT I'M NEVER GOING TO GET ON TO ALL THOSE 282 HILLTOPS, AM I?

Done 0–99 There are far too many to actually do them all, I'm just having fun on some Scottish mountains.
Done 100–199 Gosh, it's not so impossible after all, given they come in three or four at a time. I could actually do this. Of course I'm not actually ticking them off, only nerdy types do that.

Done 200 + OMG, they're almost over! What am I going to do with the rest of my life? Better start revisiting the good ones, being careful not to use them all up, because those Corbetts, they don't look quite so much fun.

AN CAISTEAL AND BEINN A' CHRÒIN (CRIANLARICH) Reasonably easy, but exciting. A high start, a lowish pair of hills, along elegant grassy ridges all twisty with rocky knolls. Hill alcopops, these two, which will get you hooked for the hard stuff...

BEINN ALLIGIN: SGÙRR MÒR AND TOM NA GRUAGAICH (TORRIDON, WESTER ROSS) You didn't just do a Munro, you just did two! But Alligin was so lovely, now you need to grow slightly stronger legs and hit Liathach (two more) and Beinn Eighe (and that's another couple).

BUACHAILLE ETIVE BEAG (GLEN COE) Again, two for the price of one. A high start point, a lovely linking ridge, and you're in the middle of all the rest of great Glen Coe.

SGÙRR NAN GILLEAN (SKYE) A real mountain, with a sharp rocky ridge, horrifying drops and real scrambling to a top that's perched in the sky like the little round bit between the rotors of a helicopter. (You say the top of Sgùrr nan Gillean doesn't go round and round at dizzying speed? You've not been there yet.)

SGÙRR NA CÌCHE, IN THE ROUGH BOUNDS OF KNOYDART A pointy rocky monster rising straight out of the sea. You can get to it in a canoe, but the half-day approach walk starts in the middle of nowhere and then just heads farther in. It's best to camp close so you can get its three

BELOW On Fionn Bheinn, northern Highlands.

BELOW On Mullach na Dheiragain. One of the huge, high schist ridges across the northern Highlands.

BELOW Ben Cruachan, inland from Oban.

BELOW Admiring Bidean nam Bian above Glen Coe.

BELOW A life without Sgùrr nan Gillean, on Skye, is a life unlived.

companion Munros at the same time.

BRAERIACH Because Cairn Gorm is a big boring path from the car park but Braeriach is an expedition, with forest paths to start with, and a bothy for the night if you take it the big way and bag Braeriach, Angel's Peak and Cairn Toul together.

BEINN MHEADHOIN It's the Cairngorm hill in the middle, so it's not just the summit but the walk along Loch Avon and the night among the mice and ghosts under the Shelter Stone. Every Munro Man needs a mousehole in his rucksack, and that applies to women as well.

BEN VANE It's the Arrochar Alp that works as a one-hill up-and-down by the rocky terraces of its east ridge. But you'll probably come back later and combine it with Beinn Ime, even better.

BEINN NA LAP, ABOVE THE WEST HIGHLAND RAILWAY AT CORROUR In later life, you'll look back on Beinn na Lap with a happy smile that you got such a boring one out of the way early on.

SHORT BREAK
Loch Ossian

The hills above Corrour Station are ordinary mid-Highland Munros: sizeable but smooth, covered in tufty grasses and bog cotton. But who cares, when what's at the bottom is Loch Ossian, with its lonely youth hostel 16km (10 miles) from the nearest public road. You lie in bed listening to the loch rippling on three sides of you – and if you're also listening to the rain on the roof, well the place has a stove to dry off in front of.

Getting there: By rail from Glasgow or London Euston, or on foot. No road access

What's there: Loch Ossian Youth Hostel (SYHA/Hostelling Scotland), B&B and cafe at Corrour Station – and that's all

Getting out: Take the train to Rannoch Station, back by an easy track along the edge of Rannoch Moor; then round Loch Ossian.

Beinn na Lap. Get that dull one done.

Train to Rannoch, then back over two more Munros, Carn Dearg and Sgor Gaibhre.

A very big day out to Ben Alder

LEFT Loch Ossian youth hostel.

A SECOND MUNRO: MEALL NAN TARMACHAN

Ben Lomond is beautiful, with its big, well-made path and gentle slopes. It has the views, yes: but by its ordinary way up it lacks the rocky lumps, the peaty pools, the scrambly moments, the sudden airy clifftop. And Ben Lomond is almost as busy as if it were somewhere down in England.

But supposing you really liked the rocky Ptarmigan ridgeline that was the more demanding route on Ben Lomond. Suppose you fancied another Munro that was like that all over, the scent of the heather and the crowberry, the feel of the schist rocks under your hands; but at the same time not too tiring, to let you take it as slow as you like and still be down by teatime. Suppose you liked the Ptarmigan so much you want to stick with the same bird, simply correcting the spelling back to the original Gaelic.

Or maybe you're renting a car out of Edinburgh rather than Glasgow.

Meall nan Tarmachan is the hill that has it all – all, apart from the long, leg-stretching ascent from roadside to ridgeline, and the strenuous slog

BELOW Heading up Meall nan Tarmachan.

WALK 11: A SECOND MUNRO: MEALL NAN TARMACHAN

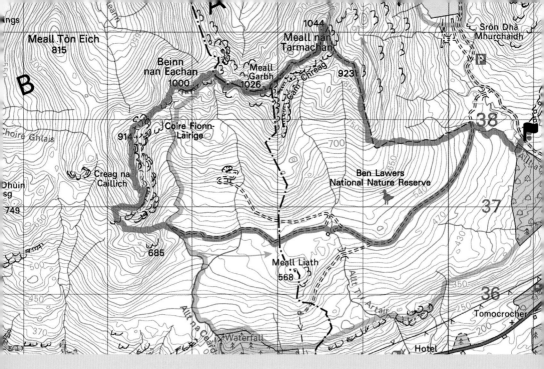

home again through the heather when you'd rather be putting damp boots in the boot and retrieving the chocolate biscuits. What Meall nan Tarmachan does have is not just a summit, but a tiny hill range: four separate tops, linked by a rambling ridgeline. And the second of them, Meall Garbh, is an absurdly pointy little thing that looks like it was drawn by a child with two sharp strokes of the big crayon. Behind this perfect

peak there's an airy ridgeline, 0.5m wide and dropping rather a long way on either side.

Beyond Meall Garbh, the path has worn down to bare schist rock, to form an awkward little scramble. Some will scamper down this bit with cries of delight. Some will – and others won't. There is a way of walking round this section, noted in the description below.

At the back corner of the car park,

This is already enough to make it a thoroughly enjoyable Munro summit, less strenuous than most. However, the continuing ridgeline is pure pleasure – assuming you avoid the dubious scramble below Meall Garbh.

a well-made path runs down to cross a stream. (The path for the A827 at Milton Morenish forks off here.) The path leads up across a contouring track (this will be the return route). Then it rises across heathery moorland to reach Meall nan Tarmachan's south ridge at about 700m level.

The clear path turns up the ridge to a cairned top at 923m. It heads down slightly left, over a ladder stile and across a damp saddle with stepping stones before the steep final summit of the main hill. The path works its way up among rugged outcrops, arriving on the north ridge. Turn back left to the summit cairn just above.

The well-worn path follows the bumpy ridgeline, passing above a couple of small lochans, to the pointy summit, Meall Garbh, the rough hump. (Just before the final cone, a small path heads down left on to the hill's south ridge – a straightforward escape route.)

Seen from Meall Garbh, rock debris

The hill is named after the bird. In its English spelling, the ptarmigan gets an initial P, as if it were a Greek word rather than Gaelic. The ptarmigan is a high-altitude kind of grouse, feeding on crowberry rather than heather and turning white in winter. With climate change, even the top of Meall nan Tarmachan is now too low down for ptarmigan, and too far south. But you will see – and hear – plenty of red grouse among the heather.

LEFT Meall Garbh.

final summit, Creag na Caillich, named as the 'old woman's crag'.

A much fainter path continues south: the route off the south end of this ridge is somewhat devious and is marked on Harvey but not OS maps. At the ridge tip, the path teeters excitingly (but unnecessarily) along the top of the east-facing crag, then bends right, south of west, to slant down grassy slopes.

down on the right is the landslip that has formed this abrupt edge. Behind the summit, the ridge narrows to an airy crest for 20m. The path then descends towards a wide saddle.

Above this saddle, the path steepens, slanting down to the right on eroded-out bare rock. This isn't altogether attractive, as the footholds are outward sloping and gritty, with few positive handholds. Fortunately for those who don't fancy it, there's an easier and more comfortable way on less steep slopes to the right. At the top of the bare rock section, a small alternative path contours to the right, to zigzag down the less steep slope facing north-west, into the saddle below.

The path continues in its wiggly way to the summit of Beinn nan Eachan, the 'hill of the horses'. After a short descent, the ridge levels. Here, a small path heads down left, a straightforward descent route in mist. Otherwise it rises again, to turn south to the uncairned

The path is quite faint; and if it's lost in mist, careful navigation or a GPS will be needed to find the little saddle at the foot of the steep southern slope. The path turns directly downhill, then slants down to the left (south-east) and contours into the moorland saddle at 670m altitude. Go through this and down the grassy stream beyond to an intake dam just below.

From here, a former track, now a grass path, contours east along the moorland. Gradually, it turns into a clear track, leading to a gate in tall deer fencing. Through this, slant down right to another intake dam with a concrete footbridge, for another track ahead. This continues around the hillside for 2km (1.2 miles) to the path of the outward route. Turn down right, retracing your steps to the car park.

The Cairngorms

The Cairngorms are special.
Everywhere else mountains rise
one at a time, with gaps and passes
between them. But away up near
Aberdeen, the Gorms are a vast, high
plateau: 35km (22 miles) of ground,
mostly above the 1,000m mark,
divided by two deep-carved glens
into three high plateaus.

Up there it's a wide,
bumpy plain, with little
bog pools, bare gravel,
and rounded granite
boulders to test your
ankles. Above the tops
of all but a handful of
the UK's mountains,
the River Dee rises in a
mossy pool, and rambles
away like any moorland
stream until, abruptly,
dropping over the edge.

And what an edge. You look down
over a mile of grey crag, down 500m
into the deep-carved valley of the
Lairig Ghru. Any walkers down there,
on the 12-hour path between Braemar
and the valley of the Spey, will be far
too small to see. And above them, the

crags rise again, and the plateau
land continues eastwards.

When the wind sweeps across the
high plateau – and when that wind
has snow in it, as it can on any day of
the year in the high Cairngorms – only
the strong and experienced will want
to be up there on Braeriach or Ben
Macdui. Just as well, then, that for the
rest of us there's the lower ground:
the ancient Caledonian pinewood of

Aviemore and the Spey. On the map,
you might mistake it for Sitka spruce,
the misnamed 'forest' of commercial
wood pulp plantations. But what's here
could scarcely be more different. Scots
pine trees, tall like cathedral pillars or
ancient and twisted like nothing else
but an ancient, twisted tree. The forest

ABOVE On Ben Macdui above Loch Avon.

BELOW Heading into the Lairig Ghru.

floor in spring is lime-green leaves of bilberry, and wide, sandy paths lead on for miles until you glimpse between the tree trunks the grey water of a lochan, or the white-on-brown of the great river itself.

The true Cairngorms are the granite lands from Braemar to Aviemore, north of Royal Deeside and south of the Spey. Downstream beyond Balmoral, Lochnagar is a lesser chip of the same granite grandeur. The land labelled as the Cairngorms National Park is, however, quite a lot larger. Commendably, the National Park designators have strived to make it as big as they could, grabbing most of the eastern Grampians on the wrong side of the A9, and even a bit of Ben Alder. Not all of this has the challenge and grandeur of the high granite under the midsummer snowstorms, the great glacier-carved valleys, the high grey lochs below their square-cut crags, the tall red trunks of the pines.

Wester Ross

North of the Great Glen, up the western seaboard, the glaciers dug deep and carved hard. Here's a whole sequence of hilly kingdoms like different magical levels in the game of Scottish mountains. The Rough Bounds of Knoydart, rising rugged above the long, narrow sea lochs and deep carved valleys. The empty quarter mapped on Landranger no. 25, a 40km (25-mile) square with a few single-track roads around the edges, the mighty reservoirs of Monar and Mullardoch in the middle, and more big, steep hills than you can shake a

walking pole over in several weeks of hard, steady walks. North again, and there's Loch Torridon, then the area known as the Great Wilderness, and eventually Inverpolly, all leading in rugged grandeur towards Scotland's top-left corner at Cape Wrath.

Back in the early Devonian period, when Scotland was getting squashed by the inexorable arrival of England, the grey schist rocks of the Central Highlands were being pushed westwards in an earth-movement called the Moine Thrust. The Moine didn't quite make it all the way over, leaving Scotland's northwestern edge a land of billion-year-old mountains standing against the grey invasion like shaggy Celtic tribes resisting the Romans 450 million years later on.

It's a moorland of bare rock and black peat and a hundred little lochans, where every second hummock was lived in by the fairies. Above this harsh base rise great,

layered cliffs of sandstone the colour of dried blood, capped with off-white quartzite whose sharp edges will slash your gaiters and twist the spike off your walking pole. For 65km (40 miles) north along the sea's edge, from Lochcarron to Ullapool and beyond, there are no uninteresting hills, and no easy ones either. A' Mhaighdean, the 'maiden', hidden within a wilderness of waterways and cold, grey lochs, with a half-day's walking even to reach the base of it. Slioch, the 'spear', its proud west face reflected in blue waters of Loch Maree. An Teallach, the 'forge', where clouds boil like blacksmith's smoke in the black, crag-circled hollow. Along the high ridgeline of Liathach you're clambering over piled towers as rough as sandpaper – which is basically what they are. The edge narrows to a flat pavement, 1m wide, but dropping either side to the peat bog and the lochans. And all the time, if you should stop and look around you, the loch is twinkling in the sunlight, and as the day fades you're clambering through rain-grey air high above a slaty sea.

There is, of course, a price to pay for all this. Not just in the miles and miles of potholed singletrack to even get to the things. Not just the years of hills

ABOVE Quartzite rock along the ridge of Beinn Eighe.

BELOW Bog path below Mòruisg.

ABOVE Am Fasarinen Pinnacles on Liathach.

before your knees and your know-how are up to their challenge. But also, on those distant countries, the lack of managed paths, the rivers not crossable after heavy rain (and rain hereabouts does tend to be heavy). Most of all, the grim peaty trods – it would be over-generous to call them paths – leading to the lower slopes. Bad in ascent, but far worse when coming down off the tops to their peat-slime and boulders on exhausted legs at the end of a long and rocky day.

It takes a certain strength, both mental and more importantly in the legs, to enjoy the special delights of Wester Ross. And there's another reason to leave them a little later in your hill career. After Liathach, An Teallach and Beinn Eighe – the little, civilised summits of the south don't quite cut it any more.

BELOW Well-made stalkers' path at the back of Beinn Eighe, Wester Ross.

The Cuillin

And so we come to Skye, and the Black Cuillin mountains. Section 17 of Munro's Tables is where Munro-baggers turn into mountaineers. Sgùrr Dearg may be one of the lowest of the 3000ft (914m) summits but it's also the most difficult:

ABOVE Lochan Coire Lagan, Skye Cuillin.

its Inaccessible Pinnacle is a full-on rock climb. The climb is technically an easy one – if you're a climber. Mere walkers will be deeply unsettled – but possibly also thrilled and exhilarated – by the huge empty spaces under our feet, in combination with the superbly rough and grippy black gabbro rock.

The rest of the range, 11 more mountains, can be reached merely by scrambling. Except there's nothing mere about Skye scrambling, with glacier-smoothed rock slabs even on the flatter ground, huge cliffs on either side, steep screes dropping to rock-rimmed lochans. And once you've sworn and scrabbled your way up the stony slopes, the notched and turreted

ridgelines slice across the sky.

But while Skye's high summits are the tops, the island also has its downside. In high summer, the one-track roads are clogged with traffic and the B&Bs are booked up solid. You can try the campsites: just make sure your tent is midge-proof and bring a protective head-net as well. And then, there's the weather. High winds and blowing cloud can keep you off the ridgeline for days or even weeks at a time. And when you're not on the ridgeline, Skye's low-level paths are black gabbro boulders and even blacker peat.

But then the clouds clear, the magnificent ridgelines of Sgùrr nan Gillean are hot under your hand, and far down below, the Atlantic stretches westwards to where the Outer Hebrides lie along the horizon like sunbathing whales.

Scotland's other islands

Take a stroll from Oban, to where a small ferry with an on-and-off timetable takes you to the tiny island of Kerrera. The walk around the island gives you a view of Oban across its

bay. Then it gives you a wild Atlantic seashore with a chance of seals. And a bit of grassy track. And then a lawn-like walk along a former raised beach. Little sea stacks stick up out of that green beach, and one of them even offers the shortest Grade 1 scramble on any Scottish island (perhaps).

Around another corner, and under a cliff of basalt cobbles, you come to Gylen Castle, a romantic ruin with – like all the best castles – not just crashing waves far down below the empty windows, but also a first-rate tearoom half a mile inland, with honeysuckle twining above the tabletops.

In a way, every Scottish island is like Kerrera. Go there not knowing what to expect – and you'll seldom be disappointed.

ABOVE Tobermory, Isle of Mull.

BELOW On Hoy, Orkney Isles.

SURPRISING ISLANDS

Islay and Jura Great for whisky, not so great for hilly terrain: the hills of Jura are big heaps of quartzite scree.

Mull Less busy than Skye (which can still mean pretty busy, especially on the road to Iona). A remarkably rugged interior with only one Munro but lots of mountain ground, and a fine coastline.

Outer Hebrides Magical lands with a unique system of thatched blackhouse hostels (the Gatliff Hebridean Hostels) and some fierce mountain ground on South Harris.

Orkneys All the islands are different but Orkney's even more different with its undulating green meadows, ancient burial sites and towering cliffs of red sandstone. The hilly ground is on Hoy.

Shetlands Rugged and remote, the place to go if you fancy being somewhere the author of this book hasn't, ever.

WEEK AWAY
Isle of Arran

Far to the south of the Hebrides, in the Firth of Clyde just off the edge of Glasgow, Arran has a greener, gentler feel than other Scottish Islands. Seals lie on the beaches, palm trees are in the gardens, and there's crazy golf on the esplanade. But Arran's small group of granite mountains, not even up at the 914.4m (3,000ft) 'Munro' height, offer rocky ridges as scrambly and serious as anywhere else outside Skye. Around the seacliffs, Arran's coastal rocks are very varied even by Scottish standards, and geologists are especially keen on it.

Getting there: Frequent ferries (passenger and car) from Ardrossan in Ayrshire, with good rail connections to Glasgow. Good bus services around the island's figure-eight road system

What's there: Bunkhouse at Brodick, youth hostel at Lochranza, walker-friendly accommodation linked with the Arran Coastal Way

Getting out: Goatfell from Brodick on a good path.

Serious scrambling on rocky ridges of Beinn Tarsuinn, Cìr Mhòr and Caisteal Abhail.

The north-west of the Coastal Way is roadside or shingle beach, but other sections offer varied clifftop walking, with buses linking the ends of each stage

BELOW Stacach pinnacles, Goatfell, Isle of Arran.

NORTHERN IRELAND

For people from the UK mainland, Northern Ireland is just different. For a start, the maps are different. No familiar Ordnance Survey here: instead it's OSNI, simpler and more colourful. That's disconcerting if you're using the OS Maps app on your phone. Suddenly this cheerful, coloured-in map appears that isn't Ordnance Survey at all!

The access arrangements are different as well. Specifically, there aren't any. No network of rights-of-way, like in England, and no right to roam, like in Scotland. As the very first sentence on the useful 'Walk NI' website puts it: 'Access in Northern Ireland is often on private land and depends on the goodwill and tolerance of local landowners.'

There are some designated long-distance paths, such as the Antrim Hills Way. Going by the map alone, those are the only walks you can be sure of. Otherwise, it's a matter of putting 'walk Ballygilbert Hill' into the internet and seeing what appears.

When it comes to being a slightly disoriented someone from the UK mainland – well, I'm one of those people myself. I've visited Northern Ireland less than it deserves. So I'll briefly describe two areas I've enjoyed and leave the rest as an exploratory exercise for the reader.

Good, vigorous exercise it'll be as well, in the country of waterfalls and small family farms, of winding lanes, quiet, rocky coastlines and soft, green hills where the cloud wafts over.

ABOVE Looking down on the Silent Valley reservoirs, Mountains of Mourne.

Mountains of Mourne

The Mournes are a small granite range that has a character all its own, quite different from anything on the UK mainland apart from being slightly like the granite hills of Arran. The Mourne Mountains are steep-sided and often cone-shaped, decorated with small rocky tors. A granite tor forms the actual summit of Slieve Bearnagh, making it one of the harder UK hills to reach the top of.

But the famous thing about the Mournes is what it says in the song. 'The Mountains o' Mourne sweep down to the sea.' Wherever you are in the Mournes, the sea shows blue in the gaps between the hills. The main base for walking them is the seaside town of Newcastle, all decorated with scraggy palm trees. On any day that's too hot for the hill, you go for a paddle on the town's long, golden beaches. Farther up, between the sea and the base of the hills, there are attractive woodland walks as well.

The hills cluster protectively around the Silent Valley with its two narrow reservoirs – they look like lakes from above, even though they aren't really. To protect their catchment area, a massive stone wall was built all around the watershed, the Mourne Wall. It links a dozen of the main summits – a route-finding aid in mist, and a lunchtime windbreak. Another treat, for those who don't appreciate the relentless up and down of these well-separated hills, is the Brandy Pad, an old smugglers' path, which weaves through them from Bloody Bridge by the Castles to Hare's Gap between Slieve Bearnagh and Slievenaglogh. And yes, the place names here are another of the pleasures.

BELOW Mourne Wall on Slieve Donard.

THE UK'S TRICKY TOPS

Sgùrr Dearg, Skye	Exposed rock climb (Moderate*) with abseil descent
Pillar Rock, Lake District	Grade 3 scramble with down-climb or abseil descent
The Cobbler, Loch Lomond	Short but exposed Grade 2 scramble
Sgùrr nan Gillean, Skye	Long, serious Grade 2 scramble by easiest route
Sgùrr Alasdair, Skye	Short Grade 2 scramble
Slieve Bearnagh, Mourne	About 40m of Grade 1 scrambling
Helm Crag, Lake District	Short but exposed Grade 1 scramble
Tryfan, Snowdonia	Clamber on to a 2m rock block
Vixen Tor, Dartmoor	40m moderate climb: all access banned by landowner

*'Moderate' is the easiest grade used for rock climbing: it's not a scrambling grade.

The group includes Northern Ireland's highest, Slieve Donard, at 850m, along with about 20 other summits. There could be a week's hillwalking here without seriously overlapping yourself.

BELOW Granite on Slieve Bearnagh.

Antrim Coast

The northern coast of Antrim is known as the Causeway Coast because the Giant's Causeway is the bit you've heard of. But over 50km (30 miles), the north-facing shore has seacliffs and spectacular rock formations: Carrick-a-Rede Island with its rope bridge,

sea stacks like the Elephant Rock, and the tall, columned crags of Fair Head. The seacliffs themselves are a strange mixture, partly pale white chalk, partly basalt as black as liquorice.

Along the top of all this is a fine footpath, the Causeway Coast Way – most of the coastline being owned and managed by the National Trust.

And in the middle of it, the Giant's Causeway itself. It's a tourist resort, with a car park and a visitor centre.

But come to it in the early morning; or after closing time, at the end of a long day along the coastal path. The crowds have cleared off, the small waves murmur against the shore, and the low sun brings out the strange hexagonal shapes of the basalt columns.

ABOVE Bengore Head, Causeway Coast Way.

BELOW Kinbane Castle, Antrim coast.

BELOW Exposed path marked for 'expert excursionists' in the Brenta Dolomites.

WIDER HORIZONS

10

LONG-DISTANCE WALKING ROUTES

Life is a journey. A progress from where you are through difficulties and challenges towards some distant dream. So why not convert this familiar self-help metaphor into an actual journey, walked through the real world on your own two feet? Travelling right across a stretch of country – from the Atlantic to the North Sea, even – watching the landscape change around you as you cross a high pass into somewhere else altogether. Checking in to some rain-stained bunkhouse, or a white-painted B&B with roses around the door, and trying to get your socks dry before walking on again tomorrow.

A long-distance walk usually takes place along a long-distance path. The UK has over 1,000 designated and named long-distance paths, with 400 of them being waymarked. Taken together, they come to 130,000km (80,000 miles). When it comes to getting from somewhere to somewhere else, the paths are almost

ABOVE West Highland Way walker approaching the Devil's Staircase.

TIPS FOR YOUR TRIP

➜ In the UK, April, May and June are the best months. July and August have higher tourism, generally higher rainfall, and the unpleasant possibility of a heatwave.

➜ Calculate your daily distance and ascent around 20 per cent less than your normal day walk.

➜ Pack as light as you can. That third pair of socks could come in handy at the end of two wet days, but the 300g of not carrying the surplus socks will help you all the way across.

➜ Happy feet aren't just for cartoon penguins. The more time you spend with dry feet, the longer it'll be before you get blisters. The best way to dry your boots is stuffing them with newspaper, then with fresh newspaper just before bedtime.

➜ Start each day as early as you can. An early start means more beer time in the evening.

➜ Day Four can be the tough one – after that, you're starting to get fitter.

three times as useful as the network of A roads and motorways. The good ones have various different kinds of wild country, a challenging bit like a high mountain pass two days before the end, hardly any corner-to-corner across farm fields, and sunshine with a cool breeze all the way along.

My favourite multiday walks

West Highland Way
(155km/96 miles)

The West Highland Way is Scotland's most popular path, by far. And those 35,000 walkers every year have chosen well. The mountain scenery is spectacular; but the route itself is mostly low-level, on a wide and well-marked path that's a former military road built to pacify the Highlands. It's well supplied with villages, bars, bunkhouses and bus stops. Meanwhile, trees and the noise of waterfalls hide the busy A82 main road and make this one feel remoter than it actually is. As a not especially sociable person, I walk the West Highland Way in March or April when it's almost empty.

Hadrian's Wall Path
(135km/84 miles)

A relatively easy and busy walk, with not too much up and down but heaps of history. Following the Tyne through Newcastle is a tarmac bike path but the different bridges are a highlight. Then along the wall itself, take time to visit at least one of the Roman forts alongside.

Jurassic Coast
(175km/109 miles)

The south coast of Devon and Dorset, from Exmouth to Poole Harbour, comes in at a more convenient length than the entire South West Coast Path (at almost 1,000km/over 600 miles the SWCP is for when you need not just a walk but a Life Changing Event). Using the South Dorset Ridgeway to bypass Chesil Beach and Portland, you introduce a high downland section among the excellent coastal walking. Another one to avoid in high summer, though; and do check the opening times of the Lulworth Ranges to avoid an unpleasant bypass.

BELOW South West Coast Path through-hiker in the Lulworth Ranges, Jurassic Coast.

ABOVE Cumbria Way in Great Langdale.

Cumbria Way
(115km/71.5 miles)

A five-day walk of lakeside, stream-side, woodland and valley floors plus a couple of high passes, through England's loveliest landscape. The only reason not to do this one is if you already know Lakeland pretty well.

Wainwright's Coast to Coast
(290km/180 miles)

When you're using your entire annual holiday on a 14-day walk, you want that walk to be as good as it gets. Which is Wainwright's one, from St Bees through Lakeland, the Westmorland limestone, the Yorkshire Dales and the North York Moors. It's the huge variety of landscape that makes this one score so highly, along with well-placed shops and bunkhouses.

It's not an official route so isn't waymarked; here and there, paths are rugged or tricky to follow. It's another busy route, so you'll need to book your B&Bs well in advance. It also helps not to start on a Saturday.

Pembrokeshire coast
(up to 300km/186 miles)

The entire Welsh coast, at 1,400km (870 miles) including Anglesey, is another one if you want a life-changing experience lasting months and months. But without going to such extremes, I've enjoyed the Pembrokeshire part of it, along the UK's second narrowest national park. A bit more rugged and remote than the bottom corner of England, it's outstandingly varied, with its limestone sea arches, warm red sandstone, rugged and ancient Precambrian rocks. Small villages offer just the minimum amount of accommodation; all of the northern section has handy bus links back to St David's. However, the industrial section around Milford Haven can, and should, be skipped.

ABOVE St Ann's Head, Pembrokeshire Coast Path.

BENEFITS OF THE SHORT-DISTANCE WALK

A reader rebuked me for describing the 100km (62 miles) of St Cuthbert's Way as a 'short-distance walk'. What was the sense behind this unnecessary walk category? And how short can a short-distance walk (S-DW) be before it becomes just a 'walk'?

Well, compared with the Pennine Way or the Pacific Crest Trail, 100km can hardly be considered long. And I still maintain it makes a sort of sense. A S-DW is too long to do in a day, and is usually a journey from A to B rather than a futile circling from A to A. At the same time, walking for less than a week has advantages:

→ You don't have to plan it in advance. It can be a weekend plus an extra day off work.

→ It's short enough to do within a spell of good weather.

→ It's short enough to do within the seven-day timespan of useful weather forecasting anyway.

→ You can do it on normal day-walk fitness, with not much more than a normal day-walk pack.

A long-distance walk is serious. You probably only do one a year. If it's the Pacific Crest Trail, you do one in a lifetime. A short-distance walk, you do it on impulse, in the sun, and for fun.

IN THE STEPS OF CUTHBERT'S CORPSE

A long-distance footpath, like a high-concept Hollywood movie, has to have a theme. Coast to coast across Scotland; the Great Wall of China; the pilgrimage to Compostela. Among all these, 'in the footsteps (as it were) of St Cuthbert's corpse' may seem less convincing. But more important than the theme is the actual entertainment value. And here the 100km (62 mile) hike from Melrose, in the Scottish Borders, to Lindisfarne in England, does rate pretty highly.

It's a lower-level route, rarely crossing the 300m contour. But each of the four occasions when it does is completely different. The steep and shapely Eildon Hills rising out of the valley of the Tweed. The grassy, folded ridgeline of Wideopen Hill above the Bowmont Water. The hillfort- and sheep-scattered pastures as you cross the Scottish border into England. And the wide, heather moorland leading down to Wooler.

The low-level sections are almost as good. The riverside of the Tweed. The goat-infested, gorse-prickly College glen. The dark, rain-washed cave where Cuthbert's dead body spent the night on its way to Durham Cathedral.

But the path saves its very best bit to the end. Officially, it crosses the tidal

BELOW On Wideopen Hill, the highest point of St Cuthbert's Way.

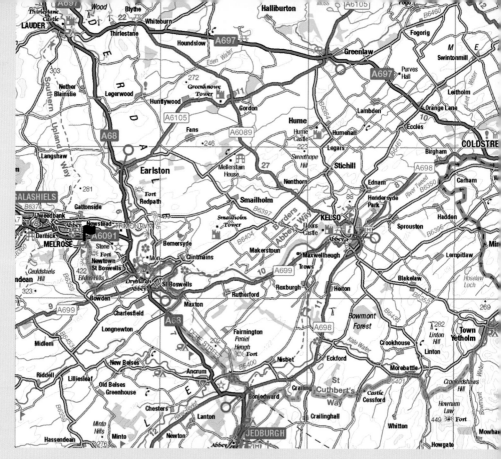

causeway to Holy Island alongside the road. The even better way, though, is the old Pilgrim Path across the sands. Check the tide tables, take off your boots, and let the mud squidge between your toes on the 4km (2.5 mile) crossing, as the castle and cathedral gradually get bigger on the island skyline ahead.

The path is waymarked, and reasonably easy to follow. After the

WALK 12 **St Cuthbert's Way**
START **Melrose, Scottish Borders**
END **Lindisfarne (Holy Island),**
   Northumberland coast
DISTANCE **100km (62 miles)**
ASCENT **2,300m**
APPROX. TIME **4–6 days**
HIGHEST POINT **Wideopen Hill, 368m**
TERRAIN **Good waymarked paths.**
   One steep ascent, on to Eildon
   Hills; paths faint in places over
   the Cheviot moors
OPTIONS **The 4km (2.5 mile)-long**
   Pilgrim Way over tidal mudflats

to Lindisfarne is much better than the official route on the road causeway
FACILITIES **Accommodation and shops**
   every 15–20km (9–12 miles)
MAP **Harvey St Cuthbert's Way**
INFORMATION **St Cuthbert's Way**
   website (www.stcuthbertsway.info)
GUIDEBOOK **If this is your first long-**
   distance walk (good choice!), then
   you may appreciate the extra info
   in Rucksack Readers' St Cuthbert's
   Way (originally by me but revised
   over the years)

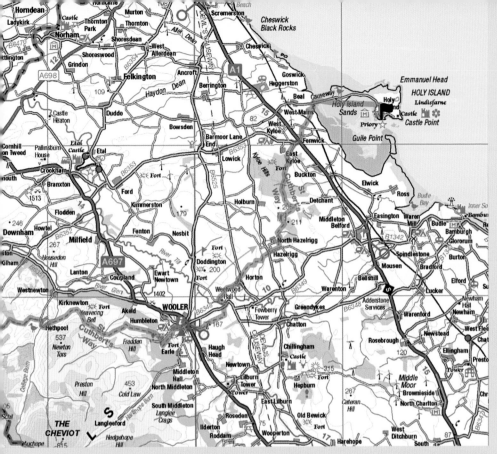

first steep climb, the going is pretty gentle and smooth. Accommodation in places is a bit thin (College Valley and Morebattle in particular). The route itself is quiet, though it seems to be getting gradually busier as its good qualities become known.

Day 1

The way starts steep, straight up and over the Eildon Hills. You can divert on to one of the summits on either side, up to 420m. There's a Roman camp round the back, a great

view from the top, and the Queen of the Fairies living deep inside. Then comes a stretch alongside the great River Tweed – follow the north bank (Borders Abbeys Way) if you want to take in the ruined

BELOW Oilseed rape and the Cheviots from St Cuthbert's Cave.

Dryburgh Abbey. The route then follows Roman Dere Street, a less interesting section of farmland tracks and paths. On a five-day schedule, you'll make a short diversion into Jedburgh for the night, thus taking in the walk's third ruined abbey.

Day 2

The way continues over higher grassland, with views opening up, to Cessford with its grim fortress tower. Then 5km (3 miles) of road – the route's only real tarmac section – lead into Morebattle. The steep-sided, grassy Wideopen Hill leads over to Kirk Yetholm.

Day 3

It's straight up again to the 300m contour to cross the border into England, then down through quiet grassy hollows to the College valley. Continue through the northern fringes of the Cheviots on gravel tracks through heather, and maybe I should have admitted it earlier, there's 400m (¼ mile) of boggy path here. Given any spare energy I would divert over the impressive hill fort of Humbleton Hill, which, if any extra inducement

were needed, is actually featured in Shakespeare's *Henry IV, Part 1* (1 I 55).

Day 4

From Wooler to the coast is low moorland, woodland and farmland that's coloured hi-vis yellow with flowers of the oilseed rape. On Weetwood Moor you could spot a cup-and-ring marked rock – very careful navigation or a GPS reckoning needed for that. But you won't miss St Cuthbert's Cave in its little sandstone outcrop.

Day 5

Pausing for the night at Fenwick lets you adjust to the tide tables for the final crossing to Holy Island. Tide times for the road causeway are found online, or on a noticeboard at the landward end. The Pilgrim Path is lower and clears about an hour later. If you get it really wrong, there are little shelter boxes raised on stilts above the high tide level.

Lindisfarne with its castle and ruined abbey is a place to linger: better still to stay, as it becomes an island again overnight.

BELOW Pilgrim Path across the tidal mud to Holy Island.

BELOW Salmon-tinted Tobermory Youth Hostel, Isle of Mull.

Hiking hostel to hostel

It was in the years after the First World War that young people from all over Britain but more particularly from the cramped, smoky inner cities, began to hit the lanes and trackways, heading for the downland, the clifftop walking, and above all for the hills. Not much money but plenty of energy, stout canvas knapsacks and even stouter hobnailed boots, sturdy knees and stout ash-sticks to support them, and elegantly compiled one-inch maps that were even surprisingly accurate.

The first youth hostel was a German invention – think '*Ach, Jugendherberge*'. By 1930, Britain's first hostel was open on the edge of Snowdonia.

So you put your bike in the bike shed or your boots in the boot room, and (provided it was after 5pm) they let you in to take your shilling, inspect your sheet sleeping bag and choose your bunk. And then you worked out where the kitchen was (the smell of sausages being a big clue), unpacked your tins of bully beef and made

yourself a nice, solid, big cup of tea.

Not all of that ethos has survived into the very different world of today. There are fewer rules than there used to be, there's hot water in the bathrooms, and you're allowed to turn up in a car. But the feeling still stays the same: a place where it's pretty cheap to stay, you can do your own cooking if you want to, and while you're stirring up your beans or slicing your more twenty-first-century-style salad, you can be chatting with young people of half a dozen different countries.

But you may need to move in quickly. Because, sad to say, youth hostels are – not threatened with extinction – but certainly endangered. And here they may be a little bit like the Scottish wildcat. Apart from the loss of habitat, the wildcat is threatened by interbreeding with domestic ones. And the rugged youth-hostel experience: it's similarly threatened by genetic mixing with more conventional and comfortable accommodation. Self-catering kitchens are getting smaller, and in England, the traditional

dormitory accommodation has largely been lost in favour of four-bunk and two-bunk family rooms. Many of us will prefer that anyway. But it does seem a shame that a cheap option for solo travellers has now been lost.

So what to expect? The accommodation will be simple, but clean and comfortable. Bunk beds are standard. All ages are welcome, from accompanied children to older people: the Scottish YHA has changed its name to Hostelling Scotland to reflect the demographic change. These days you are allowed to buy (or sometimes bring) beer or wine. The internet signal will almost always be very poor, but the common-room conversation will be of high quality. And hostel wardens are friendly and helpful to travellers.

Otherwise, they're amazingly varied. A tiny hut high in the Welsh mountains (but sadly, Rowen seems to be one of those under threat). A balconied townhouse in Bath. A seafront villa looking out over Oban harbour. A small mansion at the edge of the Peak District. A coastguard hut high on the Cornish seacliffs.

And never mind the internet: one or two of the best ones aren't even on a public road. There's Corrour on Rannoch Moor: all alone at the edge of a pine-fringed loch – but the station 2 miles away has a direct sleeper service to London. Black Sail Hut in the Lake District, and Allt Beithe in Glen Affric, are only reached by a half-

ABOVE Mounthooly Bunkhouse, Cheviot Hills.

LEFT Spot the hostel: Tintagel on the South West Coast Path.

day walk. Note that these inaccessible hostels are especially busy: at most times of year you'll need to book in well ahead.

There's good news as well. Just as the Scottish wildcat is being replenished with outsiders bred elsewhere – something slightly similar is happening with hostels. Private enterprise has stepped in with a network of independent ones, especially in Scotland. These share the youth hostel ethos, and many of them are in fact former YHA hostels. As they're run by owners who live there, they're more likely to be open in the off-season. Some are rather more comfortable than the regular youth hostels. Some independent hostels have mixed-gender dormitories and bathrooms: if that doesn't suit you, take care to check in advance.

Even so, it's harder than it used to be to link together a multiday hike from hostel to hostel.

Harder – but not too hard. A cluster of four in the Shropshire Hills (though one is currently for sale). Four more in the Brecon Beacons. Three on the Isle of Skye, though you'll need strong legs to link them all together. A series of five along the Pembrokeshire Coast Path. For urban walkers, a set of six in London. Seven within walking distance in Snowdonia (though the crucial Rowan hut, high in the northern hills, is on the market as well). Ten in the Peak District. The Gatliff Hostels, four heather-thatched black houses in the Outer Hebrides. But for density, variety, and the ease of planning paths between them, you can't beat the 17 hostels of the English Lake District.

A HUT FROM HOME

Hostel, YHA or Hostelling Scotland: Double or four-person bunk bedrooms or single-sex shared dormitories of four to eight beds. Showers. Food: dinner breakfast + picnic, self-catering kitchen. Common rooms. Drying room. Bike shed.

Hostel, independent: Similar to YHA, but may have more or fewer facilities, cheaper or steeper prices. Some may only accept larger groups.

Bunkhouse: Typically fewer facilities than youth hostels; may not offer food or kitchen, though many are attached to pubs.

Camping barn: Your 'stone tent', offering mattresses, washing facilities and not much else. Bring a sleeping bag.

Pods, shepherd's huts, hobbit-houses, glamping: Primitive but at the same time luxurious, you can expect a comfortable bed, a non-functional wood burner and a hefty price tag. Mostly require two or four people and multiple nights.

Bothy: No facilities, no bedding, no electricity, no warden, no charge. See Chapter 11.

TOUR DE SCAFELL PIKE

Seventeen Lake District hostels may give as many as a thousand possible multiday treks. Here's one of them. Instead of simply walking up Scafell Pike, you can make things a whole lot harder by walking all around it. Thus re-enacting the famous Tour du Mont Blanc.

Like the Mont Blanc walk, you'll visit seven valleys in three different countries – the former Westmoreland, Cumberland and Lancashire rather than Switzerland, Italy and France. But this one also has special features that belong only to England. The cute little rocky top of Haystacks. The ancient oak woods of Borrowdale. The 6m climbing challenge of Helm Crag. And above all, the great, empty head of Eskdale, ringed by England's highest hills.

Or, of course, you could try out one of the other 999 possible route plans.

Day 1 Grasmere to Rosthwaite

13.5km (8.5 miles), 800m, 5–6 hours

Straight away, the route confronts you with one of the difficult choices. The intimate wee valley of Far Easedale, with its waterfalls and overhanging crags? Or the high ridgeline by Helm Crag, where the summit rock, if you care to confront it, offers a technically easy but certainly scary scramble. Either way, the descent is into the empty, lonely Langstrath Valley.

Borrowdale's charming riverside hostel sits at the foot of an ancient oak wood. If you're taking a rest day, this could be the place. Day walks range from little Castle Crag to big, imposing Great Gable; or you could stroll down the riverside to the tearoom at Grange; or, if your equipment is turning out inadequate, you could take a bus ride to

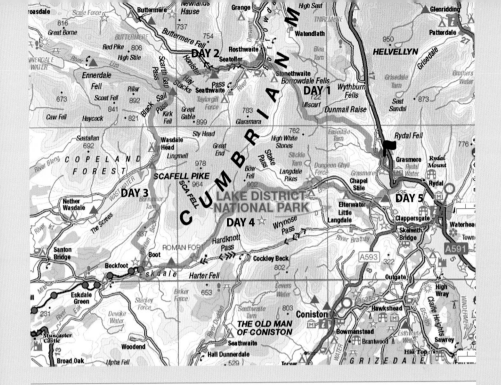

WALK 13 **Tour de Scafell Pike**
START/END **Grasmere, Cumbria**
DISTANCE **65km (40 miles)**
ASCENT **3,200m**
APPROX. TIME **3–5 days**
HIGHEST POINT **Three Tarns, 730m**
TERRAIN **Hill paths, rough and small on Day 4**

CAR-FREE **Frequent bus services Grasmere, Rosthwaite, Langdale: narrow-gauge railway to Boot (Eskdale)**
PUBS & CAFES **Lunchtimes on days 2, 3. All evenings**

BELOW The off-road hostel at Black Sail (second overnight).

Keswick's busy gear shops.

More ambitious walkers could press on to Honister Hause, adding 4km (2.5 miles) and 300m of ascent to the day – though this hostel has currently reduced itself to group bookings only.

Day 2 Rosthwaite to Black Sail

9km (5.5 miles), 650m, 4 hours

A short morning's walk brings you to the bleak, high-altitude hostel at Honister Hause. Amid the industrial ravages of the slate mining complex there's a handy little cafe: you could even take time for a tour of the underground mines (they don't have that on the Tour du Mont Blanc) or the airy terrors of the via ferrata course.

Pleasures of a more – well – pleasurable sort await on the high path above Buttermere, the two rock-fringed tarns, and the knobbly summit of Haystacks, at 597m one of England's great small hills. Then down to Black Sail, where you're alone in the green emptiness of Ennerdale. It's the YHA's only off-road hostel, and as night falls the only other light will be the moon rising above Great Gable.

Day 3 Black Sail to Eskdale

16km (10 miles), 650m, 6 hours

Two passes to cross today. But they're both low ones, and only the first one is steep. Technically Black Sail Pass, at 550m, is quite high, but still only a shortish distance above the hostel. And you'll need to take it as slowly as you can, else you'll arrive too early for lunchtime at the Wasdale Head Inn.

After the bleak moorland around Burnmoor Tarn, the best path crosses the low hump of Boat How before descending past a stone circle to the pubs of Boot. Cross the valley floor to Eskdale Church with its stepping stones, and a riverside walk to the Woolpack Inn and the hostel just beyond.

Day 4 Upper Eskdale to Elterwater

18.5km (11.5 miles), 850m, 7–8 hours

Today's the tough one, through the heart of the hills. But it starts easily enough, along the west bank of the River Esk, whose deep, greenish pools are busy spots for wild swimming. But turning off just before the stone-built Lingcove Bridge, you're on small, rough paths in harsh tussock country. The reward is the views across to the rugged side of the Scafell range as you slant up to the high pass at Three Tarns (730m).

The descent path is well used and well maintained. Just as well, as the descent's

LEFT Looking down on Buttermere (Day 2).

a long one, with Langdale, unwinding in front of you all the way down. If you're tired at this point, there's a good valley bus service. Otherwise, it's a valley-bottom ramble, the best paths being the ones used by the Cumbria Way. The advantage of Elterwater's independent hostel (formerly YHA) is not climbing to the YHA's Langdale Hostel right at the end of the day.

Day 5 Elterwater to Grasmere
6km (4 miles), 2.5 hours

From Elterwater, head up north-east through a low pass, then bend round right to cross the road north of the youth hostel, for the start of the Loughrigg Terrace path. Pass between Grasmere lake and Rydal Water. Cross the A591 up on to White Moss Common, to drop into Grasmere by the old coffin road past Dove Cottage. There's plenty of time before your bus to spread your maps across a cafe table and start planning out your next hostel-to-hostel hike.

ABOVE Wasdale Head Inn (Day 3).

LEFT Three Tarns, the highest point of the circuit (Day 4).

11

BACKPACKING AND WILD CAMPING

Why would anybody be a backpacker? Who would want to pick up a large, heavy rucksack and wrestle it on to their back before setting off on some day-long path or even, heaven forbid, up on to some high-level ridge? Why sleep on the cold, hard ground when you could have a soft feather bed or at least a youth hostel mattress? Why cook up a nasty little meal of dehydrated unidentifable meat-like stuff and burn your fingers on the stove when fate has placed pubs and inns all over the wilder parts of our country?

Well it's cheaper, for one thing. Except, of course, that it isn't. A decent two-person tent, well designed not just to keep the rain out but to let the air through so as to prevent condensation, with a groundsheet to keep the damp from coming up from underneath, and the aerodynamic design to not only

ABOVE Heading into Rannoch Moor on a two-day backpacking trip in December.

make it look amazingly groovy but also stop the wind from blowing it over quite so easily... That costs a lot more than three or four nights in a hostel.

Well, there is the convenience and the freedom. No schedule. No booking six B&Bs and a shepherd's hut with outdoor Jacuzzi and then finding the scheduled eighth nightspot's already full up. There's stopping early beside the little waterfall and spending the afternoon swimming, or feeling fit and going 13km (8 miles) extra.

But the real reason is when you come up the rocky little path after nine hours of heavy going under the even heavier rucksack, and see the little stony tarn spread out below the crags. Clouds are sweeping across the crag top like rags escaped from a washing line; but down here it's so quiet you can hear the little waves lapping against the stones. You lean the rucksack up against a boulder, enjoy the cool air on your back as you wander along the shoreline looking for the perfect patch of grass. The tent goes up first time – you've done this twice already; you know how to do it now. The sleeping bags are out to air, the water bottles are full of water and standing in a row. And now it's time to watch the colours of sunset reflecting in the little lake. The first star, then two, and then a hundred, all moving sideways in the gaps of the clouds.

And you know what? When you've walked for miles under the backpack and pitched up your tent and unrolled your little mat to sit on, and watched the little cooker glowing in the darkness – that dehydrated meat-like stuff turns out to be ten times tastier than any gastropub or fancy hotel.

Then there's the other night, not so entirely enjoyable. The cloud's come down and the rain's falling in that slow, steady way that means it can keep doing this all day and all tomorrow too, and the blister's a slow pain in a different place on each of your feet. The tent goes up (because yes, you do know how to do it now) and you ease out from under the waterproofs and leave them dripping in the entrance, and you writhe and wriggle into your carefully saved-up pair of socks. And your stove's glowing in the entrance of the tent, and the raindrops patter on the nylon overhead, and down inside your sleeping bag your feet are lovin' it in the lovely dry socks.

But ain't it a shame you forgot to have a pee before you came in out of the rain?

BELOW High camp on Ben Lui.

Tent or bivvy bag?

A bivvy bag is a waterproof, breathable bag made of nylon or some other sort of plastic, just big enough to contain a sleeping bag with you inside it. It is usually coloured brownish green, or else just green.

A bivvy bag is a lot cheaper than a tent. If you're on your own, it's also lighter than a one-person tent. It has advantages, such as not being able to blow down because it isn't up in the first place, and not needing any tent pegs, and only taking a very small space to lie down on, and being extremely inconspicuous. But none of that's really the point. As against a tent, a bivvy bag is a different experience.

On a mild summer night, to lie down with the night breeze kissing your face, and the stars circling slow above your head; to see the stag in the moonlight silhouetted against the loch below, and not miss a second of the sunrise; all this is well worth the sacrifice of not doing any cooking and having nowhere to put your stuff except stuffed back inside the rucksack.

On a nasty night, on the other hand... You zip yourself up inside your little bag, and the raindrops are hitting the nylon an inch from your ear, and how are you ever going to get up out of here in the morning without your sleeping bag and your special socks getting soaked? And right now, the rainwater on the outside is obstructing the subtle breathable membrane, so you and everything around you is slowly getting soggy.

Okay, I'll try to be a bit more positive. But I don't want to be misleading.

I enjoy bivvy bagging – I enjoy it a lot but it certainly isn't for everybody. One way to up the chances of a nice night rather than a nasty one is to wait for an encouraging weather forecast (no rain, not much wind, and a lovely full moon) and head up onto the hilltops for one night only.

BELOW Bivvy bag on Bow Fell, Lake District; overnight view to Windermere.

BOTHIES

Bothies are simple unlocked shelters dotted over the Scottish Highlands and Borders, plus nine in Wales, three in the Lake District and one on Cross Fell. They are mostly defined by what they haven't got. No beds, no food, no warden, no electricity. No charge for use. No running water, no toilet. What they do have is a wooden platform for sleeping on, a roof to keep out the rain and a door to keep out the midges.

A bothy can be a refreshment and a refuge: friendly folk who already lit the fire, candlelight on old stone walls, air and space to hang up your dripping waterproofs. Or just occasionally, a grim experience: uncongenial drunks for company, a mouse in your muesli bag, and other people's litter. What's invariable is a superb location miles from any highway or habitation.

On a backpacking trip, I take note of any nearby bothies. The tent, or maybe bivvy bag, is my intention. But if I do get three days of non-stop rain, I'll reroute to be in the bothy. And a nearby bothy is useful if you're a beginner backpacker who can't get the tent to stay up because you brought the wrong set of poles.

Many of the bothies are maintained by the volunteers of the Mountain Bothies Association, whose website tells you where they are. (www.mountainbothies.org.uk)

BELOW Rowchoish Bothy beside Loch Lomond. The string is so you can hang up your food overnight so the mice don't get it.

Packing light

Well ... you're backpacking, so you're not packing light. But packing less heavy...

The ideal bit of kit, whether tent, cooker, rucksack or waterproof jacket, has four crucial qualities. It's light in weight. It's light on your credit card. It's durable and long-lasting. It really keeps the rain out.

Occasionally, a piece of kit has three of these qualities. Nothing combines all four. When kitting up for the first time, the ones to concentrate on are the first two. Cheap, shoddy equipment can be satisfyingly lightweight. If it performs poorly, you'll know where to spend your money next time. And if it performs really poorly, and there isn't going to be a next time – well it's easy enough to carry your cheap kit off to the charity shop.

Next, sort the stuff you need into three heaps. The equipment that's absolutely necessary like the tent or bivvy bag. The kit that's desirable to assure a comfortable night. And those little lightweight luxuries that it's so nice to have along. Leave heap number three behind. Then leave heap number two behind as well.

Because no luxury is as luxurious as a lighter pack on your back.

Making backpacking bearable

Putting on a rucksack that's twice as heavy as you're used to is going to be uncomfortable. How much worse when you then try to walk 15km (9 or

10 miles) underneath it. The trick I employ is to get used to the weight in stages. If the backpack's going to be 12kg (26lb) (with care it shouldn't be more) and your normal daypack's 6kg (13lb), then spend two or three days under one that weighs 9kg (or 20lb). It'll be just about bearable, and it'll build up the rucksack muscles for the full-weight one to come.

That 9kg outing could be a one-nighter in good weather with early supper in the valley below. Which would also be a try-out on how to put up the tent.

Carry a sleeping mat? Under the principle of throwing out heap number two, for many years I didn't. If I walk far enough, I can sleep anywhere. This did lead to some uncomfortable nights, especially when the soft woodland leaf mould turned out to actually be gnarly roots.

The closed cell foam mat is cheapest and lightest, and it's also highly durable. Scoring three out of

four on the packing list! It's bulky, and if it's on the outside of the sack it catches the wind in an awkward way. If it's inside, that means a bigger, and heavier, sack.

So nowadays I treat myself to a three-quarter length, semi-inflatable one. It's only slightly heavier and could almost be described as comfortable.

Site specific

Early afternoon is the time to start thinking about wind and water. For wind, we hope to be somewhere in the range between enough of it to blow away the midges, and not enough to blow away the tent. Water is less important; I often camp high above streams or springs. You can carry up 1.5 litres per person, which is all you'll need overnight. The main thing is not to have any of it trickling into the tent.

Having found your sheltered corrie, or the lumpy outcroppy ridgeline with the grassy hollows, take time to choose

ABOVE Crummock Water on the second evening of a walk across the Lake District.

a site. Better 20 minutes wandering among the heather than a night with a boulder between your shoulders. See Chapter 2 for the discussion about the access status of wild camping in Scotland and elsewhere.

Routes round-up

One-nighters

Head uphill, or out along the coastal path, in mid-afternoon when everyone else is heading for home. In the morning, come down again, chastened and slightly more experienced: or reload the sack and make the most of the five hours between sunrise and the arrival of the other people.

Lake District

You might think backpacking here is even more pointless. Everywhere in the Lake District is within three hours' walk of a car park, and four hours of a pub and a place to spend the night. In fact, I find myself doing quite a bit of Lakeland backpacking. It's easier: there's always a valley below with a pub and a shop and a bus stop. So the pack doesn't have to be very heavy. And spending the short summer nights high up means you get the fells to yourself, and in busy Lakeland that's pretty special.

The Tour de Scafell Pike (Walk 13) is one good backpack expedition, taking two to five days. Or a trip right across Lakeland, at around three days. Penrith to Ravenglass is one that works for me.

Southern Upland Way

For a first long outing, Scotland's official coast-to-coast path makes things easier. It's waymarked all the way, a good path to follow, and there are five bothies for refuge when everything goes wrong. There are small towns and shops, but the hill country between is genuinely remote.

Mostly, I wouldn't backpack a named and recognised path. It's so depressing seeing those less heavily laden walkers zooming past you day after day. But the Southern Upland Way is almost as quiet as if it weren't an official footpath at all.

Across Scotland

Walking through the Highlands is what backpacking's all about. A fortnight of smooth, heathery east and rugged rocky west; at least two nights in the middle of the mountains far from human habitation; a route chosen by you and your map-reading eye; and if your legs are up for it, one or more of the high-level, peak-to-peak ridges that lie conveniently in the correct direction. Melrose to Shiel

BELOW Southern Upland Way on Lowther Hill.

ABOVE Beside Loch Hourn at the start of a walk across Scotland.

Bridge might be good for a first-timer; Stonehaven to Inverie in Knoydart for the even more ambitious.

Cape Wrath Trail

The trek from Fort William to Cape Wrath, through all but one of the UK's gnarliest mountain ranges, is the very best thing in backpacking within these islands. There's an official route line – in fact there's two – but snatching some summits on the way, diverting to interesting-looking sea lochs and bothies ... it could take three exhilarating weeks.

The USA

This country is for backpackers who like to think big. Big skies, big mountains, big, big heavy backpacks.

BELOW Below Beinn Bhan, Applecross, on the way to Cape Wrath.

On California's John Muir Trail you walk ten days without touching human habitation (the downside being carrying ten days' worth of food). And yes, there are bears, there are wolves – but a rigorous system of permits means not that many people. For the ultimate life-changing experience (supposing you needed such a thing) you can spend seven months along the 4,300km (2,700 miles) of the Pacific Crest National Scenic Trail.

BELOW Minimal tarp tent at Marie Lake on the John Muir Trail.

WEST OF THE WEST HIGHLAND WAY

Between Loch Lomond National Park and the Great Glen, between the sea and the West Highland Way, there's a network of quiet glens, with paths or tracks along them and big mountains on either side. This is proper backpacking country, but on a slightly smaller scale and with slightly easier going underfoot. The sketch map shows the various paths and passes. Walk 14

is just one possibility in this area, four days from Dalmally to Fort William.

West Highland is also wet Highland – those wonderful lochs and rivers do, necessarily, start off as drops of water falling out of the sky. And even more so in autumn, as grey clouds flop across the hilltops like a rain-sodden tent, and the dying leaves make the ground underneath your boots smell a bit like

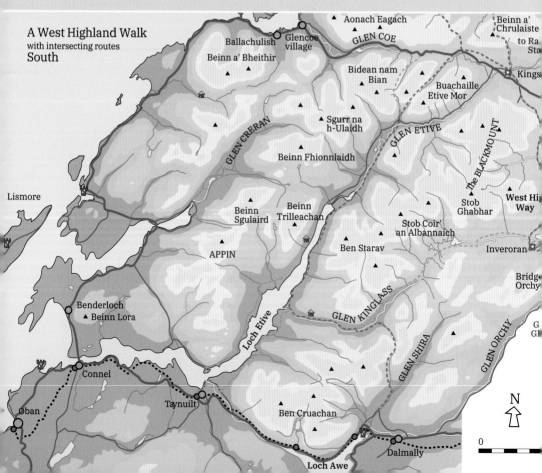

A West Highland Walk
with intersecting routes
South

WALK 14 A West Highland Walk
START Dalmally
END Fort William
DISTANCE 96km (60 miles)
ASCENT 2,500m
APPROX. TIME 4 days
HIGHEST POINT Beinn a' Chrùlaiste,
    857m

TERRAIN Tracks, paths, rough
    pathless descend from Lairig
    Dhoireann pass
OPTIONS Many alternative routes,
    easier and harder – see sketch map
CAR-FREE Start and end are at
    stations, or Citylink coaches to
    Glasgow

the socks inside them.

But autumn does have a beauty all of its own. In Glen Nevis, the grey schist rocks match the grey schist sky, but contrast in a wonderful way with the ochre beige of October birch trees. The Steall waterfall's even more super-splashy than it is the rest of the year. Short autumn days mean eight hours or less on your feet. Or if they don't – if

you only just arrived on the train from Glasgow and need to get through to the bothy in Glen Kinglass if there's to be any chance of a dry place to hang up the dripping waterproofs – well, there are other advantages then. There's the moon shining on the River Kinglass between the alder trees. The altogether interesting experience of trying to find the footbridge over that river, in the

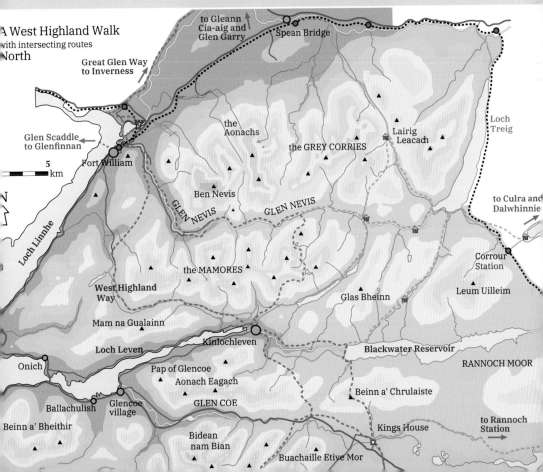

A West Highland Walk
with intersecting routes
North

ABOVE Damp morning beside Loch Etive.

dark, while rambling around among bog, bog myrtle and thigh-high tussocks of grass.

Now, as a long-standing map-and-compass man, I don't need any of this newfangled electronic equipment. Compass bearing and counting steps, that does the job here.

On the other hand – stumbling around in the dark, in a wood, in a pathless grove of bog myrtle: this is enough fun on its own, without the added interest of wondering whether it's the right wood or somewhere else altogether. So yes, I've downloaded the map into a small, yellow GPS gadget, so that its little glowing screen shall guide me.

There is also the intriguing possibility that the footbridge itself, two tiny dashes on the Landranger map, mayn't actually exist as a bridge across the real world. The path leading down to it, an equally confident line of little strokes, was merely a happy memory in the mind of the mapmaker. Well, if it exists, the GPS says the bridge is a mere 20m away. I turn towards the river noise. As the trees open out, poles probing under the heather to avoid stepping over the edge – the river water is silver under the moonlight, and I feel the cool of it on my face. And yes, a straight-edged black shape among the blobs of silver. The bridge is right here, a few steps downstream.

And across it, the start of a gravel track. Ten minutes later, a hunched shape at the end of the torch beam: the bothy is there as promised. After 90 minutes of concentration in the darkness it feels like the middle of the night. It's only 8pm. But after a quick cold supper from the meal deal section of the Sainsbury's at Queen Street station, 8pm is quite late enough to begin a satisfying night's sleep.

That late-afternoon pass of the Lairig Dhoireann was, in fact, the walk's one tricky bit. By daybreak, I was following the track out to the salt waters of Loch Etive. (This is the long, lonely access track for Glen Kinglass Lodge, and makes an easier, alternative way in to this point, starting from Taynuilt.) As day breaks, Loch Etive and its mountains emerge from a morning mist that's the colour of the bruise on your knee where you fell over on the stony path in the dark. Through a damp, pink-and-grey sunrise, an old path leads up the loch side, into the backs of the Glen Coe mountains.

Here, the obvious way onwards would be the quiet, dead-end road – which even has a point of cultural significance, as it's the brief pause on the road to destiny for Daniel Craig, Judi Dench and Daniel's Aston Martin DB5 in *Skyfall*, the Bond movie of 2012. However, the Harvey map hints at an 'intermittent path' running on the right-hand side of the river. It's old, but not

yet past it, the path along the east side of Glen Etive. It moves upslope above a craggy river bend, then zigzags down to a grassy bank, and sneaks below another woody crag.

For the afternoon, there's the ancient drove road through the gap called Lairig Gartain. It's a stiff climb, but an excellent path, restored and repaired by the National Trust for Scotland. At its top, Glen Coe is at its most evocative, with grey cloud chundering along the glen like a flock of giant-sized sheep seen from underneath. The old Glencoe road is sinking into the peat. One day, it'll be a gravel-and-tarmac fossil for future archaeologists, but for now it's a firmer footing across the moor, with the racket and stink of today's A82 drifting across the peat like an evil mist. Bar meal tonight at the Kingshouse, and a soft bed in the dripping spruce trees across the stream.

From here, the quick way to Kinlochleven is by the West Highland Way. One of the best bits of the WHW as

BELOW Glen Etive.

well. But I'm taking a wilder route. Flat-topped Beinn a' Chrùlaiste is well worth crossing for its outstanding view of the big hills of Glen Coe, Buachaille Etive Mòr and Bidean.

Well, it would be, if the cloud would only come up off it. In grey drizzle, I navigate down the hill's northern flank and find a grassy stream bank through the bog and lochans to the foot of the Blackwater Reservoir.

The Scottish Outdoor Access Code explicitly allows access across dams. From the Blackwater one, there's a view along 12km (7.5 miles) of eponymous black water; and the other way, down the grey precipice of concrete to the treetops below. And crossing the dam leads to the 6km (4 miles) of woodland path down into the village. Woodland that's especially fine in heavy rain, as you look across to the waterfalls on the southern side of the valley. And if a wisp of mist is hiding those, the north-side ones are flowing right out across your feet, adding paddling fun to the patterns of dead leaves stuck to the wet rocks

and the rhythmic tree-drips on the hood of the anorak.

A wet day in autumn is also advantageous when finding somewhere to stay without a booking.

With a long afternoon of drying out ahead, I buy a newspaper to go with my food supplies. A tabloid newspaper: not so much for the quality of its journalism, but its absorbency. The sports section gets stuffed straight into my boots, to be replenished by each of the news pages as I finish reading them.

From Kinlochleven, the easy way – but rather long – is the track by Loch Eilde Mor to the head of Glen Nevis. The short way – but rather strenuous – is to cross the Mamores range, up to the 1,000m mark on the old deer-stalkers' paths. There's also, for the truly tired out, the West Highland Way round the left-hand end.

Given three different ways to Fort William – the obvious answer is to choose route number four. Another old deer-stalkers' path weaves through the eastern end of the Mamores, past

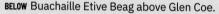

BELOW Buachaille Etive Beag above Glen Coe.

ABOVE Lairig Gartain pass, looking back down Glen Etive.

a high-level lochan big enough that anywhere else it would be a full-on loch or lake; around the head of a hidden deer-sanctuary valley; through another hill gap with another high-level lochan; and down to a small rocky knoll overlooking Glen Nevis. Leading to a compelling question that must be answered. What's so special about that small knoll on the back of Binnein Beag?

The advantage of a predawn start is the Grey Mare's Tail Waterfall in the dark, roaring like the grey-white ghost of the mighty river-demon it actually is. It's seeing whatever the grey world is offering by way of a sunrise,

as well as hopefully reaching Fort William in time for a nice, hot bar meal. The disadvantage, in the half-light underneath the oak trees, is not noticing when you've dropped your map.

Now, I'm a map-and-compass man, me. At least I was one back in 2015. But with my map somewhere in the

RIGHT Crossing Beinn a' Chrùlaiste.

WALK 14: WEST OF THE WEST HIGHLAND WAY

Einstein's relativistic speeding-up of time due to the gravitational field. Maybe I should take advantage of their efforts.

The wind howls around the flank of the mountain. Grey cloud slides steadily past, halfway up the hillsides. The path up oak woods an hour's walk down the hill, and this handy little GPS device glowing in my pocket like a magic get-across-the-Mamores card – well, maybe it's time to start trying out this modern and of course entirely unnecessary technological wonder. The Americans have gone to the trouble of setting up the 31 satellites 20,000km (12,500 miles) above my head, and even calculated in the correction for to the first high lochan is still used as the way to one of the Munro summits, so it's easy to follow. Then it fades, a green trace zigzagging down and around the hill slopes to the second of the little stony lochs. And when it comes to finding the long-abandoned old stalkers' path into Glen Nevis, the GPS gadget works really rather well.

The path ends above a shaggy slope of orange grasses, and rain-blackened

rocks, and gleaming waterfalls; and at the bottom, the silver streak of the Water of Nevis. I aim for a wider and fast-flowing reach of the river, for a crossing that's less than knee-deep. Along the rough, peaty path, patches of custard-coloured sunshine are lighting up the huge toffee-coloured hills on either side. The rain eases off. It might almost be worth stopping to squeeze the Water of Nevis out of my socks. And after 4km (2.5 miles) of enormous emptiness, the glen widens to a level meadow, and a froth of birch trees.

After two full days of literal, as well as literary, wilderness, here's another place of pilgrimage for film fans. But you know what? The 120m, stony-grey and splashy Steall waterfall looks even finer without Harry Potter's Triwizard Tournament taking place at the bottom of it.

Down through the Nevis gorge, the river roars between house-sized grey boulders. The path emerges to gleaming grey schist, and birch woods the colour of egg yolk. Grass matches leaves: rock suits the sky, in the ochre-grey tartan style favoured by Alicia Silverstone in the opening scene of *Clueless*.

Down at the road bridge, a kayak launches over the Lower Falls into the boiling, white-water pool below. It's so good to meet people who make a four-day hike through the autumn rains seem like a comparatively sensible thing to do.

A path runs down the right bank of the river, saving tired feet from the tarmac on the other side. And yes, it's marked on the Harvey map – reason being, I once wrote to Harvey and told them about it. Ben Nevis looms huge overhead, the river chatters in the dark. The long footbridge leads from what feels like night-time into the early-evening youth hostel.

BELOW Steall Falls and the Nevis Gorge.

12

RUNNING UP THAT HILL

I went on my first ski trip and got a nasty shock. At 2pm, with the lifts still running, I was too tired to carry on. I had to spend the afternoon in the sauna. So I decided to sort myself out with some jogging on the hill tracks behind our house.

The first couple of times, I just about got to the end of the drive, with all sorts of nasty stuff coming up from out of my lungs, reminding me that several years before I had been a cigarette smoker. But two weeks later,

that changed. I was running 3–5km (2–3 miles), without stopping, even on some slight uphill slopes. Even more surprisingly, I was quite enjoying it.

OK, I was already pretty fit, from hillwalking and heavy work in the garden. I was only 35 years old. (Note to you 35-year-olds: 35 is very young.) And I've got a skinny build, just right for running. Even so, I was astonished

ABOVE Glyn Jones crossing An Garbhanach, Mamores range.

at how quickly my heart and lungs and legs adapted to this new mode of travel. Four months later, I did my first half marathon. Ten thousand other runners all around, slow going at the start of the race, chat:

'Yes, I really need to get fit for skiing.'

'Me too, just the same reason.'

A pause.

'One thing though... ski season's over, two months ago.'

Which is how, three years later, I came to be heading up Ben Nevis, in the dark, the surroundings faintly orange from the streetlights of Fort William. I can't remember how long we took to get Ben Nevis; it would be more than two hours and less than three. What I do remember is the murky brown and orange sunrise on top, then off down the boulderfield,

eyes flicking ahead to the next stone below, feeling feet and eyes attached to a single spring, moving fast in focus down the stonefield.

We clambered along the skyline boulderfield that's the Càrn Mòr Dearg Arête – my friend Glyn was with me on this one – and paused for several seconds to enjoy the crags and ridges of the great north face behind us. There's a long, slow climb on to Aonach Beag, which though named as the 'Little Ridge', is Scotland's seventh-biggest. After that, a steep rocky descent that's hard to find. But then, through the morning, the almost level ridgeline above the Grey Corries, relaxed along slabs of off-white quartzite, like a city pavement if you raised a city pavement 1km (0.6 miles) into the air.

EIGHT FACTS ABOUT FELLRUNNING

→ Hillrunners don't run up hills, so on a long fell race they may spend more than half the time walking. But a runner walking uphill is faster than a walker running.

→ You're quite right, it isn't sensible running around in the rain in just your underwear.

→ But hillrunners don't hurt themselves as often as you'd expect. Sprained ankles are the commonest injury.

→ Fellrunning has doubled in popularity since the year 2000. But that still doesn't make it tremendously popular.

→ Surprising as this seems, fellrunners are having fun, especially on the downhill bits.

→ A marathon distance on hills can be easier than a marathon distance on the road, because of the relaxing uphill and downhill bits.

→ On the other hand, the 42 Lake District peaks of the Bob Graham Round, done in 24 hours, may be just a brisk walk but it's still a very, very difficult thing to do.

→ Fellrunning shoes are not trainers. They look like trainers but they aren't, they are running shoes.

At the end of the morning, there was a long, gentle slope of heather down to the head of River Nevis. You 35-year-olds won't remember Zebedee from the *Magic Roundabout*, the little chap who bounced around on a spring. But that was who we felt like on the descent. Ahead of us rose the swooping ridgeline of the Mamores, with its airy paths, awkward scree slopes and occasional scrambly rocks.

This is Tranter's Round, 18 magnificent summits on either side of Glen Nevis. And yes, this is a very specialised form of fun. The 50km (31 miles) with 5,500m (almost a Kilimanjaro) of ascent are more than challenging for any hillwalker, though Philip Tranter achieved it in 1964 wearing walking boots. But with hillrunners' footwear, fitness and stamina, it becomes a solid and very satisfying day out, not proving anything in particular but just having a good time nonetheless.

A good time, most of the time. Nightfall saw us on Mullach nan Coirean, which is the final summit. The year before, Glyn had a nasty time getting down from there, in the dark, in the forestry plantations. So we tried a different ridge, and you know what? In the dark, in the plantations, we had it even nastier.

Hillrunning is mostly a solo activity: just you and your cardiovascular system against this hill. But at the same time, when done in groups, it's surprisingly sociable. Après-race activities are as informal as any event can be, given that they involve standing around in a car park in your vest and pants.

There are also events run by the Long Distance Walkers Association (LDWA). And yes, I do mean 'run'. If you're doing 40km (25 miles) of bumpy countryside in a short autumn day, the way to do it is gentle jogging. Apart from those two blokes

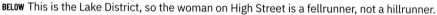

BELOW This is the Lake District, so the woman on High Street is a fellrunner, not a hillrunner.

ABOVE Runner (in blue) with pacers, on the Ramsay's Round 24-hour challenge over 24 Munros.

at the front who are very keen to beat each other, the LDWA's events aren't competitive. Jog and chat for a couple of miles, then drift into the next checkpoint for some delicious dehydrated soup and a flapjack.

The Fell Runners Association (FRA) in England & Wales, the Scottish Hill Runners (SHR) and the Long Distance Walkers Association (LDWA) all have events programmes online.

Meanwhile, if you want to get serious, the tough day (and night) out is the circuit from Keswick over 42 separate summits called the Bob Graham Round. It's the fellrunners' Everest and has almost the same amount of ascent as the world's highest mountain. The very strange thing about this is: if you're a fit fellwalker in your middle years, and you really, really want to do this, and you train yourself with lots of long hill trips, and get to know the route intimately, and recruit some loyal supporters, and get reasonably lucky with the weather – it's quite possible you could do this thing. More than 2,500 runners have now achieved the 100km (62 miles) and 8,000m of ascent within the 24-hour time limit.

RIGHT Solo hillrunner on Beinn a' Chròin, Southern Highlands.

RUNNING UP THAT HILL

13

WALKING ABROAD

Boots and bathing costumes

I've never fully understood people who go to some exotic faraway place and then lie down on some sand with their eyes closed. Baking your bones on the beach, yes OK – but not until after a morning's walk on some rugged little hills. The African continent has advanced northwards just for this very purpose, crumpling up limestone of the ocean floor into cliffs and ravines all along the Mediterranean coast. Those spectacular canyons can even offer a shady walk, so you don't have to worry about overheating either.

Shady, but also scrambly. There's going to be more bare rock and big drops than we're used to in the UK. We'll need to carry more water and a big shady hat and learn 'left' and 'right' and 'lost' in the local language.

And then boots off, swimwear on, and off into the sea.

Ways and means

When considering a mountain range to spend ten days and quite a lot of

ABOVE Mediterranean limestone on the north-west coast of Mallorca.

money in, I'll start by buying the guidebook. Nearly always, it's one published by Cicerone Press. The guidebook will suggest the most suitable map. Sometimes it's different from whatever's on the 'topo' layer of the Outdooractive app, so that gives two different views.

While the guidebook will supply the lowdown on all the logistical bits, it won't actually do the bookings. Going **self-guided** is when you get a commercial company to do everything apart from the actual walking. They will suggest your route, supply your maps, book your overnight accommodation and make sure you get a really delicious evening meal; and they'll provide comfort by being a human being at the end of a telephone to answer all your questions.

Hut-to-hut hiking

The bad part of hillwalking is walking up hills. The other bad part is walking all the way down again. Wouldn't it be grand to have a walk where once you're up you stay up, for days and days and days? And so was born the sport of hut-to-hut hiking. In Norway, in certain parts of Spain, in the High Tatras Mountains of Slovakia – but most of all in the Alps. By cool green lakes surrounded by pine trees below shaggy crags. Perched on rock knolls at the tops of glaciers. On high flowery meadows where the cowbells clank.

SOME START POINTS FOR SUN, SAND AND SCRAMBLY MOUNTAIN PATHS

→ White Mountains coast, Crete
→ West coast of Mallorca
→ Canary Islands
→ Nerja, southern Spain

And whether referred to as *refugio* or *cabane*, *hütte* or *chata* or even (in the Carpathians) as cottages, the one thing the mountain hut isn't is a hut. These days, they're middle-sized hotels, sitting surprisingly among stony wastelands miles from the nearest road.

Expect a terrace for your late-afternoon tea and cream cakes; a wood-lined common room around the stove for your beer or local wine; a hearty evening meal and simple bunk bed or, for the less well-off, a communal dormitory costing not much more than a UK youth hostel.

The highest huts have sunset views to warm the heart – but cold water only for your body's outside surfaces. The one thing mountain huts all have in common is that they are always very different from one another.

And what of the paths between? The best ones teeter along ledges on steep, high valley sides; climb through little rocky passes; wander along mountain hollows floored with glacier-scraped rock. These paths are different from the ones here at home. They're marked with flashes of red and white paint, with signposts at every junction. At any time, they may confront you with a rocky step and iron staples to clamber up on, or a wire cable to grab as you dangle above a whole lot of empty air.

There are various ways of having a long, satisfying hike. You can hump a heavy rucksack through the great empty places of America. You can rent a mule for a hot, dusty ramble through the Moroccan Atlas Mountains. You can trek across England's coast-to-coast in the rain or confront the midges on a tour of bothies in Scotland. But honestly, why bother? When nothing is so much fun as a hut-to-hut hike through the European Alps.

Switzerland has the finest mountains. But Swiss paths are strenuous, with long, long ascents and descents, and the huts are awfully expensive. In Italy, the food is better, and the Dolomites offer as much dangly scrambling as your nerves can stand up to. But before the Second World War, it was Austria that my Granny and Grandpa headed off to.

Hut-to-hut essentials

Who are the experienced hut-to-hutters? They're the ones with the smaller rucksacks. The fleece top for if there's an unexpected snowstorm? Yes. The other fleece top for when you reach the hut wet through? Yes, but that can be the same fleece as the first fleece top. On the odd day when it does get wet, it'll dry out in the cosy atmosphere around the stove.

BOOTS On a sun-and-alcohol holiday, when they lose your bags you just buy a new swimsuit or else seek out the nudie beach. On a hiking holiday, you're useless without your boots. So wear them on the plane.
WATERPROOFS Lightweight, unlined. The Alps can have afternoon thunderstorms. But you needn't prepare for day-long humid gloom like you would in Scotland.

BELOW High-level huts have the views of the Matterhorn: Theodule Hut, Tour of Monte Rosa.

SHEET SLEEPING BAG Huts supply blankets, helpfully marked '*Fuss*' at the end where previous people put their feet (assuming they could read German). But you need your own sheet-pillow-case arrangement. *Not* a full sleeping bag, which is much too heavy to carry.

VERY LIGHTWEIGHT SHOES For wearing in the hut once you've taken your boots off.

SUNSCREEN AND WOOLLY HAT These are occasionally even both needed at the same time.

BLISTER PLASTERS Of course.

INSURANCE Helicopter rescue in the Alps isn't cheap. Simple, effective insurance is included in membership of the Austrian Alpine Club (ÖAV), which has a flourishing UK-based '*Sektion Britannia*'. This also gains discounts in huts run by national alpine clubs, which tend to be higher in altitude and lower in price than privately run ones.

ABOVE Lower-level huts have the finest food and hot showers: Europaweghütte, Tour of Monte Rosa.

WATER Depending on fitness and weather, you may need 2 litres a day. Alpine air is drier than the UK, especially if you're breathing through your mouth.

CASH Many huts aren't connected to the internet (some people consider this a big advantage) and can't take card payments.

Items that could be useful

TREKKING POLES Note that they cannot be carried in hand luggage.

CARABINER-SLING SET-UP A loop made with about 2.5m of climbers' nylon tape and a carabiner or snap-link. Tie it with two figure-eight knots and tighten one of them around your waist. This can add a bit of extra

LEFT Sling and carabiner set for a bit of extra security on chained paths.

security and confidence; I use it to clip myself to the cable while taking a photo.

POWER PACK FOR YOUR PHONE This is essential, as huts don't always have charging points.

Some planning principles

From London, at least, you can get to Innsbruck in a day by **train**. But if you're travelling on an aeroplane, try not to use two of them. Get into the right country, then take the train. In a train station, you're already on your holiday. In an airport, you ain't.

Use the **chairlift**. There's nothing fun about walking uphill, under the pine trees, through the heat of a long afternoon. And walking down again is only slightly more amusing. Spend your money on the cable car and spend your time on the heights.

Learn some of the **language**. Not everyone in the world speaks English, and it's embarrassing to find you've ordered a supper consisting of picture postcards. Given the low expectations

BELOW Italian sign showing gear for full-on via ferrata scrambling.

Europeans have of our language skills, anything beyond the basic greetings will be a pleasant surprise.

And some places to go

PICOS DE EUROPA (NORTH-WEST SPAIN) A spectacular limestone range, with good huts. Expect long ascents and descents and plenty of bare rock.
TOUR OF MONTE ROSA (SWITZERLAND & ITALY) Superb high-level paths, views of the Matterhorn. The one glacier crossing

RIGHT Chained path up to Bocca di Brenta, Dolomites. Any alpine path is likely to have rocky moments above big drops. If you're happy on Grade 1 scrambles, you'll enjoy it. If you aren't, then you probably won't.

BELOW Wild hiking in Utah's Canyonlands.

is actually a summer ski piste, but still serves to put off a lot of people and make this one much, much quieter than the Tour du Mont Blanc.

TATRAS MOUNTAINS (POLAND AND SLOVAKIA) Good hut system, spectacular granite mountains, but rather busy.

JOHN MUIR TRAIL (CALIFORNIA, USA) A superb wilderness trail with no facilities – carry a tent and lots of food. Walker numbers are very restricted and it's hard to get a permit. Other trails in the Sierra Nevada are easier to get on to.

JULIAN ALPS (SLOVENIA) More fine limestone mountains with good huts, quieter and cheaper than the main Alps.

DOLOMITES (ITALY) The 'Alta Via 1' is very popular and busy but it's a huge range with wide opportunities for DIY touring as well as the other nine Alta Via routes. Many routes involve via ferrata-type scrambling.

AS WELL AS… The rest of the Alps, the Pyrenees, several other bits of Spain, and all the other places I haven't actually been yet.

THE STUBAI HIGH-LEVEL ROUTE (STUBAIER HÖHENWEG)

It was soon after sunrise when we left the hut. But – no sun. The clouds from yesterday's rain still sagged over the hillside like a damp dishrag, darkening the schisty rocks to sombre grey. We followed the red paint markers, zigzagging up on gravel and bare rock, the inner glow from the breakfast coffee subsiding into a satisfying trudge.

Then, after half an hour, I noticed my faint shadow moving alongside me. And the cloud around us split and ambled away, like a sulky crowd dispersing at the end of an uninspiring political rally. Harsh golden sunlight flashed off the rock peaks across the valley. The last

BELOW Path signposts, and decayed icefield, at the Bremer Hütte, Austrian Alps.

scraps of cloud hung around aimlessly, some at our level, some below, but still far above the grey-green shadowed valley. Within a few minutes, the rock under our fingers was dry again, and warm, as we clambered up to a perfect little pass, a narrow rock pavement slung between two towers.

Beyond, below a short rocky ramp, the ground dropped into black shadow.

But as our eyes adapted, we saw the tiny path, zigzagging across and back again down the rocks. A cable stapled to the bedrock accompanied it all the way down. And to distract us from the drop, the alpine flowers clinging to the rockface were helpfully labelled in three different languages. No need to bend down. As we stood on the narrow path, the plant labels were at eye level beside us.

Below, a little mountain lake, still in the early morning shadow. And dewy meadows led down to the Sulzenau Hut.

Just in time for another cup of coffee.

Day minus-60

I set about prebooking the seven huts, some through a collective website but mostly by emailing the huts direct. One was full up, but an alternative was available. Since the Coronavirus pandemic, huts tend to be busier and more booked up.

WALK 15 The Stubai High-level Route

START/END **Stubai valley, south of Innsbruck, Austria**

DISTANCE **80km (50 miles)**

ASCENT **6,500m**

APPROX. TIME **8 days**

HIGHEST POINT **Großer Trögler, 2,900m**

TERRAIN **Waymarked paths, sometimes rocky or exposed with cables and iron rungs**

OPTIONS **The energetic can take in some 3,000m mountains on the way round**

The Stubai High Level Route

map from 'Trekking in Austria's Stubai Alps'
by Allan Hartley
published by Cicerone Press

ABOVE Descending from Niederl pass (Stubai High-level Route, Day 4).

Day 0

Flight from Scotland to Munich, then train to hotel in Innsbruck booked via booking.com.

Day 1 Elferspitze to Innsbrücker Hütte

(11km/7 miles, 1,350m ascent)

The official route is the uphill trudge from Neder village. From the map and the tourist board website, I chose a slightly longer alternative using the Elferlifte cable car, then crossing a small limestone summit, the Elferspitze. The very top is a short but exposed scramble on metal rungs – easily bypassed by the more nervous member of the party (me).

Day 2: Innsbrücker Hütte to Bremer Hütte

(10.5km/6.5 miles, 900m ascent)

A grand traverse high above the valley floor, with some rocky sections supplied with wire cables. A dramatic ascent through crags to the hut, on ledges and short rock walls.

Day 3: Simmingjochl to Nürnberger Hütte

(6km/4 miles, 500m ascent)

This was the shortened day, of about four hours, because of the Sulzenau Hut being booked up. This worked out well as it was also the heavy rainfall day. It was rocky going on boilerplate slabs, with temporary waterfalls gushing alongside, and a little footbridge over a spate stream.

Day 4: Nürnberger Hütte to Sulzenauhütte, over Großer Trögler to Dresdner Hütte

(10km/6 miles, 1,150m ascent)

This combined Sections 4 and 5 of the guidebook map (previous page). After the narrow Niederl Pass, we descend into the shadows on the chained, zigzag path down an intimidatingly steep slope of rock and grass. For the afternoon, a tougher route option as steep chains led up to the thrilling little ridgeline of Großer Trögler. The Dresdner Hut, at the top of a cable car, is made of concrete and rather busy. There were even some other Brits there.

Day 5: Mutterberger See (lake), Grawagrubennieder (pass), to Neue Regensburger Hütte
(13.5km/8.5 miles, 950m ascent)

An easier day technically, but quite long (seven hours going), on another path contouring high above the valley. Approaching the hut, the boulderfield has the remains of a dying glacier buried inside it.

Day 6: Schrimmennieder (pass) to Franz-Senn Hütte
(6.5km/4 miles, 500m ascent)

A short day (five hours) to Franz-Senn Hütte. After a moody sunrise, the weather was clearly going off, and we crossed the pass inside cloud.

Day 7: Sendersjöchl (pass) to Starkenburger Hütte
(18.5km/11.5 miles, 700m ascent)

Not too surprisingly, as it was the start of September, we woke to see fresh snow just above the hut. The alternative route is a long descent to the valley, then up again to the final hut. However, we set off hopefully into the cloud. If the path got difficult to follow, we could use our GPS to return the same way. At the high pass, we emerged between cloud layers, for an airy traverse and descent under limestone crags to the final hut.

Day 8: Hoher Burgstall to Kreuzjoch cable car
(5.5km/3.5 miles, 520m ascent)

The official line is a 1,400m descent of the hut's access track. Despite low cloud, we took a more ambitious option to another small limestone summit, Hoher Burgstall, then a panorama path to a cable car. This still got us down early enough for an afternoon in Innsbruck, visiting the folk museum, with its insights into the life of the high valleys we'd been passing through.

BELOW Steep, exposed path on the Großer Trögler.

14

LISTS OF HILLS

To make it seem like it makes some sort of sense, even though it doesn't, many of us build our hillwalking activity around some lists of hills – the Alpine 4,000m peaks, the world's fourteen 8,000m ones, or maybe Scotland's 282 Munros.

The disadvantage is, we may end up treating our walks as if they were work. Each hill to be knocked off as quickly as possible, by the shortest possible route, from the most convenient car park. But the advantages are more important. Instead of just going up Great Gable again and again, our list gets us out into all the corners of the country. It can move us outwards and upwards even in the off-season, in rain, snow, low cloud and other interesting sorts of weather. And when we get to the end, it's time to throw a little party for all our hillwalking friends.

But beware! Hill bagging can become compulsive. If you're going to devote the next ten or 20 years to some hill list, then choose that list with care.

ABOVE Pillar Rock, the tricky 2,000-er but happily not listed among the Wainwrights.

OPPOSITE A Graham, Cruinn a' Bheinn, below a Munro, Ben Lomond.

The Munros

From 1891, this is the first and original hill list. Current surveys show 282 mountains in Scotland above the old measurement of 3,000ft, which nowadays is 914.4m. That includes most of Scotland's finest summits, along with some less interesting ones for ballast. As a lifetime project, it makes a rich and varied hill experience. There's more on the Munros in the 'Scotland' section of this book.

The Munro Tops

Sir Hugh Munro also listed 226 lesser high points, still over 914.4m but not significant enough to count as separate mountains. They're not really worth collecting in their own right. However, including them into a round of the Munros can lead to different, interesting and less frequented routes up the main mountains.

The Corbetts

Many of Scotland's lesser heights are worth visiting as well. J Rooke Corbett's list has 221 hills from 762–914m (2,500–2,999ft), with 152m (500ft) of clear drop round each one. Many choose this as a follow-up list after completing the Munros. The bonus is adventuring into the Southern Uplands, Arran, Rum and Jura. However, compared with the Munros, the Corbetts are a different and somewhat less satisfying experience. The hills are separated by their drop requirement, and also because the bigger Munros get in the way; so your day may just be an up-and-down of a single hill. They tend to be pathless, with rough and vigorous vegetation. And while some are excellent in their own right, quite a high proportion aren't.

The Munros have their 'difficult one', the Inaccessible Pinnacle of

Sgùrr Dearg, requiring rock climbing. The difficult one among the Corbetts is the Cobbler of Arrochar, a short but exposed scramble above a nasty drop, to a spectacular rock-spike summit.

Other Scottish lists

The 231 **GRAHAMS**, of 610–762m (2,000–2,499ft), are much the same as the Corbetts, only a bit less so. With some exceptions, such as Suilven, they tend to be pathless, heathery and not very high. If you live in or near the Southern Uplands, though, you could chase after the 89 **DONALDS**: hills between the Highland Line and the English border, all over 610m (2,000ft), but with a much less rigorous drop criterion. Donalds can be linked into long hill days along the grassy ridges.

The Wainwrights

Alfred Wainwright chose 214 Lakeland summits as separate chapters in the six volumes of his *A Pictorial Guide to the Lakeland Fells*. Visiting each of these is a great way of taking in all of the finest hills, as well as the far-flung corners of the area. Many of the summits are minor ones, and a hill day can easily include half a dozen. So there aren't nearly enough of them for a full lifetime. Indeed, some fellrunners have knocked them all off in a week.

The requisite 'difficult one' is Helm Crag above Grasmere, a short but exciting scramble on to the Howitzer rock. Wainwright himself never achieved it.

BELOW The Cobbler's top at sunrise.

ABOVE Tryfan, one of Wales's top summits.

The English 2000s

There are 256 English summits over 610m (2,000ft). Visiting all of them will give you a thorough coverage of the Lake District (170 of them are there) as well as the Pennines down to the Peak District, plus a moment on the border of South Wales and a day out on Dartmoor.

The 'difficult one' is Pillar Rock, not considered as a summit by Wainwright on the basis of being a proper rock climb of about 40m, graded 'Moderate' by climbers and 'Grade 3' by scramblers.

The Welsh 2000s

The 190 Welsh 610m (2,000ft) hills make for a thorough exploration of the country, from Snowdonia right down

to the Brecon Beacons. It's another very worthwhile hill list, despite not having any 'difficult one' – all can be reached by normal walking. A lot of normal walking...

The Marilyns

For listomaniacs seeking the ultimate hill list, this is it: the 1,556 points in Britain (plus the Isle of Man) that, however high or low, have 150m (492ft) of clear drop around them. This excludes Scotland's Cairn Gorm and England's Scafell, each having only 140m of drop, but takes in such gems as Arthur's Seat in Edinburgh, the Skirrid in South Wales, and Ailsa Craig island in the Firth of Clyde – along with a huge number of miscellaneous humps covered in bog and forestry plantations. Not many of us want to devote our lives to this particular list, given that most of us have jobs, families, etc. But adding in one or two of them will add a certain something to any walk.

The 'difficult ones' here are two sea stacks off St Kilda: hard to get on to, even harder to get up, and covered in bad-tempered birds.

ABOVE Hardown Hill, a Dorset Marilyn 207m high.

15

MORE APP AND MAP

Human minds and the computer screen: it's one of the great evolutionary partnerships, like the shepherd and her dog, the shark and the little wrasse fish that cleans the shark's teeth for it.

Clicking out routes on the computer

The map app, seen via the browser on your computer screen, lets you flick between Landranger and Explorer maps like a magician plucking handkerchiefs out of thin air. But that's not all. It also lets you click your proposed route on to the map, to give you an instant distance and ascent for it.

The distance figure claims to be accurate to within 10m. Measuring something as wiggly as a walk to that accuracy doesn't actually make sense. Anyway, if you're using Snap-to-Path as in the next paragraphs, the distance you get will be about 10 per cent higher than the distance you get if you aren't. Meanwhile, if you're not using Snap-to-Path, and your path makes its way around any steep hillside, then your ascent figure will be too high.

ABOVE Challenging conditions on the side of Skiddaw.

ABOVE This path below Crib Goch, Snowdon, is found by Snap-to-Path but not on maps.

The app also gives a time for your route. Even if you've put your appropriate speed in km/h into the app's settings, the OS app tends to add on too little time for the uphill bits. So it's better to use the Naismith's Rule formula, outlined in Chapter 3.

When you've clicked out your route or recorded it as a track by walking along it, you can make it public for all the other app users to admire and walk along. You can also download it as a GPX file on to your desktop. That GPX file will open in any mapping app, not just the one you're currently using. You can send it to your friends and store it for the future.

And, like walking routes that go either clockwise or anticlockwise, this too works in either direction. You can upload GPX files sent by your friends, or anywhere else you can find them. And once you've uploaded them, you can look at them on your computer screen and follow them using your phone.

All the routes on the Walkhighlands website can be downloaded as GPX files. And if you've bought a Cicerone or Rucksack Readers guidebook, its routes will also be available as GPX.

Mapping software makes a distinction between GPX routes and GPX tracks. A **GPX track** is a route that you've recorded in the real world and has lots and lots of waypoints on it. A **GPX route** is a track that you've clicked on your computer and has rather fewer waypoints. So while they're technically different, they're actually both the same thing.

Mapping on the computer: not that easy to use, then, but it can be very useful if you do. Even if it won't clean your teeth for you.

Snapping to your path

If we're walking across London, Google Maps offers us the best possible route to Waterloo Station, marked with little blue dots and a timing. We hardly think about the algorithm in cyberspace, an algorithm combining the street knowledge of a million London taxi drivers with the speed of a rattlesnake heading towards a tasty toad.

It would scarcely be possible to extend that sort of system to the open countryside, with its tangle of tracks, trails and little trods, many of them not marked on the maps, or else marked wrong. Scarcely possible – but those open source guys have done it. And with that rattlesnake perhaps in mind, they call it Snap-to-Path. You switch it on with a little horseshoe-magnet icon somewhere on your screen.

When clicking out your route line on the computer to find out how long it is and how much ascent it has, Snap-to-Path saves a lot of effort. Click your start point. Now click somewhere a couple of kilometres along your route; and your route line does a little snake dance and fits itself along the pathway in between.

But Snap-to-Path can also be used to seek out usable routes that aren't marked on maps. Do people actually walk along that airy-looking ridgeline? If Snap-to-Path will snap a path along it, then you can be pretty sure they do. On low ground in Scotland, where the map doesn't have right-of-way paths on it, Snap-to-Path can also find the walked-on ways.

Even rattlesnakes aren't entirely reliable, and neither is Snap-to-Path. If you click the two ends of the wide and popular path from Beck Head below Great Gable down to Wasdale Head, the OS Maps Snap-to-Path currently heads off sideways and takes you over the top of Kirk Fell. So there's still some space for the human intelligence. To make your route work, you may have to switch off Snap-to-Path and click a straight-line section, then switch it back on again.

A walk in the Mamores

Before walking it on your feet, walk it in the mind, and on the map.

It's a lot easier to read the map, understand the hill shapes and anticipate your day when you aren't standing on loose scree in a gale with

RIGHT Am Bodach (left) and Stob Coire a' Chairn (right).

two shivering companions who the moment you take the map out start going, 'Oh no, are we lost now?'

So: let's suppose the plan is a couple of big hills from the village of Kinlochleven, in the south-west Highlands between Glen Coe and Fort William. Which will be Walk 16 in this book.

Stob Coire a' Chairn (the 'peak of the corrie of the cairn') and Am Bodach (the 'old bloke'). Why these two? Well, the Landranger map shows them as steep-sided and pointy, but with a nice clear ridgeline between. If you'd like help visualising the shapes,

on the OS mapping app the 'standard' map layer has hill shape shading and so does 'OpenStreetMap' on the Outdooractive app. The smaller-scale Harvey British Mountain Map has altitude colouring.

The Landranger also shows a path arriving east of Stob Coire a' Chairn, and another one coming down again from the ridgeline west of Am Bodach. Looking good so far...

... So let's measure it up.

Clicking along the route while using Snap-to-Path gives 15km (9.5 miles), with 1,200m of ascent. In my book, 1,200m counts as a full-on mountain day: it's going to be pretty tiring. (If I click out the route without Snap-to-Path, I get 13.5km/8.4

ABOVE Studying the map at home pays dividends on the hill.

LEFT Wastwater, viewed from Great Gable. Confident night walking is one reward for getting on top of paper and digital navigation.

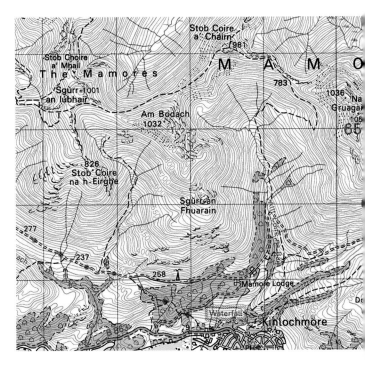

miles and the same 1,200m of ascent.) Using the Naismith's Rule (see Chapter 3), the ascent counts as 9.6km (6 miles) extra. Reckoning 3.5km/h that suggests around seven hours for the circuit. Incidentally, while I've included distances in miles throughout this book, for any serious work with today's metric maps it really only makes sense to be thinking in kilometres and metres.

What about the weather? This is proper mountain ground, so the Mountain Weather Information Service website (mwis.org.uk) is the one to go for. Let's suppose it says light southwesterly wind, occasional showery rain, cloud lifting off the tops, patches of sun, visibility excellent.

Looks like we're going for it!

Next question: which way round? The map shows complicated paths heading up north from Kinlochleven, whereas the final part of the descent, when we're tired and not thinking so sharply, will be the straightforward West Highland Way. Already, that's suggesting going anticlockwise. And now, look closely at Am Bodach. The north-east flank is steep, and not that well defined. That could be tricky to find if starting from the top. The west ridge, on the other hand, is more

gently sloped, and steep on both sides, making it easier to find and to follow. It's always easy to find the way up a hill, so it makes sense to have the less demanding south-west side as our descent. So yes: anticlockwise is going to be easier.

However, if those forecast southwesterly winds had rain in them, we might go the other way, so as to have the rain behind us up on the high ground.

Studying the route in more detail – again in a rain- and wind-free indoor environment – let's turn to the larger-scale OS Explorer. (Or the Harvey Superwalker if you happen to have one available.)

This one shows us the car park, which is a good start. Various paths lead uphill to the north, north-east and north-west; some are on both

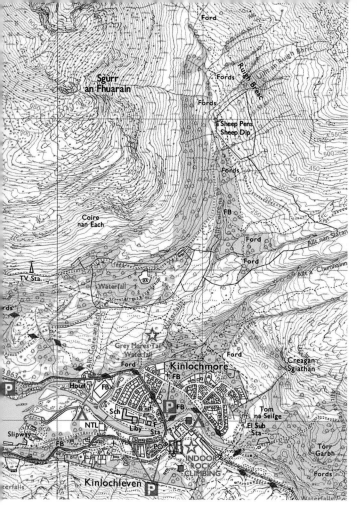

the map's possible
paths do appear to exist,
as determined by people
with phones walking
up them.

Good. We want the
one running north;
either of the ones
turning north-west will
also be fine, leading on
to the same high-level
track along the 250m
contour line. The one
running up north-east
would be a mistake. So
we'll need to cross one
fair-sized stream, the
Allt a' Chumhainn, and
then head up to the right
of the main stream, the
one with the Grey Mare's
Tail waterfall at the
bottom of it.

Landranger and Explorer scales,
some just on the larger Explorer map.

However, on that Explorer, the
various paths are the very pale grey
'well maybe' kind of dashed line.
Experience has made me suspicious
of all paths on Landranger, and also
of those pale-and-hesitant ones on
Explorer. Paths starting at a car park
and running up into the hills: yes,
those ones are likely to exist. And
if you've a Harvey map handy, the
hoped-for paths are on it as well. But
the easy way to check is to switch on
Snap-to-Path. Putting a starting click
on the car park and then clicking
around that high track shows that all

So now we're at the big bend in the
track at the entrance to the big hollow
– or is it a small valley? – to the south
of Stob Coire a' Chairn. The stream is
Allt Coire na Ba, and on the Explorer
map the hollow itself is Coire na Ba
(the corrie of the cattle, or possibly
deer hinds).

There's something a bit special
about the path from here up to the
ridgeline (783m on that Landranger
map). Most hill paths go straight up
and down, crossing the contour lines
at right angles. This one takes a long
slant out to the right and back again.
Following it onwards, it crosses Stob
Coire a' Chairn before it bypasses to

ABOVE The ridge running to Am Bodach.

the north of Am Bodach, then to the south of the next summit, Sgùrr an Iubhair, finally wandering down on to the southern slopes of Stob Ban. It is, in fact, a Victorian-era deer-stalkers' path, built for ponies and also for people with more sensible ideas of how to go up a slope than the straight-up-and-down hillwalkers of today.

On the Harvey map, the path has a gap in it halfway up. But even if we're

BELOW Mamores route – Coire na Ba: Snap-to-Path gives a different line from the path on the map.

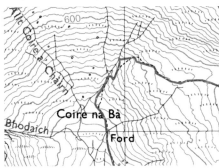

looking at the Harvey map in the first place, we shan't worry about that. Snap-to-Path confirms that all of the path exists – though if you look closely, you'll spot a couple of points where the path snapped to isn't the one on the map. Since they made that map, the path's got trodden on to a different line.

Now we're at the 783m saddle south-west of Stob Coire a' Chairn. From here, it's a sharply defined ridge, steep drops on the left, steep and craggy drops on the right. That bit's going to be fun.

According to the forecast, the top of Stob Coire a' Chairn could be in the cloud. So how do we get off it? The descent west is more of a spur than a ridgeline. After dropping three contour lines, which will take about five minutes, we'll bend a bit left, south-west, on a pretty clear spur line. That's a fairly OK bit of compass work. Anyway, the map says there's a path:

ABOVE Mamores route – Am Bodach.

and this time it's the darker black 'yes we really mean it' sort of dashed line on the Explorer. And if we're really stuck we can fire up the phone. So that should be all right.

The ridge running south-west is almost level, but with one wee bump in it. (When we get there, that wee bump's going to look like a pretty big one.) Still steep on both sides, nice.

What about if we're tired, and maybe the weather's worse than we expected. Can we get down off here? Let's have another wee peep at the Explorer map.

Aha! There's a path, just at the base of Am Bodach, down into the Coire a' Bhodaich. But looking closer, I'm not too keen on that little path. The slope's a steep one. On the Landranger map,

some of the 10m contour lines have been missed out. That's a sign of a slope that's not going to be nice to go down.

And does the little path even exist? Snap-to-Path doesn't snap to it, and it's not there on the Harvey map. Shall we just bear that one in mind, as a doable way down on to more sheltered ground, but probably not a nice one? (We shan't go far wrong if we do: in the actual world, that path happens to be another disused old stalkers' pony-path, grassed over but definitely there.)

If we wanted to dodge Am Bodach, there's also the bypass path across the northern slope, to the saddle on the other side. Confidently marked on Explorer, it's an 'intermittent path' on Harvey, and Snap-to-Path snaps to it. I've been there, and it isn't all that obvious on the ground. But the mapping app on the smartphone would keep you on track.

But while we're looking at the escape routes: what about that corrie to the north, Coire a' Mhail? It looks lovely and sheltered, the slopes down don't look too steep, and on the Explorer map there's even a little path. Coire a' Mhail leads us down into the wrong valley, of course; but maybe we'll be so cold and wet we'll be up for the expensive taxi ride back round to Kinlochleven.

Well, Coire a' Mhail is possibly the strongest argument in all Scotland for checking escape routes in advance. Track that sheltered valley down, and you find an area marked as woodland, with some very crowded contour lines. In fact, that's the Steall Waterfall, 120m tall, tumbling down slabs of bare quartzite with a few birch trees clinging on by the tips of their roots. Seventeen students tried to come down that way in the dark with only two torches between them. I know because it was me who saw the two torches and called out the helicopter.

RIGHT Mamores route – Coire a' Mhail.

Looking at the map, now, in your nice cosy home, you may be able to work out how you'd try to get out of Coire a' Mhail. Hint: it's not by going down the stream.

Next up: what about Am Bodach itself? Is there going to be a path?

The OS doesn't mark any, not on Landranger and not on Explorer. But Am Bodach is a Munro summit and, honestly, there's going to be a path. And Snap-to-Path agrees.

The OS paths are based on history, which is why they mark the Victorian

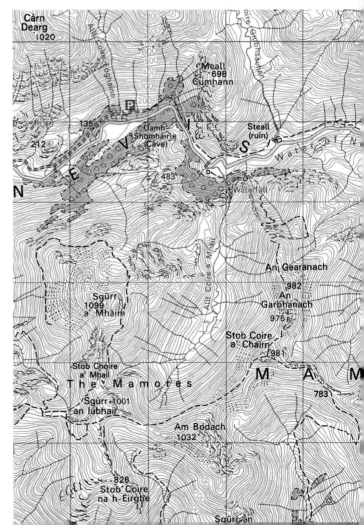

LEFT Steall Falls: not a safe way out from the corrie north of Am Bodach.

The descent from Am Bodach is a well-defined ridgeline, direction west. Shouldn't be any trouble there. Then along the level saddle until the ridgeline starts to rise. That's where we'll look out down sharp left for the descent path in Stob Coire na h-Eirghe. Which, the top of it, doesn't actually exist, according to the Landranger map. Common sense says that path comes all the way up. The Explorer map agrees and so does Snap-to-Path. And once on it, we should be cosily sheltered from that southwesterly breeze by the side summit of Stob Coire na h-Eirghe.

Whew! That was a lot of work. And we haven't even got out of the car yet...

deer-stalking routes. Harvey maps are based on photos taken from aeroplanes. But the paths on the crowd-sourced OpenStreetMap are the ones from tracking people's phones. The OS 'standard' map layer and Outdooractive OpenStreetMap layer both mark the path we'd expect across the top of Am Bodach; and Snap-to-Path snaps on to it. So yes, it's there.

Oh, and how to get out of Coire a' Mhail? As it narrows, and starts to steepen downhill, you'd head up slightly north of east to join the path coming down from An Gearanach. That's 200m of ascent, and it's a tricky bit of navigation, especially in the dark.

STOB COIRE A' CHAIRN AND AM BODACH, MAMORES

B ack in the Scotland section, I suggested not going up on Ben Nevis by the wide and busy 'Mountain Trail'. The route in the Mamores whose maps we've been examining is just that: the Not Going Up Ben Nevis walk. And it's

what Scottish mountains are all about. Birch woods and a waterfall to get you started. A well-laid zigzag ascent on an old path. High, airy ridgelines. Exhilarating views – including across to Ben Nevis itself. And if you're up for it,

WALK 16 **Stob Coire a' Chairn and Am Bodach, Mamores**
START/END **Grey Mare's Tail car park at the north edge of Kinlochleven (NN187622: nearest postcode PH50 4QU)**
DISTANCE **15km (9.5 miles)**
ASCENT **1,200m**
APPROX. TIME **7 hours**
HIGHEST POINT **Am Bodach, 1,032m**
TERRAIN **Hill paths, sometimes rough and stony**

OPTIONS **Scrambling (Grade 1) on a short out-and-back to An Garbhanach**
PARKING **At start**
CAR-FREE **Buses to Kinlochleven from Fort William and Ballachulish on the A82**
TOILETS **South end of the bridge over the River Leven**
PUBS & CAFES **Several in Kinlochleven: cafe at Ice Factor indoor climbing wall**

LEFT Grey Mare's Tail waterfall, Kinlochleven.

already implied by the map discussion on the previous pages. The path starts at the back of the car park, with a junction where you turn left. Soon the path descends to a footbridge over a stream. Now you should divert left to admire the nearby Grey Mare's Tail waterfall.

Return past the path junction and take the path bending left, uphill, to the edge of the birch woods. Keep right at the path junction here, up to a gate in deer fencing. The path contours north above Allt Coire na Ba, across two streams, to another junction. Again, keep ahead, on a rather faint path, climbing gradually to the contouring track shown on the map.

Turn left briefly, and just before the bridge over Allt Coire na Ba, turn off

the out-and-back to An Gearanach is airy scrambling on good, grippy rock.

If you like this one – well, there are seven more Mamores to enjoy, without even leaving Kinlochleven.

Most of this route description is

right, passing left of sheep pens into the upper valley. At the valley head, the path makes a wide zigzag up right: it can be unclear over damp ground here. Then it turns back left to reach the high ridgeline. Take the ridgeline path up left towards Stob Coire a' Chairn.

Want to try the ridge to An Garbhanach? Arriving at a small shoulder, look out for the path marked on Explorer and Harvey maps, slightly downhill round into a little hollow then up to the saddle north of Stob Coire a' Chairn. Follow the spur crest, on paths and clean, well-used rocks, over An Garbhanach, whose name means the 'rough one'. An airy ridge continues to An Gearanach, the 'steep one'. Return over An Garbhanach, for the path up the northern spur to Stob Coire a' Chairn. This adds 2km (1.2 miles) and 150m ascent, a good hour including the scrambling in both directions.

The path leaves the summit west, soon swinging down south-west on to the ridgeline over the 909m hump. At the next col, the bypass path could be taken slanting slightly downhill to skirt the north side of Am Bodach – it's not so clear as the map suggests. (And check the warning a couple of pages up about not descending into Coire a' Mhail.) Otherwise, take the steep and stony path up to the commanding summit of Am Bodach.

English has a disparaging term, 'hag', for women who are no longer young. But it takes Gaelic to add the equivalent, 'bodach', for man-hag. His female partner across the valley is Beinn na Caillich, the 'witch's hill'.

The ridgeline path leads down west, slightly left of the crest line, then bends round towards north-west, to the next col. At a cairn, the descent path turns down left (faint at the very top) into Coire na h-Eirghe. It's a reasonably gentle descent, but a long one, to the track across the hillside at the 250m contour. Turn left, and bear right down the wide path of the West Highland Way to the edge of Kinlochleven.

BELOW An Garbhanach, the 'rough one', and Stob Coire a' Chairn.

16

MORE MAP AND COMPASS

Mostly, we're going to be using modern digital navigation with the smartphone (you did pack that back-up battery pack, didn't you?) Old-style compass work is interesting in itself and can come in useful as well. Plus, back when I was last caught in a whiteout, the smartphone didn't actually exist.

What is a whiteout? The word gets used whenever the cloud's down and it's snowing. But a real whiteout is worse than that. When the cloud's down, and it's snowing, and also the ground is completely covered in fresh snow so that you can't see where the ground ends and the sky begins and you can't tell what you're about to tread on and you can't even tell which way is downhill – that's a whiteout.

I was on Merrick, the high point of Galloway. The Merrick's a hill I know well, but still, let me tell you, this was an unsettling experience.

ABOVE Stob Ghabhar, Southern Highlands.

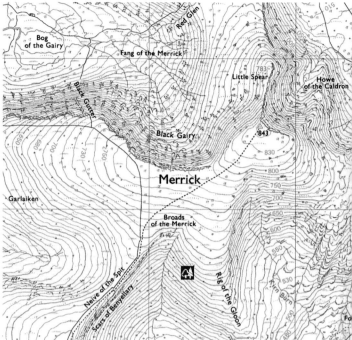

The path off Merrick slants down a wide, gentle slope called the Broads of the Merrick. At the bottom corner it meets a drystone wall and runs beside it along the grassy ridge to Benyellary. The wall would be a guide; and to get to it I just needed to descend south-west. Not that difficult. Not difficult at all. I wouldn't have been that far up there otherwise, not in those conditions.

However, the right-hand edge of the wide slope is a crag dropping to the north called the Black Gairy. The top of Black Gairy would now have a cornice of soft snow. If I ventured too far to the right, by the time I spotted those crags dropping to the north I'd be dropping to the north myself.

For the first time in several years, I placed the compass against the map and took an accurate bearing, aiming a bit above the bottom corner of that wall. It was back in the 2000s, so I adjusted for magnetic variation. Then I put the compass

between my teeth – come to think of it, that's another use for that square chunk of plastic on the compass – because I wanted both hands for my walking poles. When you don't know whether your next step's going to be

down or up, poles help. Every few steps, I checked my bearing; I even turned round and back-checked it against my footprints.

After 20 minutes, I found the drystone wall and followed it down out of the cloud.

Nowadays, GPS makes it a whole lot easier not to walk out onto that snow cornice above the Black Gairy. Even so, the compass clasped between the teeth is the way to do it without getting your phone wet or taking off your gloves.

LEFT Map and compass, Place Fell. About to take a bearing from Place Fell summit along the path heading roughly north-east. (Map: Harvey Superwalker)

BELOW Binsey, Lake District. Turning the map around until it matches the countryside can help. This is 'setting the map'. On the phone, you can do it with a single touch.

WHY DIVIDE THE CIRCLE INTO 360?

For lovers of pointless factoids: the degree, for angles, is the oldest unit of measurement still in use today. We've abandoned the megalithic yard and the cubit, not to mention the rod, pole or perch. (As a lover of pointless factoids, you're already aware that the rod, pole or perch is 1/40th of a furlong, or 5.03m.) The degree was devised by Babylonian astronomers: one degree is approximately the amount the stars move round the night sky between midnight tonight and midnight tomorrow. Also the gods of the Babylonians counted in 60s.

The military, not being beholden to any blooming Babylonians, divide the circle into 6,283.2 mils. Except if they're in NATO, where (to confuse the Russians) there are 6,400 of them.

So, how to take a bearing?

Back in Chapter 4, I suggested ignoring all the little numbers around the edges of your compass. Now we're going to start looking at them.

For finding your way across the Atlantic, you need something more precise than 'a wee bit east of south'. So we divide the circle into 360 degrees, counting clockwise. East becomes 090, South becomes 180, West becomes 270, and North becomes either 360 or 000. With care and a compass you can steer to the nearest degree, which means that after 1km you'll be out by just 20m (or after 1 mile, by 35m).

There are two stages to taking a bearing. First, use the rectangular hunk of plastic and the twiddly bit in the middle to measure your desired direction off the map. Next, consult the compass needle itself to point

ABOVE Taking the bearing off the map. (The measured bearing is 45 degrees, exactly north-east.)

out the desired direction across the ground.

Measuring the bearing

For this first stage, you'll ignore the red-end white-end moving needle. Instead, note the two different arrows on the compass itself. Outside the blue twiddly bit, on the plastic rectangle, the arrow next to my forefinger is the

direction of travel arrow. Obviously, the long edges of the plastic will have the same effect. The other arrow, the one underneath the moving needle, is the **north arrow**.

I'm at the summit of Place Fell, and my route is along the path running roughly north-east. So first I line up the long edge of the plastic, and the direction of travel arrow, with the path I want to go along. Then, holding the plastic in place with the thumb you see in the picture on page 273, I twiddle the central circle so that the north arrow, and the lines alongside it, run parallel with the north-south grid lines on my map. In the picture I've just finished doing that.

Magnetic variation

There are two main sorts of north: magnetic north, where the compass needle points, and grid north, which is the north–south lines on the map. If

you are reading this in the UK, in the decade of the 2020s, then **skip this step!** For you are an all-time fortunate individual. The 2020s were when, in the UK, magnetic north and grid north were both in the same direction. If you happen to be reading this in Hebden Bridge, Yorkshire, in August 2024, then magnetic north and grid north are exactly in alignment. Happy indeed is Hebden Bridge on that day! If you're unlucky enough to be living in, say, 2035, then you will need to make an adjustment for **magnetic variation**. You'll need to remember: **The compass is smaller than the map. To get from map bearing to compass bearing, subtract a bit.**

In 2035, in the UK, the amount to subtract will be 2 degrees. The exact figure is found on the edge of your map; or search for 'grid magnetic angle calculator (UK and Ireland)' on the internet.

Following the bearing

The second stage is to lift up your compass and rotate the whole thing until the red-end white-end needle lines up with the north arrow underneath it. And now the direction of travel arrow will be indicating your direction of travel.

If you need to follow this bearing for a while, just walking along while holding the compass as steady as possible works surprisingly well. Otherwise, you look ahead and choose a tuft of grass. Walk towards it, then stop and choose another tuft.

Also, a good trick is to use the

LEFT Lining up the compass needle.

compass bearing in reverse to check your position against a path signpost or other landmark you're currently walking away from – or even your footprints behind you in the snow.

Pole-planting procedures

For really tricky situations, there are complicated procedures you can do using walking poles or your companions. Plant a pole, walk as far as you can see, and look back along your bearing to adjust your position. (If you took off the little basket on the end, the pole you planted probably won't have fallen over.) Plant the second pole and go back and retrieve the first one. That means walking everything three times.

With a companion and plenty of poles, there's a more efficient way to do it. You, the compass reader, take all the poles and walk ahead as far as you can see. Adjust your position and plant one pole. You can now walk on, while at the same time your companion advances to the pole you just planted.

But honestly, it's easier just to use the GPS.

BELOW Tricky conditions on the Fairfield Horseshoe, Lake District.

Aiming off

You're on a long, rough slope, and at the bottom there's a river with a crucial footbridge. Unfortunately, there are trees all along the river and the footbridge can't be seen. So you take a bearing.

When you get to the river, you might have hit the footbridge exactly. Neat! But if not, which way do you turn? (The tiresome answer would be, 100 paces left, then 200 paces back right, then 400 paces left again, and so on...) So instead, you take a bearing 5 degrees to the left of the bridge. Now, when you get to the river, you know to turn right.

Aspect of slope

You're lost in the mist, and OK the compass is pointing north. But that just tells you which bit of mist is the bit of mist to the north of you. Well, you do have one more bit of information. You're on a fairly steep slope, and the compass can tell you which direction is the downhill one. The direction that's downhill is called 'aspect of slope'. But skiers call it the **fall line** because it's the line you fall down if you fall over. And it's the line that's at right angles to the local contours.

So now you're searching the map for somewhere you could plausibly be, which also has fairly close-together contours with the fall line pointing down south-west.

This kind of thinking, combining compass and contour lines, can become almost instinctive. As an example, suppose you're in the mist, on Carnedd Llewelyn in northern Snowdonia, and you want to get to

ABOVE Crossing Rannoch Moor. Careful reading of the contours is going to help here.

Yr Elen because it's the next of the Welsh 3,000-footers – those 914.4m summits. This means you need to be on the spur line I've marked with pink dots on the map below, leading to the col above Ffynnon Caseg.

What you do is: you take the bearing down the spur line, which is 300 degrees, and set that on your compass. Now if you're walking downhill, and that downhill direction is the 300 degree pre-set on your compass, then you're on that spur line. On the other hand, if you're too far down to the left, towards where I've drawn the red asterisk, then the fall line is pointing down westwards. This is to the left of the bearing marked on your compass, which you need to ease round to the right. Alternatively, if you're too far to the right, then the fall line will be north, down towards Cwm Caseg. This is to the right of the bearing on your compass, and you need to ease up to the left.

If what I've said so far makes sense, you could stride forwards into the next two paragraphs.

Now let's suppose you came in from the north-east, along the Cambrian Way. Contour to the right around the slope of Carnedd Llewelyn; and when the fall line dropping to your right matches the 300 degrees bearing on your compass, then you're on

the spur line for Yr Elen.

Coming in from the south and contouring to the left, it would be a bit more complicated. If the fall line on your left is 300 degrees, then yes, you're on the spur line with the pink dots, and you turn down left along it. But what if you're a bit too low? Then you'll find the fall line swinging round to the south-west; and at that point you turn directly uphill, north-east, to arrive at the col. A bit farther round, the fall line's down south: you're at the point I've marked with a cross, or else somewhere directly below or above it. Now, straight uphill will get you on to Yr Elen.

So in thick mist, and whether you start on top of Llewelyn, or from either of its approaching ridges, you can find your way to Yr Elen using only the compass and the fall line. If you're with someone who doesn't know how it's done, this seems just like magic.

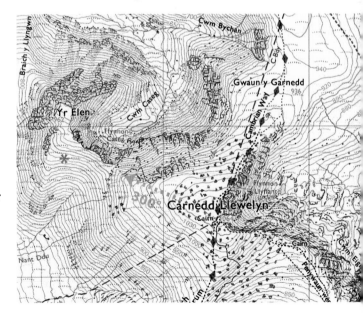

RIGHT Carnedd Llewelyn (direction of slope).

Grid references

The Ordnance Survey's 'national grid' is a system for specifying any point in the UK. It's sort of like what3words, but with numbers. It's still used by many walkers and is ideal for telling the rescue services where the casualty is if you're phoning from somewhere else. Also, if you have failed to upload the map into your phone, you can use the OS Locate app (without a phone signal) to mark up your position onto a paper map.

I'll use Bwlch Mawr, on the Llŷn peninsula, because it's conveniently at the bottom-left-hand corner of the Snowdonia map.

The grid reference (GR) starts with a pair of letters, which specify a 100km

BELOW To be above the cloudsea, you have to come up through the cloud...

RIGHT Bwlch Mawr – grid references.

square of territory. That's the 'SH' in the corner of the map. The rest of it comes off the blue grid lines that cross the map. Each of these squares is 1km across – and this is true on any walking map of any scale, whether OS or Harvey.

The memory line here is: you walk across the ground and then you climb the tree. Look along the bottom of the map: Bwlch Mawr is in the square starting 42. Looking up the side, it's in the square starting 47. So SH4247 is Bwlch Mawr's 1km grid square.

For the third and sixth digits, you estimate the distance across the square. Going sideways, we're **seven** tenths of the way across from line 42; going up, we're **eight** tenths of the way up from line 47. That gives us SH427478. This is accurate within one tenth of a grid square, which is 100m.

Just one mystery remains. Why is this hilltop called Bwlch Mawr, when *bwlch* is the Welsh for a pass?

Finding the way Stone Age-style

When it comes to the wind, sun and stars, we're never going to match the skills of a Stone Ager, let alone an Arctic tern or a migrating wildebeest.

BELOW Night navigation on Helvellyn.

MORE MAP AND COMPASS

Even so, natural navigation encourages us to see and feel what's going on around us. Also, it leaves the hands free for the walking poles.

Wind

The wind is not a reliable guide – but it's a guide. If you're heading down the south-west ridge with the wind in your face, and the wind on the summit was a brisk easterly – well, this suggests you aren't heading down the south-west ridge after all.

Sun

If you're aware where the sun should be shining from, that's another easy, phone-free check on your direction. The sun rises in the east and sets in the west, correct? Exactly so, just so long as it happens to be the last two weeks of either March or September. Otherwise, the sun compass below gives a rough guide. The winter sun rises at 8am, nearer to south-east than east; and sets in the south-west. The summer one is adjusted for British Summer Time, so that midday, with the sun in the south, occurs at 1pm.

Following yonder star

You can read up on how to identify the Pole Star. And if you're lying out on a hilltop, it's almost cosmological the way the Great Bear, or Plough, rotates around it like a half-speed clock. But when I'm walking in the dark, the stellar navigation that works for me is: first, get the right direction with compass or GPS; and then select a star that's in the correct direction and follow it for a while. This saves switching on the torch again and lets the eyes adjust to the moonlight, for a slightly more Stone Age walking experience.

After half an hour, the star will have shifted round a bit, and it's time to take out the torch and the map and choose another star.

BELOW Sun compass.

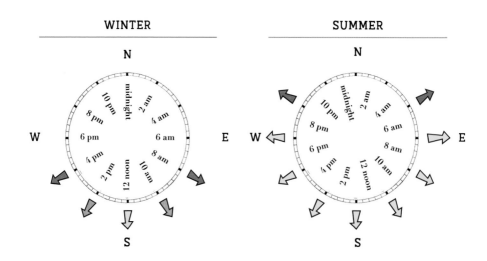

WINTER

SUMMER

17

WINTER SKILLS

The purpose of the ice axe is not for axing ice. Instead, it's an example of a tool that's changed its function while staying exactly the same. The ice axe, for us ordinary hillwalkers, is for stopping us sliding down snow slopes.

I was about 12 when my Dad and his friend took me off up Liathach in the snow. Somewhere in the back corrie we reached the first patch of hard snow, and we spent a quarter of an hour practising what's rather grandly called the 'self-arrest technique'. A few hours later, when it came time to descend off the ridgeline, I discovered what a difference that 15 minutes had made. What should have been an intimidating slope of hardened snow became a shiny white playground for trotting down with effortless ease – just from the confidence of knowing how to stop.

Here's how it works. When walking on a steepish snow slope, the axe, in the uphill hand, is held with the pick pointing backwards. Then, if you're sliding down the slope, you hold the axe against your shoulder and lean down on to it.

Obviously, if the pick were pointing forwards when you fell, at this point it stabs deep into your shoulder. But

ABOVE Descending Swirral Edge, Helvellyn.

if you were holding it the right way round, you'll now come quickly to a stop. Even, possibly, too quickly. If the snow is hard and icy, you'll need to lean the spike into it quite gradually.

On your safe snow slope, having discovered how well this works, you can practise falling head first, or on your back.

The spike on the bottom end is for plunging the ice axe into the snow slope and using it as a super-secure walking stick. The item behind the pick is the adze. It was designed for cutting steps into hard snow. It can still be used for that, though as you're wearing your crampons you won't need to. Meanwhile, the pick was for cutting steps in glacier ice. And if you do use it for cutting through a frozen lake to get some drinking water, you'll find that it's very good at that. With the axe-head in your hand, you can also

ABOVE Ice axe self-arrest:
1 Being glad the pick isn't about to go into my shoulder
2 Shoulder drives the pick into the snow.
3 If wearing crampons, you'll need to keep your feet up out of the way.

RIGHT Walker's ice axe on Ben Lomond.

Ice axe in use: pick pointing to the back.

drive the pick into hard snow or frozen turf for a handhold.

Ice climbers, incidentally, carry much shorter ice axes. They carry two of them and poke the pick into the ice overhead before pulling themselves up on the shaft. An ice axe for walkers will have a straight shaft; a good length for it is, with the head in your hand, dangling to the anklebone.

And just to repeat: the key to confidence on steeper snow is playing about in advance, somewhere safe, on some snow that isn't steep.

Crampons

When snow thaws then freezes again, that's the firm surface known as *névé* (French) or *Firn* (German) or just 'good snow' (winter climbers). That's the time to put on your crampons. Or rather, that's slightly too late. The time to put on your crampons is just before

RIGHT Soft snow in the Lake District, where good, firm snow is fairly rare. Crampons won't help here and would get blunted on the stones underneath.

you get to that special snow.

And even before that, when you're still safe and warm at home. First, work out which crampon is which; usually the clip or fastening is on the outside. Practise putting them on – you'll be doing it with cold fingers or with gloves on. With a new pair of crampons, I walk around on my lawn. It's a good way of checking they're properly fastened. It's also good for the lawn.

Good snow for crampons is quite rare. For every dozen days when I'm carrying the things, I actually put them on once or twice in a winter – on the big Scottish mountains it'll be oftener than that, hopefully. As a walker rather than a winter climber, I go for the most flexible crampons I can find. High-performance crampons for high-

ABOVE Crampons on Ben Lomond.

BELOW Using ice axe and crampons on Striding Edge, Helvellyn.

performance ice climbers require a special set of extra-stiff boots to strap them on.

On a snow slope without crampons you kick your foot in to make a step. Or stamp down your heel, if coming downhill. With crampons, the technique's different. You want all eight of the spikes stuck into the snow, flat footed. On steeper slopes,

this means going uphill in zigzags. Downhill, it's a slightly unnatural knees-forward posture, with the ice axe behind as a stabilising third leg. On slopes where there isn't a risk of sliding out of control, so that you won't need an ice axe self-arrest, crampons plus walking poles work together well.

Winter and rough weather

Winter has great rewards, but also its own special disadvantages. I've described the whiteout in Chapter 16; my attitude to one of those is to get the heck off the hill. Cornices are the overhanging shelves of snow that form at the top of steep slopes on the downwind side. They're easy enough to spot and to avoid in clear conditions, but in mist you can be standing on top of one before you're even aware of being anywhere near the edge. My Grandpa discovered this when looking for a route down off Beinn Achaladair above the Moor of Rannoch. Grandpa lost his car keys and his spectacles but not, I'm glad to say, his life. And it was back in the

RIGHT Cornice on Helvellyn.

BELOW Avalanche debris in the Galloway Hills. A cornice collapse has set off the slope below.

days when you could start up your car with a piece of wire under the bonnet.

In mist or blowing snow, navigating alongside a cornice is easier and safer using GPS. Just so long as you can keep your battery warm and your phone dry.

The remaining special hazard of the winter hills is the avalanche. These can happen even on quite minor hills: the UK's most lethal one so far came off the South Downs into the town of Lewes in 1836.

Avalanches mostly happen:

→ on steep (but not very steep) slopes
→ on the downwind side of the hill
→ during heavy snowfall and for about two days after
→ plus, cornices may collapse when the snow begins to thaw

The best way to build avalanche awareness is to consult the SportScotland avalanche forecast at www.sais.gov.uk, ideally for several days before your trip. In the Lake District or nearby, the Lakeland fell top conditions, including avalanche risk if any, are reported daily at www.lakedistrictweatherline.co.uk.

All this sounds like a whole lot of winter-specific hassle and precaution, and it is. But once you're up there – with your crampons on the correct feet

and the ice axe the right way round – on a sunny afternoon on crisp, firm snow when you scuttle around like a spider on a Christmas cake, with more snowy mountains stretching to the edge of the world, well, it all makes the stony slopes of summer seem ever so slightly ordinary.

18

A BIT ABOUT BEDROCK

'J'ai besoin de connaître la géologie, comment Sainte-Victoire s'enracine, la couleur géologique des terres, tout cela m'émeut, me rend meilleur.'

I need to know geology, how Mount Saint-Victoire is rooted, the geological colours of earths, all that moves me, makes me better [as a painter].

PAUL CÉZANNE, WHO PAINTED THE LIMESTONE MONT SAINTE-VICTOIRE 83 TIMES

Rocks are dark grey, which is pretty boring. Where do they come from? They don't come from anywhere, they're just there. They lie around on scree slopes, but do also make nice big crags which, when you come to climb them, are covered in little handholds.

That's when I was a teenager. Well, my Granny did live in the Lake District. But then I got taken to Stanage Edge in the Peak District. And suddenly, rock came in little cliffs, 0.5km (0.3 miles) long but only 50m high. Rocks were yellowish brown, and had cracks instead of handholds, and were gritty and grippy under the foot. Very odd. And not that easy to climb up.

A few years later came Torridon in Wester Ross. And now the rocks were in three different colours, like

ABOVE Gabbro coastline, Loch Scavaig, Skye.

a Neapolitan ice cream. Streaky gneiss across the moorlands, purply-brown Torridonian sandstone rising above, all topped off with angular, off-white quartzite.

Which is when I got interested in this stuff I was clambering about on. And it was a bit like people in a novel, or even in real life. Friendly or stand-offish, honest and open or tricky and treacherous and dark – what, if they were people, we'd call their personalities. Their moods and behaviour all formed by traumatic experiences in early childhood, hundreds of millions of years ago.

Different sorts of stones

Mangled volcanics

The Lake District and Snowdonia are made from volcanic rocks: lava-flows, underground sills, ash fallen from the sky. This doesn't mean you'll find any volcanoes today. These favourite national parks started as two chains of volcanic islands, which then got

mashed and broken by the collision of England with Scotland 400 million years ago.

Having cooled from a molten state, these rocks are firm and compact, containing crystals of various sorts whose sharp little corners make them grippy underfoot. The great earth movements created the many cracks, chimneys, gullies and miles-long fault lines through the ranges, as well as the overall chunky look.

Grand for looking at, grand for climbing and scrambling, but the complexity of the mangled rock types means they're not so easy for making sense of the geology of it all.

SCRAMBLABILITY? Scrambler's heaven. Ashfall tuffs are rough-textured with plenty of small holds. The lavas are more compact.

Granite

Rocks are grey – but granite rocks are white, or yellowish white, or even pink. And not just pink, but pink with little black specks. Granite boulders are round and blobby, like the droppings of some primordial giant rabbit. Granite cliffs look just like piles of stone pillows.

Granite is magma that has cooled, slowly, deep underground. And not just any magma, but the stuff melted from pale, sticky, quartz-rich continental crust. Seen close up, the rock has three different crystals: glassy quartz, pink or off-white feldspar, and a dark, iron-rich mineral. Hence the speckles.

The feldspar and dark mineral break down in the rain, giving the granite boulders their rounded shapes. So there won't be any handholds, you just have to learn hand-jamming in the cracks. But the hard quartz remains, sticking out from the surface. So basically you're scrambling on sandpaper.

Some granite mountains – the Galloway Hills and especially the Cairngorms – stay with the shapes of the original huge blobs of underground magma. Wide, barren moorlands and plateaus, slabs of rounded bare rock. Others go pointy and steep-sided, like the Isle of Arran and the Mountains of Mourne. And on Dartmoor, the Mournes and the Cairngorms, just to relieve the grimness, the tops are sprinkled with little granite tors.

SCRAMBLABILITY? Deliciously solid and rough, but the rocks are rounded and holdless. Scrambles that look easy can be impossible.

BELOW Confronting the granite on Goat Fell, Isle of Arran.

Gabbro and basalt

While pale, continental magma makes granite, dark magma from the Earth's mantle, when it cools and crystallises deep underground, gives us gabbro, and the crags of Skye's Black Cuillin range. Those big crystals mean Skye's rocks are rough enough to wear out the climbers' fingers. The iron-rich magma lends the grim black colour – some of the rock is actually magnetic. Incidentally, any kitchen worktop marketed as 'black granite' is actually some sort of gabbro.

ABOVE Basalt intruded into gabbro, Ardnamurchan Point.

BELOW Basalt lava flows at Chimney Tops, west of the Giant's Causeway.

The same dark rock-melt, emerging into the open as lava flows, cools with no crystal structure at all. That's basalt. Basalt is slippery and brittle. It forms wide, flat terraces with little crags at the edge of each flow. Experience basalt in northern Skye, and along Antrim's Causeway Coast. Flat layers of lava, shrinking as they cool, can give the hexagonal structure of the Giant's Causeway itself.

> SCRAMBLABILITY? Gabbro's the best. Rough, black and grippy, even in the wet. Basalt? Not so great. Smooth underfoot, while holds are either big or not there at all.

ABOVE Wiggly schist, Cruach Ardrain, north of Loch Lomond.

Schist

The mighty Caledonian mountain range was formed when Scotland and England crunched together 400 million years ago – it must have been good while it lasted. All that's left of it now are its roots: squashed and crumpled, heated by friction, baked and half-melted deep underground. Schist is the changed, or 'metamorphic', rock formed of this mangled mix.

Schist forms Scotland's Central Highlands, from Ben Klibreck in Sutherland down to the Cobbler alongside Loch Lomond. The rocks are knobbed and wrinkled like the hide of an elephant that's 400 million years old. Platy mica minerals were formed in the underground pressure cooker.

The mica is shiny and smooth: you might notice the schist slipperiness as you climb to the top of the Cobbler, shown in Chapter 14. The mica also gives a sinister gleam on dull afternoons.

Schist breaks down fairly easily and forms lumpy ground rather than huge, spectacular crags. Where the original rock involved limestone, the decayed schist grows the lovely wildflowers on Ben Lawers.

> **SCRAMBLABILITY?** Few handholds, much plant life, and because of the mica, can be treacherous when wet.

Quartzite

Beach sand is made of the tough mineral called quartz. When grains of tough quartz are cemented together with that same quartz mineral, that makes the off-white rock called quartzite. The quartzite that tops off the mountains of Wester Ross formed in ancient seabeds. But across the Central Highlands, a different sort of quartzite comes from the compression and melting down of something that was originally sandstone. So quartzite, confusingly, can be sedimentary (at Torridon) but also metamorphic (across the Grey Corries).

Quartzite is slippery, blocky and brittle. Where it breaks up, its square-cornered boulders make truly tiresome walking. But where it doesn't, along the tops of the Grey Corries, it forms smooth, flat surfaces that are quite delightful.

As well as the highest tops of Wester Ross, small areas of quartzite are here and there all over the Highlands, and

BELOW Quartzite boulders, Grey Corries ridge east of Ben Nevis.

also on the Stiperstones in Shropshire. White, shiny and square-cornered, it is interestingly different from whatever rock you're passing over immediately before and after.

SCRAMBLABILITY? Smooth and slippery, but with lots of tiny sharp holds. Even gently sloping rock slabs can give good scrambling.

Deep-sea sediments

Sludge piles up in ocean trenches, and then, given the necessary earth movements, comes up again as compact grey rocks whose main attribute is being nondescript. Being made of mud, they're rather smooth and slippery to walk on. They form no mighty crags, but rounded grassy uplands, with streams cutting little ravines into their sides.

This can make attractive, steep-sided hills, as in the Howgill Fells. Or it can just make hills, as in the northern Lake District (the Skiddaw Slates) and Scotland's Southern Uplands. In the Rhinogs of southern Snowdonia, underwater mud avalanches have formed thick, chunky rock slabs.

SCRAMBLABILITY? Any crags are scrappy ones; Sharp Edge and Halls Fell on Blencathra (Lake District) are where ocean sediments have been hardened up by the arrival of nearby hot granite.

Sandstone

Sandstone is grains of quartz sand, cemented together with the limestone mineral called calcite. So it's much the same as the lime mortar you use to repoint your house, if you're a fussy sort of person living in an old house made of stone.

And where did the sandstone's sand come from? As often as not, eroded out of some previous sandstone: a repeating cycle that pioneer geologist James Hutton described as 'no vestige of a beginning, no prospect of an end'.

Sandstone is laid down in flat layers on the seabed, in lakes or rivers, or in a desert. Its texture and layering can tell us which – the Millstone Grit of the Peak District is from a big, vigorous river delta that formed and reformed across Middle England during the Carboniferous or coal period.

Two special sorts of sandstone rise as important UK hills. The Old Red Sandstone formed in outwash rivers from the Caledonian mountain range, that crumple zone where Scotland met England. Lifted and tilted by a later set of earth movements, the Old Red crops out all the way across South Wales as the north-facing escarpment of the Brecon Beacons National Park. The summits are flat and slabby. The rocks are worn down and rounded,

ABOVE Lakebed ripples in Old Red Sandstone at the summit of Pen y Fan, the high point of South Wales.

but sandpaper rough underfoot.

Then in the far north-west, there's a sandstone that's five times older again than the Old Red: the Torridonian. It forms the grim, purple-brown walls and terraces of the area's mightiest mountains, including Liathach and An Teallach.

SCRAMBLABILITY? Sandstone can be soft, with rounded handholds. Hand-jamming can be a useful technique. Watch out for loose blocks.

Limestone

Limestone is what makes Yorkshire, Yorkshire. It's creamy white in colour, lumpy and rounded, forming wide scar cliffs, cave systems, and the dissected, flat limestone pavement. It's formed of shells and other sea life, dissolved in seawater then precipitated out again as calcite mineral, or sometimes straight and unchanged in the form of fossils.

Limestone dissolves in water. This means that eroding streams not only wear it away, but also add it back again, to build stalactites, stalagmites and other weird formations found in caves. The rock erodes to thin, lime-rich soil, so that walking on limestone is smooth, green and grassy. In the Yorkshire climate, the rock grows an invisible layer of algae, making it slippery to walk across. If you climb around underground, on the other hand, you'll find it rough and grippy.

One thick layer of almost white, fossil-rich limestone forms much of the Yorkshire Dales, as well as the Mendips and many parts of South Wales. It used to be called the Mountain Limestone, but now, less excitingly, the Carboniferous Limestone.

> **SCRAMBLABILITY?** Rounded and smooth, and slippery underfoot unless you're underground. Requires care.

BELOW Shells and coral in Carboniferous Limestone, below Carreg Cennen Castle, Brecon Beacons.

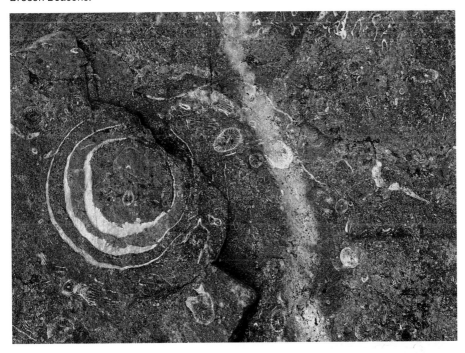

Seacliffs

There have been two earth-moving episodes in Britain's history. The Caledonian one, the Scotland–England collision of 400 million years ago; and 150 million years later, the Variscan, as Africa nudged into the corner of Europe. Any rocks more recent than the Variscan haven't been raised upwards to make mountains. So no hillwalking on the New Red Sandstone, the Jurassic limestones and mudstones, the Chalk, and the soft clays of the last 50 million years. The place to see all those is around the edges of this country.

The seacliffs of England, Wales and Northern Ireland are a showcase of geology. The Dinosaur Coast of North Yorkshire, the Jurassic Coast of Devon and Cornwall, Antrim in Northern Ireland and the Pembrokeshire Coast National Park are just the highlights. And the particular treat of the younger rocks is the fossils: shells, coral and ammonites plus the very occasional dinosaur. And the sea keeps knocking down the cliffs, exposing fresh ones all the time.

SCRAMBLABILITY? Loose, friable and liable to sudden collapse, even sitting down underneath some seacliffs is slightly risky.

BELOW Robin Hood's Bay, Yorkshire, endpoint of the Coast-to-Coast walk, with ironstone and mudstone cliff.

Ice

Is ice a rock form? If so, it's a short-lived one, hardly enduring even for a brief million years. Plus, of course, it moves as glaciers a lot quicker than the standard 4–5cm a year of the shifting hills.

It took until 1840 for geologists to realise it: all the mountains of the UK have been carved and shaped by glaciers that have only just gone away. Once you've seen those absent glaciers, the signs are all around. The grey mudstone boulder sitting on limestone bedrock. The rock-scratches exposed along a newly eroded path. The deep, U-shaped valleys with all the side spurs chopped off; the scooped-out corrie hollows, always on the north or eastern slope, the downwind side where the snow piled high; the little hillocks of moraine rubble left along the valley side.

SCRAMBLABILITY?
Requires crampons.

ABOVE Spot the absent glacier: moraine hummocks low down on the side of Bow Fell, Lake District.

BELOW Rannoch Moor granite dumped by glacier on schist of Beinn Pharlagain, Perthshire.

FINAL WORDS

The best geologist, said pioneering geologist Professor Herbert Harold Read, is the one who's seen the most rocks. Which means that all hillwalkers are, potentially, great geologists.

And can we take this further? Given the benefits to our health, the strength of legs and hearts and lungs, the confidence and self-reliance, the friendships we build inside the rainclouds, the sheer fun and enjoyment of it all – is the best human being the one who's seen the most seacliffs or made it up the most mountains?

Obviously not. Cyclists, astronauts, scuba divers – they can be very fine people too. What we can be sure is that folk who go up hills are healthier, happier, and will be building life skills like resilience and self-reliance. As well as being thoroughly wised up on the ways of drying out our socks.

BELOW Ronald enjoying Lord's Rake gully, Scafell.

GLOSSARY

Abseil: (Climbing) Roping down; descending using a doubled rope and a friction device

Arête: Narrow ridge, steep on both sides, sometimes scrambly along the top

Ascent: (In 'distance and ascent') The accumulated uphill height gained in the course of a walk

Backpack: American term for rucksack

Backpacking: Walking with overnight gear such as a tent and cooker

Base layer: Underclothing with logos on

Beanie: A bobble hat without the bobble

Bearing: A direction of travel expressed as an angle (see Chapter 16)

Bearing, grid: A bearing measured from the map's north–south grid lines

Bearing, magnetic: A bearing measured from magnetic north

Belay: (Climbing) Attaching yourself, or your climbing rope, to the rock face

Bivvy: A night in the open using a breathable bivvy bag rather than a tent

Bothy: An informal shelter in the mountain, typically with sleeping platform but no other facilities

Boulderfield: Ground (sloping or flat) formed of broken-up chunks of rock, formed *in situ* by frost action at the end of the Ice Age

Bridleway: A legal right-of-way line for walkers, horse riders and cyclists in England or Wales; may not involve a visible path on the ground

Broken ground: Sloping ground that's a mixture of vegetation and rocky outcrops

Buff: A scarf with the ends joined together or a hat with a hole in it

Cairn: Pile of stones to mark a summit or path or (sometimes) for hiding litter inside; in Gaelic, a stonepile sort of mountain

Carabiner: Metal snap-link used by climbers

Chimney: (Climbing) A crack in the rockface wide enough to climb inside

BELOW Col: Hause Gate, the ridge foot below Cat Bells. 'Hause' and 'Gate' both mean col or saddle.

Col: Saddle point such as a pass or a low point on a ridge

Contouring: Moving around a slope rather than upwards or downwards

Coomb, combe, cove: English (rather than Welsh, Scots) term for corrie

Corrie: Hollow in a hillside, normally ice-carved with steep headwall, facing north or east, and often with a small lake

Cwm: (Welsh) Corrie or valley

Exposure:
1. The technical expression for Argh-huge-scary-drops-below
2. Old-fashioned term for hypothermia, getting dangerously chilled (the other one being hyperthermia, formerly known as heatstroke)

Fall line: An imaginary line drawn directly downhill

Gabbro: A black, rugged, superbly grippy rock found in the Skye Cuillin

Gaiters: Sturdy nylon coverings for the lower leg

Gill (ghyll): A steep, rocky stream typically with waterfalls and enclosing rock walls

GPS point of interest: A fancy GPS waypoint with added data such as a name, description or photo

GPS route: A digital file recorded on screen, specifying the line of a planned journey; typically with far fewer waypoints than a GPS track

GPS track: A digital file that specifies the line of a journey, recorded in the course of that journey: typically with a recorded waypoint every 20m or so

GPS waypoint: One of the individual location points making up a GPS track or route

Granite: A pale, speckled, crystalline rock, often forming distinctive tors on summit plateaus

Grid reference: A code of two letters and six, eight or ten digits indicating precise location (see Chapter 16)

Grid square: A 1km x 1km square of the National Grid marked on Ordnance Survey and other walkers' maps

Gully: Rocky slot running up through a crag, often with loose rock in the bottom. Gullies are uncomfortable to go up, but scenic

Handrailing: Navigation along a linear feature such as a stream, forest edge or fence

Harness: (Climbing) Nylon webbing around the body for attaching ropes to

Index contour: On maps, a thicker contour line, typically every fifth one, making it easier to reckon altitudes and height changes

Klettersteig: German term for via ferrata

Linn: (Scots) A river or stream, typically slow-moving, between rock walls

Lochan: A small loch

Naismith's Rule: Simple algorithm for calculating expected time and tiredness from the distance and ascent, see Chapter 3

Névé: Thawed and refrozen snow, firm enough for crampons without being icy

Pitch: (Climbing) A stretch of roped climbing between two belay points

Public footpath: A legal right-of-way line for walkers in England or Wales; may not involve a visible path on the ground

Re-entrant: A descending valley-line cutting into a slope (see Chapter 2)

Runner: (Climbing) A running belay: a protection point with metal snap-link allowing the rope to run through it

Saddle: A saddle-shaped land formation such as a pass or the low point on a ridge; same as a col

Scrambling: Climbing up or down on rocks with the use of hands, but not serious enough to constitute roped climbing

Scree: Slope of loose stones below a cliff, formed from its break-up under frost action

Spot height: A precise height measurement, typically on a summit, marked on maps but without a trig point

Stance: (Climbing) A ledge where one climber can stand while using the rope to protect their companion

Talus: US term for scree and/or boulderfield

Tor: A small, picturesque rocky tower

Traverse: (Climbing) Climbing sideways across the rockface rather than up or down it

Trig point: A low concrete pillar on a summit or other viewpoint, formerly used by the Ordnance Survey for surveying, now a useful marker and camera stand

Via ferrata: In the Alps, a route across rock equipped with cables and artificial footholds

Waymark: An arrow or other marker to indicate the route, typically on a public footpath or bridleway

Waypoint: See GPS waypoint

Whiteout: Combination of mist and deep snow so that neither the ground nor the skyline can be distinguished

Wicking: Technical undergarments designed to carry sweat away from the body

Wind slab: A hard-frozen layer lying on top of softer snow; on steeper slopes, wind slab is an avalanche risk

BELOW Scree: awkward going over the Wastwater Screes, Lake District.

INDEX

A

abroad, walking 244–54
  hut-to-hut hiking 245–7
  places to go 248–9
  planning principles 248
  Stubai High Level Route
    250–3
  in the USA 231
  ways and means 244–5
  what to pack 246–8
access rights 54
access tracks, mountain 64
adders 95
ancient paths 64, 87
Apple Maps 69
avalanches 76, 112, 287

B

BAA avalanche forecast
  app 76
backpack child carriers 93
backpacking and wild
  camping 224–31
  bothies 227
  Dalmally to Fort William
    232–9
  packing tips 228–9
  routes round-up 229–31
  tents or bivvies 226
  in the USA 231
bedrock/geology 288–97
  deep-sea sediments 293
  gabbro and basalt 291
  granite 290
  ice 297
  limestone 295
  mica minerals 292
  quartzite 293
  sandstone 294
  schist 292
  seacliffs 296
  volcanic rock 289–90
Blencathra by Halls Fell
  97–100, 104–6
boat trips 22
Bob Graham Round 243

boots/shoes, walking 33–4,
  246
bothies 227
British Red Cross first aid
  app 76

C

Caledonian mountains
  292, 294
care of the environment,
  mountains and 86–9
cars/car parks and traffic
  87, 89
Cat Bells 20, 22, 134
children and toddlers 90–3
Church Stretton,
  Shropshire Hills 123
clifftops 60
clothing 28–9, 33–5, 37,
  114, 246–7

coastlines
  England 152–3, 296
    Cleveland 'Dinosaur'
      Coast 142, 296
    Jurassic Coast 154–7,
      210, 296
    Porlock and the Three
      Peaks of Somerset
      153
  Northern Ireland 202–5,
    296
  Wales 175-6, 211
compasses 31–2, 66–7,
  85
  how to take a bearing
    275–7
    aiming off 278
    aspect of slope 278–9
    following the bearing
      276–7
    magnetic variation
      276
    measuring the bearing
      275–6
    pole planting
      procedures 277
  incorrect readings and
    remagnetisation 68,
    85
contouring mountain
  paths 64

cornices, navigating 286–7
corries 64
cows and sheep 94, 95
crampons 285–6
cycle paths 54

D

Dartmoor 204, 290
denes and coombes 61
Derwent Water boat trip
  22
digital maps see mapping
  apps; maps, paper and
  digital
dogs and hillwalking 94–6
downlands/grassy hilltops
  61
duty of care, walkers'
  116–17

E

Emergency SMS
  registration 77, 118
England see coastlines;
  Lake District; long-
  distance walking routes;
  Peak District; Shropshire
  Hills; Yorkshire Dales
English 2000s hills 257

F

farm animals 94, 95
Fell Runners Association
  (FRA) 243
first aid 36, 76, 118
food and water 36–7, 247

G

geology see bedrock/
  geology
Google Maps 69
GPS (global positioning
  system) 32, 71–3
ground nesting birds
  94–5

H

hill running/fellrunning
  240–3
horseshoe routes,
  mountain 63
hostels 217–19

K

kit/equipment 28–42, 114

L

Lake District 133–41, 204, 289, 293
  backpacking and wild camping 229–30
  Borrowdale 135
  Cat Bells 20, 22, 134
  Great Gable 77–8, 137, 139–41
  less busy times 136
  long distance hostel to hostel walk 'Tour de Scafell' 220–3, 230
  Scafell Pike 13–14, 138
  the Wainwrights 256
littering 86–7
Long Distance Walkers Association (LDWA) 242–3
long-distance walking routes 208–12
  Cumbria Way 211
  Dalmally to Fort William 232–9
  Hadrian's Wall Path 210
  hiking hostel to hostel 217–19
  Jurassic Coast 210
  Pembrokeshire coast 211
  Scotland 209–10, 230–1
  St Cuthbert's Way 213–16
  top tips 209
  Tour de Scafell Pike 220–3
  in the USA 231
  Wainwright's Coast to Coast 211
  West Highland Way 209–10
lost, getting
  author's experience 77–85
  checking your compass 85
  what to do 79
low level routes, locating UK 56–8

M

mapping apps 67, 68–70
  on a computer 68–9, 259–61
  following a route online 261–8
  GPX files 260
  for smartphones 69, 70–6
  Snap-to-Path function 259, 261
maps, paper and digital 66–7
  black dashed path lines 52–3
  bridleways 54
  contour lines 44–6, 54
  grid references 280–1
  Harvey Superwalker maps 51, 52, 53, 54, 263, 266–7
  OpenStreetMaps 51–2, 53, 68, 69, 262, 268
  Ordnance Survey Explorer maps 50–1, 52, 53, 68, 263–7
  Ordnance Survey Landranger maps 49–50, 52–3, 54, 68, 262
  Ordnance Survey Northern Ireland 202
  phones *vs* paper 29–30, 69
  public footpaths 54
  rights of way 53–4
  summits and saddle points 46–7, 54
  see also mapping apps
Marilyn hills 258
metric *vs* imperial 56, 263
midges and ticks 179
mobile phones *see* smartphones
moon phase apps 76
Morton Mains Hill 13
Mountain Rescue 76, 77, 96, 115–19

N

Naismith's Rule 59, 263
navigating by nature 282

Northern Ireland 202–5
  Antrim Coast 204–5
  Mountains of Mourne 203–4, 290

O

OpenStreetMaps 51–52, 53, 68, 69, 262, 268
OS Locate app 75–6, 280
OS maps, digital 70, 71, 72, 202
Outdooractive app 70, 74, 262, 268

P

Peak District 122–32, 294
  Dark Peak 125
    Kinder Scout 130–2
  Edale 124, 125
  White Peak 124–5
    Hartington Valleys 126–9

R

remagnetised compasses 68, 85
ridges, mountain 63
right of way networks, UK 56–7
rights to roam (UK) 54
riversides and lakesides 61
routes, choosing 55–64
  estimating your route time 59
  finding attractive routes 60–2
  guidebooks 58
  internet research 57–8
  locating UK low level routes 56–7
  mountain ground 62–4
  routes to avoid 62
rucksacks 36

S

safety precautions
  being prepared/vital advice 114–15, 118
  duty of care 116–17
  hillwalking with children 90–93

hillwalking with dogs 94–6

see also Mountain Rescue

Scotland
 backpacking and wild camping 230–1
 Ben Lomond 184–6
 Ben Nevis 182–3
 bothies 227
 Cairngorms 195–6, 290
 Cape Wrath Trail 231
 Corbetts 255–6
 Galloway Highlands 180–1
 geology, Central Highlands 292, 293
 Grahams and Donalds 256
 hill running 241–3
 islands 199–200
 Isle of Arran 201, 290
 Kerrera 199–200
 Loch Lomond and the Trossachs National Park 183, 204
 Loch Ossian 190
 low level routes 57, 177–81
 Mamores - Stob Coire a' Chairn and Am Bodach walk 261–8, 269–71
 Meall nan Tarmachan 191–4
 midges and ticks 179
 the Munros and Munro Tops 181–92, 255–6
 Peebles 180
 Pitlochry 178
 Skye Cuillin 199, 204, 291
 Southern Uplands 177–81, 230, 293
 Wester Ross 196–8, 293
Scottish Hill Runners (SHR) 243
scrambling
 Blencathra by Halls Fell 97–100, 104–6
 gill 100
 grades 1 to 3 101
 guidebooks 103

site recommendations 102
 strategems 99
 suitability of rock types 290–7
 wild 100
sheep and cows 94, 95
short-distance walks, benefits of 212
Shropshire Hills 123
smartphones and apps 30, 31–3, 67, 69
 airplane mode 71
 back-up power 70–1, 111, 118, 247
 emergency SMS registration 77, 118
 following pre-set routes 73
 missing the scenery 74
 for navigation 70–3
 other useful apps 75–6
 saving maps offline 71–3
 see also mapping apps
snow 96, 107–13, 283–7
 see also winter walking
socks 37
stellar navigation 282
Streetmap 69–70

T

tents vs bivvies 226
ticks 96
toileting/toilet paper 87
torches 37
Tranter's Round 242

V

Vixen Tor, Dartmoor 204

W

Wales 158–76
 Brecon Beacons (Bannau Brycheiniog) 169–74, 294
 Black Mountains 170
 Pen y Fan 169–70, 171–4
 Waterfall Country 170
 Snowdonia (Eryri) 160–8, 289

Cadair Idris 164
 Capel Curig 164
 Glyder range 78, 80–5, 160–1
 Moel Siabod 165–8
 Rhinogs 164, 293
 Snowdon (Yr Wyddfa) 161–4
 Welsh 2000s hills 257–8
 Welsh coast 175–6, 211
 St David's 176
 Welsh language pronounciations 159, 162, 163
walking poles 38–9, 247, 277
 pole planting procedures 277
Walla Crag 20–5
waterproof clothing 34–5
weather forecasts 76, 108–9, 112, 114
whiteouts 272–4
wild camping see backpacking and wild camping
wildlife 13, 94–5
winter walking 107–13
 author's snowy experience 110–11
 avalanches 112, 287
 navigating cornices 286–7
 top tips 109
 using ice axes 283–5
 weather forecasts 108–9, 112
 where and when to go in the snow 112–13
 whiteouts 272–4

Y

Yorkshire Dales 143–53
 Ingleborough walk 146–51
 Settle 145